Forest of Tigers

Forest of Tigers

People, Politics and Environment
in the Sundarbans

Annu Jalais

Routledge
Taylor & Francis Group
LONDON NEW YORK NEW DELHI

Reprint 2011
First published 2010
by Routledge
912–915 Tolstoy House, 15–17 Tolstoy Marg, New Delhi 110 001

Simultaneously published in the UK
by Routledge
2 Park Square, Milton Park, Abingdon, OX14 4RN

Routledge is an imprint of the Taylor & Francis Group, an informa business

Typeset by
Star Compugraphics Private Limited
D–156, Second Floor
Sector 7, Noida 201 301

Printed and bound in India by
Avantika Printers Private Limited
194/2, Ramesh Market, Garhi, East of Kailash,
New Delihi 110 065

British Library Cataloguing-in-Publication Data
A catalogue record of this book is available from the British Library

ISBN: 978-0-415-54461-0

Contents

List of Maps and Illustrations

Maps

All maps drawn by the author and digitalised by Manuel Montañez Martinez Manolo. The copyright rests with the author.

Illustrations

All photographs courtesy the author.

Acknowledgements

It is impossible to name all those who contributed to this book based on my Ph.D. thesis which was successfully defended in 2004. My deepest gratitude is to the people of the island of Satjelia, especially those living 'on the river's edge' who welcomed me into their lives and homes. Foremost amongst them are Leelabati and Haren Mondal, their sons, nieces and nephews — particularly Tukai — and their respective families who provided a warm shelter and a much needed sense of inclusion. I am also deeply grateful to Lokkhi and Binod Bera and their daughters who opened their home and heart to me. To them and to Bimal Adhikari, Parikshit Bar, Ranjit Ghosh, Sasadhar Giri, Sudhansu Mondal, Probhas Mondal, Murari Mondal, Putul Mondal, Sudha and Sasanka Mridha and Chedor Nityananda, who introduced me to the various aspects of politics, literature or theatrical plays of the area, I shall forever remain grateful.

I could have never undertaken this work without the guidance and protection of Tushar Kanjilal. 'Mastermoshai' — as he is affectionately known — greatly facilitated fieldwork by generously including me in the veritable 'movement' for social change he has initiated in the Sundarbans through the NGO, the Tagore Society for Rural Development. There I was fortunate to have met Ganesh Misra who always took good care of me in Rangabelia, Isita Ray who invited me to her Kolkata flat where our evocations of the Sundarbans always ended with making me want to return, Dr Amitava Chowdhury who many a times made the Sundarbans bearable by providing good literature and a warm enclave of 'Kolkataness' in Rangabelia, and finally Protima Misra, Satyabati Mondal, Sumati Mondal, Jharna Panda, Bijoli Sarkar, and Dr Gita Sen who conveyed to me their deep sympathy and energetic struggle with and for the women of the Sundarbans.

I owe an immeasurable amount of gratitude to P. K. Sarkar who has supported me in countless ways throughout the duration of this research. This research would have been much poorer without his deep insightful comments and corrections as well as those by late Babu Beckers — who was one of those rare people whose fabulous generosity matched his vast knowledge; I will always hold very dear the afternoons spent at St Xaviers listening to his stories about his time in the Sundarbans. Shyamoli Khastgir, my Shantiniketan green-living artist aunt, and Marie-France Martin, grassroots educator extraordinaire, have been inspirations since my early days and I thank them as well as late Pannalal Dasgupta and Rakhal Chandra Dey for their warmth and faith.

I am also very thankful to Amitav Ghosh whose visits to and questions about the Sundarbans taught me how to do better fieldwork and gain a deeper insight into what he called the 'gateway cults' of the Sundarbans. His sound advice and our stimulating exchanges about the region have been of immense support. I shall always remain indebted to Manju Guha-Majumder and Professor Anindya Datta for their great generosity and encouragement. I am also thankful to Fr Roberge for inviting me to discuss the Sundarbans with his students; to William R. da Silva for sharing his knowledge on folk studies on the tigers of the Malabar coast; and to Nazes Afroz for clarifying doubts and correcting mistakes. My deep appreciation for lively conversations on the Sundarbans also goes out to Pradip Bhattacharya, Rathindranath De, Dr Basuri Guha, Dr Ratna Gupta, Sirajul Hossain, Bonani and Pradip Kakkar, Shobhana Madhavan, Sanjay Mitra, Biswanath Mukherjee, Susanta Mukhopadhyay, Pranabes Sanyal, and Ajoy Tarafdar.

I gratefully acknowledge the support received from the London School of Economics (LSE), and its generous bestowal of two studentships and research travel grants. I am also very thankful to Madame Bernès-Lassere, Pascale and Bertrand Figarol, Jenny and Raphael Gay, Savitri Jalais, les Amis de l'Arche for financially supporting me. The writing stage of the thesis was helped by financial assistance from the Royal Anthropological Institute's Radcliff-Brown Trust Fund and the LSE Malinowski Award. The thesis would have been impossible to complete without the economic support of these kind friends and trusting institutions.

I am profoundly indebted to Professor Henrietta Moore for her insightful wisdom, constant encouragement and help in choosing this book's title. I have been extremely fortunate to work under the supervision of Professors Chris Fuller and Jonathan Parry. Their suggestions throughout the research have provided the much needed focus and background for many of my arguments. I have also greatly benefited from comments and suggestions made by Professors Martha Mundy, Maurice Bloch and Dipankar Gupta; faculty members of the

Department of Anthropology of the LSE; and Dr Shabnum Tejani and Dr Daud Ali of the History department of the School of Oriental and African Studies for having invited me to present a paper based on a version of my chapter which deals with the connection between tiger-charmers and Sufi saints. My heartfelt thanks to the panel organisers of 'Aw(e)ful and Fearful Knowledge' (Association of Social Anthropologists [ASA], Manchester, July 2003), Alberto Corsin-Jimenez, and 'Forgetting Bengal' (American Anthroplogical Association [AAA], Chicago, November 2003), Tahmima Anam, for inviting me and with whom, along with my co-panellists, it was such a pleasure presenting papers. I am also greatly indebted to Professors Partha Chatterjee, and Ralph Nicholas and Drs Gautam Basu and James Carrier for having been such insightful and encouraging discussants.

Most of Chapter VII, 'Unmasking the Cosmopolitan Tiger', was published in the journal *Nature and Culture* (vol. 3, no. 1, 2008) and portions of Chapter VI, 'Sharing History with Tigers', appeared in the *Economic and Political Weekly* (vol. 40, no. 17, April 23, 2005, pp. 1757–762) under the heading 'Dwelling on Morichjhanpi: When Tigers Became "Citizens"', Refugees "Tiger-Food"'. Some of the arguments which appear in Chapter VIII were penned for *Conservation and Society* (vol. 5, no. 4, 2007) under the title 'The Sundarbans: Whose World Heritage Site?' I am indebted to the editors of these journals for permission to include them here.

It would be impossible to list all those whose reactions have contributed to improving the work. I shall name here just the most important: Mahesh Rangarajan was the first to read my thesis manuscript, offer many valuable suggestions and suggest that I should publish it — without his encouragement this book would have never seen the light of day; Piya Chatterjee offered thought-provoking comments and gave invaluable advice concerning publishing. I thank Nilanjan Sarkar and Rimina Mohapatra of Routledge, New Delhi, for taking on my manuscript and their solicitude through it all, and Jaya Chowdhury for her patient copyediting. I am also thankful to Routledge's anonymous referee who made a number of useful suggestions.

Early in my fieldwork I had the chance to meet Dr Bikas Raychaudhuri. I remain eternally grateful for his excellent advice to follow his fieldwork experience in the Sundarbans which was to 'bite the earth like a tortoise and stay clinging to it for dear life'.

During my fieldwork I was affiliated to the Anthropological Survey of India, Kolkata, where I benefited greatly from discussions with Dr Ranjit K. Bhattacharya, Dr Jayanta Sarkar, Dr Tushar Kanti Niyogi, and their colleagues. This study owes a great deal to Dr Gopinath Barman whose passionate narratives introduced me to the fascinating side of Gosaba's Hamilton Estate history. I also thank Dr Ajit Kumar Banerjee of Arabari experiment fame for sharing his commitment to the Joint Forest Management scheme which was the first to involve the local population in a redistribution of forest resources.

The energy which sustained me during the both lively and lonely field months was generously provided by Damayanti Lahiri aka Dodo and her magical limitless materialisation of both tickets for cultural shows and amazing dishes which kept me tuned in and fed while on my 'breaks' in Kolkata. I remain grateful to her and to Bithi Bera, Nivedita, Kunal Kaku, Shyam Barua and his cousin Sanjay, Stefan Ecks, Laurent Fournier, Shyam Goswami, Arnab Lahiri, Biswajit Mitra, Stefan Moulin, Iraban Mukherjee, Amal Pandit, Isita Ray, Savitri, Prem, and my parents for taking the trouble to visit me during fieldwork and for having been such good sports. I thank my friend late Bhavana Krishnamoorthy, as well as Jai Motwane, Stephen Vella, Fatema Ibrahimi and little Vasanthi for providing some much needed moments of fun and recreation in London.

Mita Dutta, Roseanna Pollen and Isabella Lepri for very helpful comments, references and footnotes; Savitri Jalais, Shyaam M. S., Mandira Kalra, Viji Rajagopalan, Amitava Chowdhury, and Laurent Fournier for their attentive reading of my thesis and/or insightful suggestions; Manuel Montañez Martinez Manolo for the perfect digitalising of my maps and Margaret Bothwell and Yan Hinrichsen for their kind assistance — to all of you and to Mao Mollona, Kate Wood and Zubaer Mahboob, a big thank you. Needless to say, surviving errors and eccentricities remain my own.

I cannot thank enough my dear friend Amites Mukhopadhyay who provided much needed support both in the field and during the writing in London. Few anthropologists are blessed with a colleague with whom exchanging field notes and ideas is such a pleasure. These exchanges were made all the more enjoyable through Amites' wife Anindita's warm and restorative invitations, constant encouragement and wonderful sense of humour.

To Kriti Kapila for giving me numerous opportunities to hone my skills in argumentation and critical thinking; to Moushumi Bhowmik who kept me going with her songs and her faith; to Murali

Shanmugavelan for bringing back passion and enthusiasm in debates on political and social issues; to Naeem Mohaiemen who patiently went through the final drafts of this book, gave vital advice and made me promise I would write a Bangladesh sequel; and to Beverley Brown for her excellent copy-editing, generous sarcasm and remarkable patience which often extended into the wee hours of the morning — I shall remain forever indebted.

This work is a tribute to my childhood friend Toofan, named after a typhoon, and to the countless others who lost their lives or loved ones to tigers, crocodiles, snakes, and cyclones; to them and to those who during my fieldwork in the Sundarbans infused life and love; and to the two persons who sensitised me to it all in my young age:

My father, for introducing me to the Sundarbans through his extraordinary stories and his passion to put right some of the social injustices of the world, and for always believing in me.

My mother, for her loving presence and wonderful letters and for exclaiming in dismay, when coming across my first ever attempt at story-writing, 'but darling, why didn't you write about the tiger?'

It took a long time to write again; now more than twenty years later, I would like this renewed attempt, finally also about the tiger, to be a mark of love and gratitude to both my mother and father.

Note on Transliteration

The main language spoken in the Sundarbans is Bengali. Like many north Indian languages, Bengali is derived from Sanskrit and Magadhi Prakrit and is, along with Urdu, the closest North Indian language to Farsi. The vowel sound 'au' as in the English word 'austere' in most north Indian languages is retranscribed as 'a' but in Bengali it is closer to 'o'. Convention dictates that commonly used terms such as 'panchayat' and 'zamindar' be written in their anglicised version with an 'a'. However, these terms are pronounced 'pɔnchayet' and 'jomidār', going by the International Phonetic Association (IPA) alphabet in Bengali. But as these terms have found their way into the Oxford English Dictionary in their anglicised form, I have left them as such.

I have, however, not been completely consistent with this system. For popular local terms such as *bādh* or *jɔŋgol* which have both been included in the English dictionary as 'bund' and 'jungle', I have preferred spelling the first as 'bund' while for the second I have alternated between 'jungle' and 'jongol'. This is because if 'jungle' conjures up the idea of an impenetrable thicket of tropical vegetation, 'jongol' commonly used with the word 'bon' for 'forest' in Bengali brings to mind ideas of 'wilderness' and in the Sundarbans, the 'sphere of non-humans'. Also, where I italicise local terms and give their phonetic pronunciation the first time they are mentioned, I have done away with both italics and phonetics the subsequent times and have provided their definition, along with that of acronyms, in the glossary.

I have avoided the usual use of diacritical signs when re-transcribing an Indian language. This is because even though some of the Bengali words derived from Sanskrit have kept a Sanskritic spelling when written in Bengali, they are nevertheless pronounced more according to a popular oral form. So, for example, even though the goddess of wealth has her name usually spelt as 'Lakshmi' and is written with diacritic signs as 'Lakśmī' by Indologists, the word in Bengali is pronounced as 'Lokkhi' — I have therefore preferred to write such words without diacritics and as close as possible, with simple roman alphabets, that is, to their local pronunciation. Also, even though I have kept to usual spellings in English when writing people's names, I have sometimes given a spelling phonetically closer to the islanders' pronunciation of the word. There are no capital letters in any of the Indian alphabets, I have, however, used capital letters for proper nouns but have tried to avoid adding an English 's' to denote the plural.

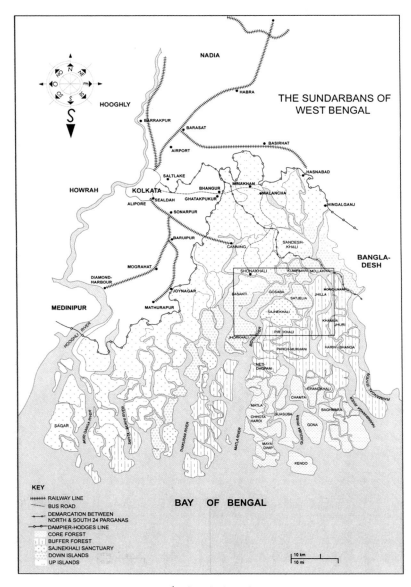

1. Sunderbans I

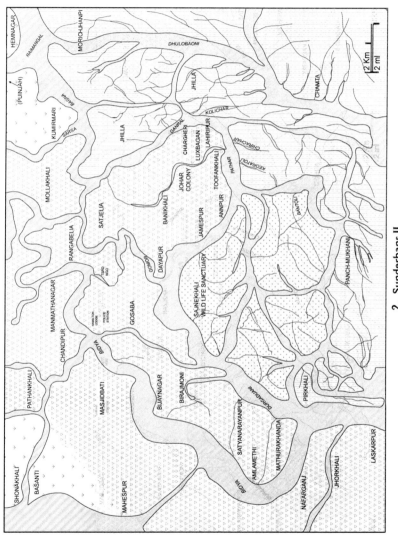

2. Sunderbans II

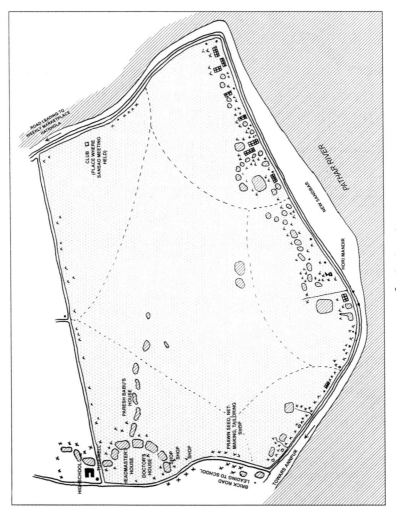

3. Garjontola

I

Introduction

Sundarbans: Between Land and Water, a Forest and a Region

The Sundarbans, literally 'beautiful forest' in Bengali, is an immense archipelago situated between the vast Indian Ocean to the south and the fertile plains of Bengal to the north.[1] Created by the confluence of the Ganges, Meghna and Brahmaputra rivers and their innumerable distributaries, the Sundarbans constitutes the southern end of both Bangladesh and West Bengal (WB). The Ganga–Brahmaputra delta stretches several hundred miles, from the shorelines of Orissa in the west to those of Chittagong and Burma in the east; it is the largest delta in the world. It is animated by two opposing flows of water: fresh water coursing all the way down from the Himalayas towards the Bay of Bengal and salt water streaming up with the tide from the Indian Ocean into the Bengali hinterland. These fast-moving salty muddy waters are the locale of crocodiles, sharks and snakes of the most dangerous variety and of thousands of mangrove-covered islands. Born of these current-driven waters, the islands seem to cling on to their vegetation for their very existence. Muddy sandbars, washed up into existence one moment, are immediately eaten away if left bare of mangrove vegetation. Thus the rivers, along with their allies, the tides and storms, continually redesign island topographies, destroying some parts, adding to others, sometimes reclaiming them completely only to reassemble them a few kilometres away. These forested islands, the littoral fringe of the Bay of Bengal, cover around 10,000 sq. km.

However, the reason why the region is famous today is not so much because of this constantly changing environment and the way humans live with it, but the fact that it is the largest remaining natural habitat of the Bengal tiger, providing a home to an estimated 600 tigers (from both sides of the Bengali border). In fact, it is mainly because of the existence of tigers that the Sundarbans has gained renown and popularity: first in 1973 when 'Project Tiger' was launched and then again in 1987 when West Bengal entered the International Union for Conservation of Nature and Natural Resources list of World Heritage Sites. Its forests also host many other endangered species of wild animals such as estuarine crocodiles, otters, gangetic dolphins, Olive Ridley turtles, water monitors, cheetals, rhesus macaques and wild boars; once upon a time even leopards, wild water buffaloes, Javan and Indian rhinoceroses, hog and swamp deer could be found. A number of rare plants also survive here. But it is the tiger that has put the Sundarbans on the global map.

The total area of the Sundarbans — water, forested islands, inhabited cultivated islands, and some parts of the Bengali mainland — is 40,000 sq. kms. Of this whole area, the total *land* area of the WB Sundarbans is about 9,630 sq. kms, of which the un-inhabited portion is just under half. 'The forest' refers to those un-inhabited islands to the south that constitute the southern end of the Sundarbans region.[2]

There are two kinds of inhabited islands: those closer to the mainland, which were deforested and cultivated largely between 1765 and 1900, and those on the fringe of the mangrove forest, reclaimed between 1900 and 1980. These two kinds of islands have distinct geographies. The former, located to the north and west of the region, are bigger, have an elevated ground level and are thus safer from the vagaries of storms and tides. Part of the 'stable delta', their fertile soil is well-irrigated by canals that are not as broad, nor as saline, as those of the southern islands. Being nearer the mainland, these northern islands also have better access to the facilities offered by the city of Kolkata.

By contrast, the more southerly inhabited islands, part of the 'active delta' are far more subject to the 'whims' of the environment in making, unmaking and remaking the terrain. Reflecting this, they are characterised by the defensive earth embankments — raised mud quays called 'bunds' (*bādh*) that protect the cultivated areas from the saline rivers and hold back the twice daily high tides — erected around their perimeters. (Totaling the length of all these bunds, they amount to some 3,500 km.) Often referred to as *ābād*, the reclamation these islands have known is perilous: the threat of the salt-water rivers in turn 'reclaiming' entire villages in a few minutes is ever present, and the regular occurrence of storms and cyclones which are usually accompanied by huge tidal waves called 'bores' causes much loss of life and damage to property. The long monsoon months bring a halt to social and economic activities. And, for islanders living on those most southerly islands closest to the forest, the fear of being killed by a tiger or a crocodile makes it one of the more inhospitable terrains on the globe.[3] It is these islands — which form a region inhabited by 50 lakh people — that are the subject of this book.

The first maps of the region inform us that the early inhabitants deserted the place due to the depredations of pirates, and the most recent accounts are of East Bengali Hindu refugees seeking shelter on the island of Morichjhanpi in the late 1970s. In-between lies a forgotten history of migrations and settlements and of hard-won reclamation of land from the 'hungry tide'.[4]

Inhabitants of the Sundarbans

In the modern period, these islands began to be peopled after 1765 when the East India Company (EIC) acquired the civil administration of Bengal. However, the main migration did not occur until after the middle of the nineteenth century, when the colonial state, anxious for new revenues, brought in groups of landless labourers and Adivasis to reclaim the region's swampy ground for agricultural purposes.[5] The new inhabitants came from far-flung places, such as Chotanagpur, Hazaribagh, Manbhum in present-day Jharkhand, from Balasore in Orissa and from the Arakan coast in Myanmar, as well as from various districts of Bengal, such as Bankura, Birbhum, Midnapur, Nadia, Jessore (Chattopadhyaya 1987: 59–60; 1999: 14).[6] The most important group came from villages north of the Sundarbans region itself, from the 24 Parganas. There are no population estimates for the period prior to the mid-nineteenth century and very little mention is made of the Sundarbans population before the first census was taken in 1872.[7]

However, these migrations were not the first human habitation of the Sundarbans. Earlier, in the seventeenth and eighteenth centuries, it appears that the Sundarbans rivers were inhabited in semi-permanent ways by fishermen, woodcutters, pirates, paddy cultivators and salt-makers who lived on boats. And even before that, it is believed that this region had been settled, destroyed, abandoned, and then resettled, for thousands of years.

One of the remarkable features of the region — the maritime frontier of Bengal — is how it is intrinsically linked to the early spread of Islam, from A.D. 1200 when Sufi holy men cleared the forests in the northern and eastern parts of the delta and introduced agriculture

(Eaton 1993: 310). This region thus also marks the agrarian frontier of Bengal. Even earlier than this phase, before the thirteenth century, the area was thriving with small wealthy kingdoms, visited by ships trading with South-east Asia and the Middle East (Chattopadhyaya 1999: 17–19). However, such tranquillity was to be broken: maps and travellers' accounts document how the Portuguese, who had started off as traders in the region's riverside markets in the 1520s, soon became infamous, along with the Arakan/Marma from Burma, for their brutal piracy. The population was terrorised into leaving and the region fell into obscurity. All through the sixteenth, seventeenth and eighteenth centuries the Sundarbans was referred to by the derogatory term *moger muluk* — literally meaning 'pirates' homeland/kingdom/den' and, more generally, 'anarchic place' — due to the lawlessness and violence that characterised it.[8]

However, the history of the island where I conducted most of my fieldwork was slightly different from that of the rest of the Sundarbans. Satjelia, along with the islands of Gosaba and Rangabelia, was bought at the beginning of the twentieth century by a Scotsman by the name of Sir Daniel Hamilton who wanted to use the islands for his experiment on starting a co-operative society. After paying off the creditors of the indentured labourers who agreed to come to these islands, he tried to convert these three islands into self-sufficient havens of peace and justice. People who settled there were not allowed to buy or sell land; he established a banking system with a one-rupee note issued for business transaction. Schooling, training (in agriculture and animal husbandry) and healthcare facilities were free. He did not want divisions of caste or religion and so disallowed pork and beef and alcohol from being consumed on his islands. The running of Hamilton's islands was taken over by the government in the late 1960s upon the abolition of the *zamindari* system and his trustees were left with managing Hamilton's personal estate on Gosaba island.

Even though Hamilton's venture in the early twentieth century is documented, little is known about the human history of those people who were either brought there or those who were living in the vicinity of the forest prior to the coming of the British. There are no records of the first 100 years of reclamation. The later snippets on the population provided by the gazetteer writers Hunter (1875), Pargiter (1889), Ascoli (1910), and O'Malley (1914) are frustratingly brief.

The Sundarbans forest has always been a source of endless fascination. W. W. Hunter, writing in 1875, devotes an entire book to the Sundarbans where, after writing at great length about the forest and wild animals, he only mentions the people in passing, referring to a 'few wandering gangs' and classifying them after long lists of wild animals and plants (1875: 317). Greenough identifies Hunter as inaugurating a tradition that continues to this day (1998: 240). The Sundarbans thus has two parallel but segregated histories, one relatively well-endowed relating to wildlife; the other, rather sparse, concerning the region's human inhabitants and their transformation of a forested landscape into a cultivated one. Present-day studies of the Sundarbans follow the lopsided structure of their nineteenth-century precedents very closely: fascination with the natural aspects of the Sundarbans but an unsettling silence on the social and human facets of the region.[9]

Social Geography of 'Up' and 'Down'

Encompassing differences between north and south, a stable and active delta is a distinction that, at the highest level, locates the Sundarbans as a whole in relation to the rest of WB and, at the local level, distinguishes between 'up' and 'down' islands.[10] These are the terms — used in English, inserted within Bengali speech — that the Sundarbans islanders use to navigate a geography comprising far more than the natural environment. The Sundarbans region as a whole is considered 'down' because it is infamously one of the poorest and least well-connected regions of WB. Following this logic, the most 'top up' places (again, these English words are inserted within the Bengali spoken in the Sundarbans) are the areas nearest Kolkata; living on islands nearer the mainland rather than on those further south, and living in Kolkata or even in the towns of the Sundarbans (Hasnabad, Taki, Joynagar or Canning) is more prestigious than living in villages (see Maps 1 and 2).

The very geography between the two is different. If the stable delta, just south of Kolkata, has agglomerate, compact settlements; the active delta contrasts sharply to it with its semi-nucleated, dispersed settlements (Banerjee 1998: 184). From the most 'top up' places, meaning the areas nearest Kolkata, people living in the Sundarbans will list islands in order of preference, the last being the ones furthest south and directly opposite the forest. These ultimate islands are also referred to as those 'at the tiger's lair'. Counted amongst such islands are the ones of the Gosaba Block, which includes Satjelia island, where I did most of my fieldwork (see Maps 1 and 2).

What is characteristic of the basin-like inhabited islands on the margins of the forest, the ones which are the concern of this book, is that they, like the forest islands, seem to be animated by the tidal rivers of the region. At high tide, when most of the vast expanses of forest go under water, these inhabited islands come alive through communication with each other as sailing between them becomes possible once again. In contrast, during low tide, the forest re-emerges and many of the inhabited islands become isolated once again as riverbeds are left with insufficient water for boats to ply.[11] There are no bridges between the down islands and commuting between them is possible only when the winds and tides permit. Even travelling and living within these islands is difficult; brick roads are few and far between, electricity is practically non-existent and drinking water rare.

Most of the Sundarbans region falls within the districts of the South 24 Parganas and of the North 24 Parganas with the active delta mainly in the south and the stable delta in the north. The differences between the stable and active delta are marked. In the stable delta the prevalent modes of transport are autos (motor-driven three-wheelers which operate as shared cabs), rickshaws, buses and trains. However, in the active delta, or in the 'down' islands, the only modes of locomotion are mechanised boats, locally called *bhotbhoti*, and simple country boats rowed with oars, called *nouka* or *dinghy*. On those islands that have proper roads, three-wheeled cycles with raised platforms, called *cycle-vans*, carry goods and people. Vital products like kerosene oil (which is widely used for lighting purposes as there is no electricity), cooking oil, bricks, cement, paddy, even many vegetables and fruit, are brought by bhotbhoti.

In many of the islands furthest south, land cannot be cultivated more than once a year due to lack of fresh water. The river water is salty and of no use for drinking or for irrigating land. Often the only fresh water, other than the rainwater collected in ponds (which is commonly used for drinking after boiling), has to be fetched by boats from islands which have tube-wells. Also, bunds frequently break. This causes the river to engulf houses and cultivated land. When lucky, the islanders are able to reclaim the drowned land back from the river by rapidly erecting, during low tide, a bund around the newly submerged area. However, even when such land is recovered from the river, it remains barren for at least three years. More often than not, it is impossible to retrieve the sunken land and each year hundreds of people leave to seek refuge elsewhere. The geography of these southern islands is literally 'on the move', with the relatively frequent breaking of bunds and disappearance of land on the one hand, and the deposition of silt and appearance of mud sandbars on the other.

This peculiar geography is often cited as an excuse for the lack of effort on the part of the authorities to improve the material conditions of the islanders through programmes such as strengthening bunds, building roads or installing electricity. This is not only because such ventures are costly and difficult to implement but also because of the widespread belief held by those in power that these islands are best 'left to nature'. It is known that tectonic movements between the twelfth and sixteenth century initiated a west-to-east tilting of the Sundarbans, causing the greater part of fresh water to be diverted towards the east. Indeed, the eastern part of the Sundarbans — the part that lies in Bangladesh — supports a more varied vegetation. By contrast, the growing brackishness (further increased since the construction of the Farakka dam) of rivers in WB is a direct threat to the livelihood of those who depend on the rivers as it means a significant decrease in crab, prawn, fish, and certain types of wood.[12] The conclusions of scientists are that these islands should never have been reclaimed and that strengthening the existing bunds will only cause greater environmental degradation. This, however, is also used as an excuse by the various administrative bodies who hope that, by leaving these islands underdeveloped, the inhabitants of the 'down' islands will be encouraged to seek refuge elsewhere. Even social scientists and people deeply committed to working for the welfare of the underprivileged of the area believe that they are fighting a losing battle and that the Sundarbans is best 'returned to tigers'.[13] But which tigers?

'Here in the Sundarbans, the Tigers and us Connive Together'

If in the literature on the region a rather crude opposition is built between tigers and humans it is because the two have never been studied together. A growing body of work shows how people's interactions with animals are not only embedded in their relation to the environment as a practical experience but also as narratives, giving them scope to elaborate on their ideas of the social.[14] This book will highlight the engagement with the actual daily material 'taskscape' (Ingold 1993: 158) as well as elaborate on how symbolic 'representations' (Descola 1996: 85) of tigers as 'non-humans' help explore social relations in the Sundarbans. While drawing on these themes, this will not involve an elaborate unpacking of theories on human/animal relations.[15] Nor will all the relationships people in the Sundarbans have with different kinds of 'non-humans' — a group which is vast and includes crocodiles, snakes and a wide range of 'spirits' and 'demons' — be discussed. The focal point will be the people–tiger relation as a tool to understand both social relations in the WB Sundarbans, and to focus on how tigers have been appropriated into urban literature as one of the most prominent trademarks of global conservation, as well as the absence of humans in the literature on the Sundarbans.

Inspired by Descola's (1996) symbolic approach and Latour's (1993) political angle on the non-human, this book identifies how economy, religion and politics bring about conceptual and ethical changes in the Sundarbans islanders' multiple understandings of tigers and how this impacts on lived and understood 'relatedness'. Deeply entrenched in the way people understand their relatedness to animals is the way they situate themselves in their environment. The inhabitants of the Sundarbans could be called environmental determinists, so strong is their belief that the environment affects them. The relative barrenness of the land (especially in contrast to the rest of Bengal's luxuriant vegetation), the constant threat of losing land and homestead, the violent cyclonic storms, and the lack of potable water, they explain, transform them into short-tempered, irritable and aggressive people. What is interesting, however, is that not only is the environment seen as having the potential of acting on their 'mood' and 'character', but also as having an impact on tigers. Moreover, they see themselves as similarly endowed with the capacity to affect the environment and tigers' natures. For example, the islanders argue that poaching and brutal political dealings 'pollute' and transform the forest into a violent place. Similarly, tigers' natures are said to have changed after the perceived betrayal by the WB government of the underprivileged after the massacre of Morichjhanpi in the late 1970s.

Today, the tiger's image is used to frame moral and ethical debates around wildlife by various transnational animal-centric charities and development agencies like the World Wildlife Fund (WWF) or the Asian Development Bank (ADB) in bids to fund projects. This global 'cosmopolitan' tiger, as opposed to the local 'Sundarbans tiger', has become the rallying point for urbanites' concerns for wildlife protection. By calling attention to two different representations of tigers in recent history, one colonial and the other national, the book highlights how representations, even of wild animals, are ultimately linked to power. Such images perpetrate the coercive and unequal relationship between those who partake of the 'global' tiger view versus those who live with 'wild' tigers. The two pictures cannot be explored separately from each other. The media's glamorous portrayal of the Sundarbans forest is seen by the islanders as potentially jeopardising their very existence in the region. Indeed, throughout the recent history of the Sundarbans, the very presence of people in the region has been seen as a hindrance to its development as a 'natural' haven for wildlife. Present-day discourses such as those on the 'environmentally degrading prawn seed[16] collectors' or the 'thieving locals' are in line with a history of discrimination against the poorest and most marginalised.

Organisation of the Book

This book is divided into seven chapters. Chapters II and III will underscore the specificity of land in the Sundarbans and illustrate how it is the locus of status. The two chapters will introduce the four main communities of the 'down' islands, as described by the islanders — Midnapuri, Muslim, East Bengali, and Adivasi — and their inter-actions with each other around questions of land and forest. This will lead to explanations of social differences at the village level: those of *jati* and *dharmo*, those between 'forest workers' and 'landowners' and between 'gramer lok' and 'bhadralok'. Following local understanding, Chapter II will highlight how the distinctions between people are reflected in the kind of localities they live in and distinguish what is meant by 'up' and 'down'. Chapter III will highlight Sir Daniel Hamilton's vision of establishing a co-operative society in three 'down' islands (Gosaba, Rangabelia and Satjelia) at the beginning of the twentieth century. What is interesting is that the forest fishers of Garjontola saw Hamilton's ideals of a classless society as doomed to fail because they were based on an economy of land — land being seen as inherently corrupting.

Chapter IV will be about the forest and about the ways in which the ethos of the forest is lived out in day-to-day life. It will discuss how forest fishers see themselves and tigers as 'brothers' — representatives of both groups having been adopted by Bonbibi (literally 'the woman of the forest'). Bonbibi is the 'divine power' sent by Allah to protect those who enter the forest. It will also draw attention to how the forest is seen as the realm of Islam and how there is an obligation to equitably distribute the forest products. If the harsh environment of the Sundarbans is to be blamed for their 'cantankerousness' argued the islanders, it is also this environment which brings about an element of 'complicity' between people and tigers and, by extension, between people and people. This connivance is expressed in the way tigers are seen to be invested with human attributes (emotions, feelings, thoughts) and in how the Sundarbans islanders see themselves as sharing the 'bad-temperedness' of tigers. In Bengali, words used were short-tempered (*khitkhite*), aggressive (*hingshro*), easily angered (*ragi*). This sharing of a 'common cantankerous nature' and of complicity will also be explored in forms of relatedness popularly described as 'fictive' kinship — a system which often overrules religious and caste affiliations. I will call it 'elected' kinship.

Chapter V will look at how the islanders situate themselves within the tension between, on the one hand, trusting Bonbibi and tiger charmers and, on the other, having faith in the state's powers of protection. This will be done through a discussion of prawn seed collectors' perceptions of their position vis-à-vis the forest. Unhappy with the ethos of the forest elaborated by the forest fishers who are predominantly middle-aged and male, the prawn seed collectors — by which I mean those who pulled nets along the river's banks (as opposed to those who fished from their boats) — some male but majority female, took up the worship of Kali as they saw in her a deity more appropriate to be the patron of their 'violent' occupation. The contrasting versions of the appropriateness of cosmologies in relation to one's chosen profession will be elaborated via the conundrum caused by a mixed Hindu–Muslim marriage.

The objective of the first part of Chapter VI is to situate the history the islanders believe they share with tigers. Tigers have changed from meek to ferocious animals, argued the islanders, not only because of the harsh environment, but also because of the history they have had to go through. The narration of the tigers' history of migration was interesting because of the parallels it drew with the islanders' own history. The chapter will also underscore how the forest's position as the domain of Islam can be interpreted in relation to historical records about Sufi saints and their 'symbiotic' relations with tigers. The second half of the chapter will underline how representations of the Sundarbans which portray it as a biosphere reserve fit only for tigers are challenged by the islanders. For them, such an image is propagated to jeopardise any real commitment on the part of the state, well-wishing NGOs or bhadralok citizens to recognise that the gramer lok might have aspirations and needs for greater social justice. The riverside islanders feel that they are wrongly blamed for the environmental ills of the Sundarbans; in this context, their version of the bloody story of Morichjhanpi and their belief that tigers radically changed after this episode and became 'uncontrollable' man-eaters, takes enormous importance. Through this narrative, the islanders voiced their fears about being, for the state, mere 'tiger food' — that is, dispensable citizens — while tigers had become, through the various programmes on the part of the government to increase their numbers, 'first-class citizens'.

Chapter VII, 'Unmasking the Cosmopolitan Tiger', explores issues around different representations (colonial, national) of tigers in recent history and how such representations are ultimately linked to power. This allows one to challenge a 'scientificity' which identifies the Sundarbans tiger as 'man-eater' and questions a 'science' which seems to be used as an instrument for establishing both state rule and international conservation agencies' hegemony, especially when 'scientific reasons' are comforting justifications for the lack of any master plan for the inhabited part of the Sundarbans. Are today's Western-dominated ideas about tigers — those that do not allow an engagement with alternative ways of understanding animals and wildlife — ultimately causing the death of the more local tiger?

Chapter VIII looks at the extent to which tigers 'are good to think with', à la Descola, and reflects on what it means for the islanders that their region should be a 'World Heritage Site'. Through the contrasting images of fishermen being evicted from Jambudwip on the one hand and the Sahara India Group's advertisement of their project on 'virgin islands' on the other, I look at the current implications (continuing from the past), for the islanders of the Sundarbans, of the oft-repeated phrase that humans do not or should not fit in the Sundarbans.

Entering the Field (and the Forest)

My first encounter with the Sundarbans occurred when I was eight. My mother had taken us to meet friends who lived on the island of Basanti — the most important of the 'down' islands where there were a few training centres, high schools and a hospital. The family we stayed with consisted of a grandmother, her two sons, her two daughters-in-law and their respective daughters, who were my age. We had come for the winter break and I remember being able to run wild, play and swim with other village children, and also spend many nights watching plays. The ones I recall best were those with stories of goddesses coming down to earth to collect worshippers and the tribulations they faced in the process. There was Manasa, who protected against snakes, Shitala, who saved from smallpox, Behula, not really a goddess but who was just as popular, as well as characters from the Puranas and the Bible which were sung about when a person died and were called Hori-nam or Jishu-kirtan respectively. However, the story I liked best was that of Bonbibi, the woman of the forest, who came to earth not to gather devotees but because she was sent by Allah to save people from tigers. I remember that a part of the family we were living with were Hindus and the other half Christians. I also remember that during the big religious occasions, both sides of the family celebrated the relevant deity. These memories started to stir up questions only years later. In 1996, while studying Bengali literature in Paris, I was shown a text by my professor, France Bhattacharya which urged people to worship the Hindu Dokkhin Rai and the Muslim Gazi Khan together as they were only different expressions of the same God. In the context of the Ayodhya riots and the dangerously growing communal tensions between communities in South Asia, my childhood memories started engendering unsettling questions.

For most of my childhood, I had lived in the professionally and economically mixed locality of Howrah, which is on the opposite side of the river Hooghly from Kolkata. Some of our neighbours were fishers, and some of them were from the Sundarbans. One of them was a fisherman working in the Sundarbans and from him I came to learn about tigers and life in the forest. Some time in 1982, his nine-year-old nephew Toofan came to live with his family. Toofan and I became playmates as we were the same age. I eventually came to know of how his uncle had adopted him, as his father had been killed by a tiger, and his mother had died in the violent 1981 cyclone. From them, and my father and his colleagues who were involved in building cyclone shelters in the Sundarbans, I heard about the island of Morichjhanpi and how the East Bengali refugees who had gone to settle there had been ruthlessly evicted on the grounds that they were contravening the Forest Acts. It was my neighbour who had first said, 'You know, tigers seem to have become more important than us people now'.

All through my growing years, the Sundarbans would appear from time to time in newspapers. Always in the form of a tiny snippet: a woodcutter who had been killed by a tiger, an area destroyed after it was hit by a cyclone, the collapse of a bund or an embankment and how this had caused the homelessness of a few hundred families. I remember receiving a book published by the Children's Book Trust called *The Man from Sundarbans*. It was about a naive and courageous man from the Sundarbans who, after having been saved by a forest official, had shown his gratitude by becoming his man-Friday. After a few episodes in Kolkata where he was duped into parting with his money, into believing that the Victoria Memorial was Indraprastha (the city of the gods) and the women he saw there were *apsaras* (nymph-like semi-divine creatures found in the city of the gods), he accompanied his master back to the Sundarbans where he helped him expose an evil tiger-charmer and saved his life from a band of poachers. His debt to his master and to civilisation now repaid, he leaves his master's launch (an enclave of bhadralok sociality) and returns 'to the forest unable to resist its call'. For a Kolkata child this was tremendously exotic and I imagined that beyond the island where I had spent my holidays lay the 'wild' people of this book.

In the late 1980s, articles by various experts were published in the leading Kolkata newspapers which debated whether the Sundarbans tigers were 'natural' man-eaters.[17] The high numbers of islanders killed by tigers was a fact no one could ignore. But the reasons why tigers were seen to prefer humans to animals such as deer and monkey were the subject of long, acrimonious debates between natural scientists, various experts and wildlife conservationists from all over the world. Here it was not Jim Corbett's old man-eaters of Kumaon attacking humans out of desperation, but young tigers seeking out humans by swimming over to villages and lifting people off boats.[18]

Some experts argued that the Sundarbans tiger's man-eating propensity was caused by the increasing brackishness of the rivers. They argued that this transformation forced Sundarbans tigers to depend on the 'sweetness' of human blood to obtain a certain dietary balance. Others added that, because the tide washes away the boundaries of the territory that the tiger marks with its urine, the Sundarbans tigers have no idea what constitutes a specific territory and that this is why they swim into villages and kill people and cattle. The inordinately aggressive character of the Sundarbans tigers might also be because they have to keep swimming for hours to stay afloat when the tide is in. The difficulty I had in those days in trying to separate 'natural' reasons from 'unnatural' ones has remained to this day.

In 1988, I had occasion to visit the Sundarbans again. This time it was while attending a 'Nature Study Camp' with my high school. We lodged in the only tourist spot of those days, which was the government-run guest house on the forested island of Sajnekhali. In those days, in order to combat the tiger's predilection for human flesh, the government had devised ruses such as electrified dummies placed in strategic spots in the forest, digging fresh-water ponds deep inside the jungle (to 'sweeten' the nature of tigers) and issuing masks free of charge to the islanders. The masks were given on the assumption that, as the tiger normally attacks from behind, they should be worn on the back of the head; this would puzzle the tiger who, seeing another pair of eyes peering out at him, would abandon the idea of preying on that person. Their foolproof status was guaranteed by scientists, who commended the government highly for its widespread distribution of masks to the islanders. I remember the guards enthusiastically showing us the masks while enumerating their merits. Intrigued by them and already convinced of their infallibility, a friend and I had asked if we could venture out of the tightly fenced sanctuary wearing masks to watch wildlife out in the open. The only places we had been allowed entry were the watchtowers of the sanctuary. The sanctuary itself was enclosed within grilled netting, like a big cage with an open roof (only we were inside the cage).

Slightly surprised by our keenness to explore the forest with the masks on, the forest guards explained that the forest was forbidden to us and there was no question of our being allowed to step outside the wildlife sanctuary without a dozen guards armed to the teeth. We argued that we had been told by the experts that the official thirty or so tiger victims of the previous year had all been islanders who had been too superstitious to wear the masks and that we should be allowed out as we weren't superstitious. Suddenly realising that the guards never moved without their rifles and thick plastic torso shields, even when straying barely 50 m away from the gates of the sanctuary, my friend cheekily suggested that they should start wearing masks and pointed out how that might convert the islanders to accepting them. The guards' response was that the masks wouldn't work for us, as we were 'healthy' kids, nor for them, because tigers were used to seeing them with rifles and wouldn't fear them if they wore masks. This bizarre, convoluted explanation triggered my first tentative steps towards questioning the validity of a 'scientific mask', which is supposed to work for the village folk or gramer lok but not for forest guards and plump Kolkata high school children.

A few weeks after this trip, on 29 November 1988, the Sundarbans was affected by one of the strongest cyclones ever to hit the area. This cyclone officially killed thousands — the majority from the southern islands of the Sundarbans — and damaged crops worth Rs 83 crore. Some people I had met on the Nature Study Camp and the vice-director of the Tiger Project, Barun Sengupta, whom we had met and who had gone there for the tiger census (which takes place every second winter), were killed. Afraid of being swept off, those who had been taken by surprise by the cyclone while still outside had crawled back home or had held on to trees; those who hadn't were blown or swept away. The next day the few branches of those trees which were still standing, and the rivers, were littered with corpses of humans and animals. The houses seemed to have been cut horizontally into two, the top half lying kilometres away.[19] As I had been there barely a few weeks before, the violence and devastation of this cyclone remained deeply etched in my memory. What was even more shocking was to see how, even after this disastrous cyclone, the Irrigation Department (the government body responsible for the condition of embankments and bunds) subsequently did not bother to devote a single page of the budget proposal to the problem of bunding or land erosion in the Sundarbans. In October 1999 I witnessed similar indifference when, a couple of months into my fieldwork, a 'super-cyclone' was announced to be heading towards the Sundarbans. The only precautionary measure the government undertook was to dispatch three motorised boats to Sagar island — one of the more prosperous islands — as relief; nothing was sent to the poorer islands in the south-eastern part of WB. The cyclone got deflected to Orissa and killed 20,000 people there.

In the light of what I knew about state negligence and buoyed by the writings of Guha (1989a, 1989b), Peluso (1992), Scott (1985, 1998), Sivaramakrishnan (1995, 1999) and Tsing (1993). I was keen to learn about peoples' resistance to state policies on conservation. I had many questions: How did the islanders perceive tigers and explain the disparity between the amount of public money spent on forested islands versus that spent on the inhabited islands? How did the islanders make a living in the dangerous and difficult locale they lived in? In our increasingly dividing world, was Bonbibi's story still narrated? How 'shared' were the beliefs about Bonbibi? I was also very keen to learn, after all these years, what had been the reasons behind the islanders' refusal to wear the masks that had been so generously distributed by the government. This study is not only a record of 'dialogical' encounters; it is also to a certain extent based on a childhood fascination for a region, sustained by years of collection of newspaper articles and bits of information from people who had links to the Sundarbans.

Katy Gardner, in her narrations of fieldwork experiences, highlights how fieldwork, usually in some far-flung location, is anthropology's centrepiece, the ultimate transformative experience through which students of the discipline must pass if they are to call themselves anthropologists (1991: 49). Though the island of the Sundarbans where I went to live for my fieldwork was in a far-flung location, the place had an air of familiarity, one that had roots in my childhood bucolic holidays. I spoke the language and knew the codes of proper behaviour, and often met people who had known me as a child.

When I went to do fieldwork, the island where I had spent some of my holidays had become an 'up' place where people were not going to the forest on a regular basis. My mother's friend had moved, like many successful Sundarbans islanders, to the suburbs of Kolkata. I wanted to stay in a new place. This is when, in the first month of fieldwork while still in Kolkata, I came across a weekly column called 'Gramer diary' (village diary) on life in the Sundarbans written by Tushar Kanjilal and published in the Bengali daily *Aajkaal*. Kanjilal was famous for having started, with his wife, an offshoot of the NGO Tagore Society for Rural Development (TSRD) in the Sundarbans in the late 1970s. When his wife was still alive, they had both been living and working there as school teachers and social workers relentlessly raising public consciousness towards improving the socio-economic conditions of the area. I was very eager to meet him. He generously invited me and suggested that I meet his health workers who came twice a month to his NGO on the island of Rangabelia and who were from the villages situated 'at the tiger's lair'.

The first women's health meeting after my arrival happened to take place in Garjontola. I accompanied a group of women from Rangabelia. We arrived at one of the NGO's health workers' houses situated directly opposite the forest. Our hostess Maloti was the contact point of the NGO for that area. Her husband Hori soon returned from the forest bearing crabs and Maloti proceeded to cook them. On my way back, reminiscing over the delicious meal, the empathy and confidence with which Maloti, a woman in her mid-thirties, had spoken to her neighbours who had gathered for the meeting and the gentle ease with which she had included me, an urbanite from Kolkata, in her distribution of household tasks, I asked the two women I was accompanying if they thought Maloti would be terribly inconvenienced if I were to settle in her place for a few months. Maloti generously accepted and when I returned I started living with Maloti, her husband Hori and their three teenaged sons.

Maloti soon adopted me into her family as a younger sister and I gradually entered the vaster web of kinship with the islanders and the more specific responsibility of being an 'aunt' to her three sons. As she worked for the TSRD as a health worker, she regularly conducted surveys in her village as well as on other islands. While I lived there, cut off from the world except for a radio (which only gave Bangladesh or Kolkata news), she would be the one updating me on what was happening in the *desh* — the 'country', by which she meant the Sundarbans islands. Her self-assured yet non-obtrusive health advice made her a very popular person in that part of the Sundarbans and I benefited enormously from her advice, comments and our conversations.

When I arrived, the local high school's English teacher had just left for a few months' training and the headmaster graciously suggested I become part of his team of dedicated teachers. I taught there twice a week for three hours for about six months. This work plunged me into being a person with bona fide reasons to be in the Sundarbans instead of a detached, impersonal researcher. Later, when the missing teacher returned, I was happy to spend more time accompanying the forest fishers on their forays and Maloti on some of her visits around neighbouring islands. I was also warmly invited to attend various literary meetings where I read out papers I had written and in general became, to use Marcus' words, the sort of 'circumstantial activist' who is questioning and renegotiating identities in different sites (1995: 115).

Notes

1. 'Sundarbans' is the anglicised version of the Bengali *shundor* (beautiful) and *bon* (forest); the region could also have got its name after the sundari tree (*Heritiera fomes*). There are different transliterations of the word in English — Yule and Burnell write it as *sunderbunds* as they believed that the etymology of *bund* lay in 'embankment' or 'mound' and not in 'forest' (1903: 869). The 'beautiful forest' notion is probably a retroformation, created by current valuations of forests under a pervasive ecological romanticism; it seems that 'indigeneous perceptions were closer to *jungal* than *ban*' (Herring 1990: 5, in Danda 2007: 28).

2. Following common practice, when referring to the forest the plural will be used and when the region, the singular; *jongol* means 'forest' or 'jungle' and *abad* the reclaimed Sundarbans islands. When I refer to the Sundarbans, I am referring mainly to the WB part of the Sundarbans region unless specified otherwise. Between 1829 and 1830 the forested littoral was surveyed and delineated as a special forest cover by Com-missioner Mr Dampier and Surveyor Lieutenant Hodges and its boundary called the Dampier-Hodges line after them. Of the twenty-two Blocks of the South 24 Parganas District in WB, eight Blocks fall within its boundary. One has to add here that in Bangladesh the 'Sundarbans' refers only to the remaining forest and not to the erstwhile region of the Sundarbans as delimited by the Dampier-Hodges line.

3. This bleak situation persists despite the fact that a specialised agency — the Sundarbans Development Board (SDB) — was created in 1973 to increase the socio-economic development of the area. It was initially under the Planning Department of the Govt. of WB; in 1994, to enhance its outreach, the SDB was placed directly under the state minister-in-charge of the newly created Sundarbans Affairs Department (SAD) (Danda 2007: 4–5).

4. The apt title of acclaimed writer Amitav Ghosh's recent novel on the region.

5. 'The sight of potentially fertile land lying wild and idle was an affront to the progressive-minded revenue officers of the Bengal Civil Service' (Richards and Flint 1990: 20, in Danda 2007: 3).

6. In 1865, F. Schiller even offered to import labour from China, Madras and Zanzibar to reclaim all the remaining wasteland of the Sundarbans (De 1990: 17).

7. For census-taking reasons, the entire Sundarbans region was partitioned and assigned to the administrative districts of 24 Parganas, Jessore and Bakarganj. Jessore and Bakarganj are today in Bangladesh, the 24 Parganas were further divided into North and South in 1983.

8. The Arakan/Marma are called *Mog* in Bengali. The term has a negative connotation because it evokes an association with piracy. James Rennell (1742–1830), geographer and marine engineer, explored the Bengal river basins and mapped them for the first time. Rennell was employed with the special objective of finding a shorter passage suitable for large vessels from the Bay of Bengal to old Calcutta. His daily journal gives a detailed account of his expedition through the delta where he records how he was repeatedly attacked by tigers, reptiles, dacoits, and 'hostile people'. His *Atlas of Bengal* (1761) was acclaimed in commercial, military and administrative quarters and remained important until professional maps were made available in the mid-nineteenth century. Sheet no. XX of his *Atlas* marks the entire Bakarganj district as a country whose population has been wiped out by the Arakanese pirates. Bernier, a French traveller who passed through the Sundarbans in the mid-1600s, mentions them as the 'Corsaires Franguys de Rakan' (1891: 442).

9. See the book by Nandi and Misra (1987) devoted to the bibliography of the Sundarbans, where most of its entries are in reference to flora and fauna. Notable exceptions to this trend are O'Malley (1914), Mitra (1963); De (1990); Niyogi (1997); Banerjee (1998); Kanjilal (2000); Mondol (2007); Danda (2007); and the conference organised by the Smithsonian Institute on the Bangladesh Sundarbans (1987).

10. The Sundarbans are often called *tatbhhoomi*: *tat* refers to the bank of a river or sea, and *bhoomi* to the earth or land; in the local dialect it means 'sunken land' or the 'land of the sea-coast'. It is also called *atharo bhatir desh* — the land of the eighteen ebb-tides — and also *bhardesh*, *astadash*, *rashatal*, *patal*, *paundrabardhan*, *gangaridi*.

11. The distribution of water is not as schematic as presented here. During the highest tides every twelve days (*bharani*) the rivers have more water than usual, when gradually the waters recede rivers which are usually full are bereft of water (*morani*). Some rivers called *duania* are horizontal and always full as they have water flowing in from both sides at both high tide and low tide.

12. The most famous example of a decrease in certain types of wood is the near disappearance, especially from the WB part of the Sundarbans, of the *sundari* tree.

13. 'Unfortunately, before the normal delta building process could proceed further, human beings started interfering with the natural environment. In this premature stage of land formation, the normal geomorphic processes proved to be completely incompatible with the prospect of Human Settlement. Since priority and immediacy prevailed over futuristic desires, nature had to be tamed, environment changed and ecology disrupted, to meet the requirements of the human habitation' (Banerjee 1998: 31). Pannalal Dasgupta (pers. comm. May 1996), a highly esteemed leftist activist turned Gandhian, who devoted most of his life towards improving the conditions of

the poor, also voiced the belief that people in the Sundarbans were fighting a losing battle and that the islands were best 'returned to tigers'.

14. See works by Franklin 1999, 2002; Rival (1996); Bird-David (1992a, 1992b, 1999); Descola (1992, 1996); and Ingold (1993).

15. The different approaches reflect key trends in the study of social analysis: these include concerns such as the relation between anthropology and colonialism and the construction of race, class and gender identities. See studies by Mullin (1999); Shanklin (1994); Ohnuki-Tierney (1987); and Ritvo (1987).

16. This refers to the hatchlings of 'tiger prawn' — scientific name *Penaeus monodon* — which is the most delicate in taste and largest Indian marine paneid prawn to be farmed. It is called *bagda* in Bengali. To facilitate reading, I shall refer to the tiger prawn hatchlings (which are usually at the postlarval stage PL 20, 9–14 mm) as 'prawn seed', even though the literature also refers to them as 'shrimp', 'post-larvae', 'juveniles' or 'seedlings'. I also use 'shrimp' and 'prawn' interchangeably.

17. Chowdhury and Sanyal (1985a, 1985b), Chakrabarti (1986), Rishi (1988) (to name a few) who all accept the findings of the first study of its kind which was undertaken by Hendrichs in 1975.

18. Jim Corbett (1875–1955), a famous hunter turned conservationist, wrote many exciting accounts of tracking and hunting man-eaters in the Kumaon region of the lower Himalayas. In his famous *Man-eaters of Kumaon* (1946) he argues that tigers are not born man-eaters but only become so with age or when struck with a disability.

19. I am very grateful to Nazes Afroz, who was then present in the Sundarbans to report on the progress of the tiger census, for having shared his first-hand experience of the cyclone and its aftermath.

II

The Village and the Forest

At last I was on my way back to the Sunderbans, this time as an anthropologist conducting fieldwork on the island of Satjelia, and to one of the southern-most inhabited islands. I would stay in a one-room hut next to Maloti's place in Garjontola, an area of Toofankali village. Travelling to Garjontola takes about seven to eight hours from Kolkata, which is about 130 km away. The first stage was a three-hour bus journey to the southern extremity of mainland WB — Shonakhali. Already I had passed from the 'stable delta' to the active delta, and had travelled from the north of the District of South 24 Parganas towards its south. Now, standing on the stepped quays of Shonakhali, opposite the island of Basanti, childhood memories of the Sundarbans returned, especially of Basanti itself. The little strip of river between the two jetties marks a huge rupture: once you crossed over, you were cut off from the mainland, forced to drink water with a salty edge, travel on cycle-vans and know that you had entered a time zone ruled by tides and the timings of passenger boats. Yet, at the same time the coming and going of boats leaving the jetty and heading towards Basanti was a continuation, an extension of the mainland and its broad tarred road, urging me onwards.

The place feels criss-crossed by different lines of communication projecting in different directions, propelling one into great lengths of travel. Buses leaving from Kolkata call out 'Basanti' or have 'Basanti' written on their windows when technically they are going to Shonakhali; at Basanti, autorickshaw or cycle-van drivers do not call out 'Godkhali' which is at the end of the Basanti island but 'Gosaba', which is the next destination by boat. Similarly, at Gosaba, cycle-vans call out 'Pakhiralay' and 'Dayapur' and not 'Arampur'. It seems as if the limits of an island, ever susceptible to disappearance are never really demarcated by their own perimeter, but rather by the edges of islands lying right across.

Coming in the other direction, if a traveller got off at Shonakhali jetty and walked towards the bus stand and caught a bus, she would be driven 'up' towards Kolkata, Sonarpur, Jadavpur, and the other places which stood for urbanity and middle-class civility. If she headed for the Basanti jetty and its boats then she was pumped 'down' towards a geography of shared cycle-vans and autorickshaws heading for Mahespur, Jharkhali or Godkhali, or towards the extremities of Basanti island from where she could take boats again and journey further towards the more remote islands of Gosaba, Pakhiralay — or Satjelia, my destination.

The river, and its jetties at Basanti, not only thrusts the traveller in or out of the Sundarbans but also allows one to branch east or west along its watery channels. From Basanti you can take a trip over the Gomor then the Matla towards the faraway ports of Sagar, Haldia and Cuttak in the west or travel via Harinbhanga and Raymongol to the border islands of the east and even, if one has the nerve, all the way to Bangladesh. Basanti allows one to imagine an illegal but possible voyage via the banned core forest towards the south, beyond the deep dark mangroves, until one would leave the grey and brown rivers of the forest and reach the vast expanse of the bottomless blue sea of the Bay of Bengal.

Basanti's centrality to the islanders' understanding of geography was what positioned their respective islands along a scale of 'up' and 'down'. Those English words encapsulated the islanders' notions of both geographical and social positionalities. If an island happened to be easily reachable from Basanti then it was an 'up' place (albeit 'down' in comparison to Basanti) but if it was difficult to access, or far from Basanti, then it was termed 'down' or even, like for those islands cursed with little convenience of access and no fresh water, 'downer down' (lowest of the low). One of the main indicators of social status in the Sundarbans is therefore where one lives. This is why, in the hierarchy of geographical locations, the worst place one could choose to settle on are the peripheries of islands adjoining the forest, in the downer down or at the gate of 'the tiger's lair'.

The inhabitants of Basanti naturally took great pride in being from there — seeing themselves as living in the perfect zone between places 'up' and 'down' arguing that they were better than Canning, considered 'up' by islands such as Patankhali and Gosaba, Basanti's immediate, albeit weaker rivals. They even went so far as to say that the inhabitants of these rival islands actually envied their position more than that of those living more 'up' places such as Canning because of their fresh air and the reputation that their women were less 'corrupt' than those of Canning. The reason is because Canning, being the last stop on the train line from Kolkata, is of course an envied place. When travelling from Kolkata, up to Canning, this can be done in style. But beyond Canning, and especially when the tide is low, men have to strip waist-down and women have to hitch up their sarees to their hips in order to be able to cross the fast-flowing Matla river (see photo number 7 on page 107). It is understandable why the objective of those who are successful is to move to the next stage of 'up' from wherever they live. Those who, like the school teachers, have a salaried job buy a plot of land in the suburbs of Kolkata; the others content themselves with buying land 'inside' (*bhetore*), either in the interior of their own island or on another one.

The islanders of Basanti believed that their island is the un-challenged centre because their river, if not as broad as the Matla, was always deep enough for boats to ply on. So they felt their river provided the dependable link connecting the great divide between the mainland and the Sundarbans. Basanti also prides itself as being a better-off down island because it has hospitals, missionary schools, NGOs, and university teachers. Besides, it is one of the oldest islands even though part of the 'active delta' as opposed to the more northern islands, some of which have now become part of the mainland called the 'stable delta'. By contrast, the geography of the southern islands is literally 'on the move', with the relatively frequent breaking of bunds, the sudden disappearance of land from one end of an island and the depositing of silt or the appearance of mud sandbars at the other.

Despite their apparent disconnectedness the cultivated or *abad* islands of the Sundarbans are not little monads. In fact, they seem like puzzle pieces all fitted into each other through rivers — drawing in the tiniest of islands into a vast web of connectedness. In the same way, within each island, the Sundarbans roads tie hamlets to each other: tarred and brick roads lead to the more important spaces such as market-places and schools, and beyond these lie smaller brick roads which in turn direct one to mud paths which finally split into tiny little dirt tracks separating fields and leading to the huts of those who, either through their own choice, or that of others, live away from the rest of the village. These modest huts, rising from the fields on their mud platforms, are accessible only through tiny paths, paths so narrow that at times one feels like a trapeze artist walking on a tightrope strung in the middle of rice-fields. Hidden between what appears like endless miles of fields and beyond the unrelenting intricacies of tidal rivers, little paths and tiny boats carry the traveller all the way to the smallest of mud homes.

Satjelia Island

Eventually I reached my destination, the island of Satjelia, shaped like a heart and one of the southern-most inhabited islands of the WB Sundarbans; indeed, one of the last islands to have been reclaimed and inhabited. Part of Hamilton's 'Gosaba Block' of islands, Satjelia nestles between the populated islands of Gosaba to the west, Rangabelia to the northwest, Mollakhali to the north and Kumirmari to the northeast. Directly to the southwest lies the forest island of Sajnekhali which houses the famous Sajnekhali wildlife sanctuary. Bordering directly on the forest, Satjelia ranks, in the hierarchy of geographical locations, in the downer down or at the gate of the tiger's lair. But this does not mean that it is completely isolated. The Pathar river, flowing along the south of Garjontola (the area of Toofankhali village where I stayed), connects the islanders to the more important channels of communication, which are the rivers Raymangal, Durgaduani, Bidya, and Matla. Garjontola is served by a bhotbhoti which carries people and merchandise daily to and from Gosaba island. It leaves every morning at 6 a.m. from Lahiripur, at the extreme east end of Satjelia island, and travels west to Gosaba, the administrative headquarters of Gosaba Block (of which Satjelia is part). The boat reaches Gosaba at noon and takes the reverse route home each evening.

I lived in the Garjontola locality of Toofankhali village on a more or less continuous basis for nineteen months between August 1999 and February 2001 and again briefly, for a couple of weeks each time, every year between 2002 and 2009 (see map 3). I lived in a hut next to the river and directly opposite the forest as a member of Maloti and Hori's household. Their relatives — both blood and elected kin — included landowners, forest workers and prawn seed collectors, the three main occupational groups described here. The inhabitants of Toofankhali were mainly Bengali Hindus whose forefathers had come from Koyra-Bedkashi, a Sundarbans region of the then eastern wing of Bengal in the late 1920s and 1930s. The Sundarbans area divisions have, from zamindar days, been referred to as 'lots' and people generally refer to their 'lot number' rather than the name of their village.[1] Also, the village is usually more of an administrative unit than a social one. So 'Toofankhali', a village of about 3,500 inhabitants, is usually referred to by its lot number.

The houses of Garjontola run along the river in the south, along the road leading to the interior of the island in the west, along the bazaar road in the north, and those to the west of Duttapara in the east, forming a rectangle (see map 3). To the west of the village lies Annpur, peopled chiefly by East Bengalis of the Malo fisher caste and by Adivasis. The mud track on the east of Garjontola runs parallel to the Duttar canal, which enters deep into the island. On the eastern side of this track lies Duttapara where many relatives of the inhabitants of Garjontola live, along with Adivasis. The mud track to the north of Garjontola separates the area from Mriddhapara, a locality composed mainly of landowners. This track leads to Hatkhola, one of the more important commercial centres of the island. It is a place with only about twenty shacks and shops, a couple of doctors' surgeries, and no houses. If dead for most of the week, Hatkhola suddenly teems with excitement on Fridays, when people throng in from kilometres around for the weekly bazaar.

The whole Garjontola rectangle represents 975 people and 209 households; it is inhabited mainly along its edges, with the centre left nearly bare, with fields and some small water tanks. The total population of the island of Satjelia is 42,000 and its area is 152,000 acres (about 615 sq. kms). This is very low in comparison to the rest of WB: According to the 2001 census, WB is the most densely populated state of India with a population of 8 crore, which means 904 people per sq. km.

About half the households of Garjontola consist of only four or five members and nearly a fourth consist of only one to three members. Even if different households sometimes live on the same broad homestead or *bhite*, they are usually nuclear. The marriage pattern is virilocal, with wives usually coming to live in their husbands' homes. However, young men, once married, rarely share cooking units with their parents or brothers. The only two generations that usually live together are parents and their unmarried children. People who lose their spouses usually live alone. In certain situations, however, a family unit may be recreated along the lines of the following example . When I was in Garjontola a widow in her early thirties was sharing a hut with her brother-in-law who was about the same age as her, was unmarried and had a leg affected by polio. He supported her and her two school-going teenage children by organising private tuition classes for the neighbouring children, and she cooked for him. Sometimes old people also live with their grandchildren or great-grandchildren to 'keep them company' until they have children of their own. Old or widowed people, young married couples, divorced or separated men or women (who elsewhere in rural Bengal are usually attached to a household headed by a male figure), all cook and live in their own huts.

Most children below the age of ten go to primary school. At secondary school level, half of them drop out of school to work as prawn seed collectors (see later in this chapter) or in people's fields; at this age they rarely work as forest fishers (see later in this chapter). Marriages take place between the ages of sixteen and twenty-three for most women and eighteen to thirty for most men. One of the important conditions when marriages are being arranged is that it should be with someone not living in the same village. Marrying somebody from within the village is seen as incestuous and is usually avoided. Young women work as prawn seed collectors both before and after marrying. The young men work either in the forest, or in big landowners' fields, or leave the village to work as labourers in the suburbs of Kolkata, North 24 Parganas or Uttar Pradesh, and even as far away as the Andaman Islands. These migrations are usually undertaken for six to eight months annually, and often over a period of two to five years. When the men come back (usually with money), they get married and construct a boat, invest in big nets for prawn seed collection, and build their own hut — either on their parents' homestead, or on that of a neighbour or an 'elected kin' (more on this in the next chapter). Most young married couples do not have automatic access to their parents' land. They have to help in the process of sowing and reaping for a share of the crops, so usually the main part of their income is made from prawn seed collection/dealing or, for the more intrepid ones, the forest.

The vast majority of the inhabitants of Garjontola are, as they prefer to call themselves, 'SC' (for Scheduled Caste), while the other communities they closely interact with are the 'ST' (Scheduled Tribe), the 'OBC' (Other Backward Caste) and Muslims.[2] The SCs are mainly of East Bengali origin and belong to the Pod and Namasudra castes (considered two of the lowest groups in the Brahminical hierarchy of castes).[3] The STs are mainly of Oraon and Munda origin, from Chotanagpur, and the OBCs are of Midnapuri origin. The islanders understand these categories as based on jati and usually maintain the jati through separate religious customs, food habits, house architecture, and marriages, which are usually between people of the same caste and socio-economic level. The Bengali term 'jati' is used especially, like 'caste', to mean 'genus', 'kind' or 'ethnic groups'. It can also encompass other collective identities, such as religion, regional affiliation and gender.

Social hierarchy, however, allies jati differences with those of economic and social status. Economic status, in the Sundarbans (as probably in most parts of rural Bengal) is mainly derived from land and/or from holding a government job (usually one accompanies the other). Generally, landowners have the political contacts or the means to pay the heavy bribe needed to get their sons or daughters a government job as a school teacher or a clerk and those who get such jobs receive salaries which permit them to buy land. Social status is conferred by one's level of education. Landowners and 'service holders' (those with government jobs) are usually educated, as they have the material means to obtain primary and secondary schooling. The prawn businessmen, even though they are increasingly well-off, lack social status because many of them have never gone through any kind of formal education, even at the primary level. The lowest on the scale of both economic and social status are those who work in the forest. In Toofankhali, the majority of the islanders are roughly from the same castes.

While people of different castes at times live alongside each other, there are very few instances of people of varying economic and social statuses living together. The salaried, businessmen and landowners who are SC, ST, OBC, Brahmin, and Muslim and who live on the school road of Garjontola, for example, participate to a certain extent in each others' social and religious ceremonies but are reluctant to attend the ceremonies organised by their poorer relatives who live beside the river. Nor do they live next to those who work in the forest even when they are from the same blood family. The village is geographically divided into two main socio-economic groups — those living in the south on the edge of the river (where I stayed) who work as forest fishers or in the prawn industry (collectors, dealers and businessmen), and those who live along the road which leads to the school and are wealthy and landed and therefore have status. I will often refer to these two groups as, on the one hand, the 'riverside people', 'people from the river's edge' (*nodir kuler lok*) or 'village people' (gramer lok) and, on the other hand, the 'people from the locality of the school' (*iskoolparar lok* — i.e., those who live along the school) or the 'bhadralok'.

Bhadralok and *Gramer Lok*

The term 'bhadralok' ('gentle-folk') comes from *bhadra*, translatable as a mix of 'polite', 'civil' and 'cultured', that is, bearing resonances of middle-class sensitivity to culture and refinement, and *lok* which is 'group' or 'people'. 'Bhadralok' carries connotations not only of landed wealth but also of education, culture and anglicisation and of upper-caste exclusiveness (Chatterji 1994: 5). It refers to the rentier class who enjoyed tenurial rights to rents from land appropriated by the Permanent Settlement. This was a class that did not work its land but lived off the rental income generated. Shunning manual labour, the bhadralok maintain their status by keeping a careful social distance between themselves and the *nimnoborgo* (social inferiors) or the *nimnoborno* (literally meaning 'inferior colour' and denoting 'inferior caste'). 'Nimnoborgo' or 'nimnoborno' denote those belonging to occupational castes considered of low status such as leather workers, liquor dealers, boatmen or fishermen, that is, those who were classified as 'Untouchables' in British Bengal. Though Joya Chatterji (in her seminal book *Bengal Divided* [1994]) refers to them as *chhotolok* — literally 'small people', I refrain from using this word as it is a derogatory term commonly used as a term of abuse (e.g., as in the sentence, *'erokom chotoloker moton byabohar korcho keno?'* — 'why are you behaving like a mean-spirited person?').

The village bhadralok, however, do not refer to the fishers with these class- and caste-connoted terms but with the neutral term of gramer lok — 'villagers', literally 'village people'. This latter term, when used exclusively for one's non-literate counterpart, is a demonstration both of one's superior learning or education and one's distance from those involved in 'rural occupations' such as river or sea fishing, or working as a cultivator or in the forest. The educated and landed elite are usually addressed by the title *'Babu'*, seen as a badge of bhadralok status and commonly used as a term of respect all over WB when addressing a Hindu social superior. The riverside people usually add Babu to the first names of the male school teachers as a sign of respect; however, they call the women of these households by the customary kinship terms used all over Bengal for non-kin people. Because I am educated and from the city I was considered a social superior and Hori (my host) sometimes gently poked fun at me by calling me 'Annubabu'. This was a play on the word 'babu', a marker of distinction and in my case a gender reversal to mark hierarchy, as well as a term meaning baby or small child. This is often what he complained I was, with my unending questions and curious ways.

The terms 'gramer lok' and 'bhadralok/babulok' are never used in direct address between the two groups, nor do they refer to themselves in these terms. However, when talking about the other group, especially in a derogatory fashion, the islanders often use these terms. Otherwise they talk of each other as 'people from the river's edge' or 'people from the locality of the school'. I also often heard people refer to the first group as 'those who live *nodir dhare* (along the river), or disdainfully as *chorer lok* (people from the sandbars), versus those who live along important roads/paths or jetties and are the *bawrolok* (rich) or the 'babulok'. In other words, social hierarchy in Garjontola is mainly along the lines of whether one is, on the one hand, a forest worker or prawn seed collector or, on the other hand, a landowner and/or government service holder, and usually what you were was directly measurable by the amount of dirt, mud and sludge you were exposed to whilst travelling from your occupation to your home.

To conclude, in Garjontola, the framing of community consciousness is articulated mainly along a gramer lok/bhadralok divide — a divide which, as we shall see, is expressed through local narratives of tigers and rooted in practical experiences of the forest. What will be demonstrated is how economic and social differences are linked to occupations which have different experiences of forest and land as well as dissimilar socio-religious worldviews. The islanders imagine their interactions with each other around the symbolisms of land and forest through narratives about tigers.

The next section offers a brief description of this land/forest opposition in relation to the three key occupations that are discussed in this book.

The Three Main Socio-Economic Groups

The nature of the distinction between forest and land relates to the fact that those islanders who work in the forest and along its rivers risk losing their life to wild animals: tigers, crocodiles, sharks, snakes. Those who are landowners, on the other hand, remain relatively safe from these animals as they rarely go into the forest. Moreover, the distinctions are also of a symbolic order. Land, argue the islanders, especially the riverside people, leads to hierarchical relations and divides people. In contrast to land, the precepts of the forest are seen as instilling 'an ethos of equality' between humans and animals, men and women, Hindus and Muslims, rich and poor. In describing the islanders' relationship with these two entities, the land and the forest, what I highlight is that social relations in the Sundarbans are perceived along the lines of whether one's livelihood depends on the forest and rivers or on agricultural land. I argue by extension that the ways in which the islanders negotiate their interactions with each other has more to do with the way they perceive their 'personhood' in its connection either to land or to the forest.

This is not to suggest that the islanders do not use conflicting explanations. In fact, they all possess, in varying degrees, access to both land and forest and draw sustenance from both spheres as well as sharing overlapping cultural repertoires. The schema proposed is merely a starting point and not to be understood as identifying watertight social compartments. The points of reference on this socio-ecological continuum make sense not so much to distinguish various groups' means of establishing community identity but to focus on elaborations about understandings of self and others. I would like to suggest that the plurality of representations that such a continuum reveals about tigers and the forest on the one end and land on the other leads to an exploration of how the islanders perceive and practise relatedness in a world where they have to juggle between adhering to the communitarian identities of religion, caste and ethnicity, and to the differences construed along the lines of their occupations' respective cosmologies.

Forest-Workers and Poachers

Those who work in the forest can be divided into the following groups: *(i)* the 'forest fishers' who catch crabs and fish and who see themselves as entering the forest with 'peace'; *(ii)* those who 'do the forest' and work primarily as honey collectors and woodcutters, as well as those who work as poachers and are called 'black parties'.[4] Although they work in the forest, the poachers are ideologically similar to prawn seed collectors because they do not see themselves as having to (or being able to) adhere to 'the rules of the forest' (more on this in Chapter IV).

The Forest Fishers

The forest fishers leave home for about ten days, twice a month, in groups of three to five. Even though they mostly catch crab and fish, they also occasionally collect honey and wood. However, the difference from those who 'do the jungle' (used alternatively with forest) is that they are seen as collecting honey and wood only on an occasional basis and therefore not with the same disposition as those who do so regularly. The forest fishers enter the forest under the protection of the forest goddess Bonbibi and see their line of work as 'respecting' the forest as it neither 'depletes' nor 'disturbs' it. By contrast, they see the activities of prawn seed collectors and honey and wood collectors (used alternatively with 'woodcutter') as troubling the wild animals, especially tigers, and as exhausting the forest. They explain how they respect the forest because they enter it 'with peace', consider tigers to be their 'brothers' and consequently share the products of the forest equitably between wild animals and themselves.

Those Who 'Do the Forest'

The honey and wood collectors describe themselves as people engaging in 'violent' activities. Even if occasionally they also work as crab and fish collectors, they are seen by the other islanders as being threats to the forest animals and therefore bringing upon themselves (and others) the forest animals' wrath. Sometimes, they also work as poachers. Honey and wood collection, along with poaching, are seen as high-risk, high-gain occupations that go against the principles of peace and equality associated with the forest. It is believed that those who undertake these occupations either lose their lives or 'make it big'. Usually, the more daredevil poachers worship the goddess Kali. Kali is perceived in the Sundarbans, as in many parts of Hindu WB, as the deity most appropriate for those practising violent and bloody occupations, which are listed as the police, taxi-drivers, poachers, and local thugs who operate as dacoits and stave-wielders (*lathiyal*).[5] Those who 'do the jungle' are composed of people from varying socio-economic backgrounds. These are the marginalised and landless, such as the East Bengali Hindu migrants from the 'down' islands as well as rich landowners from 'up' islands who possess fire-arms and are in search of cheap thrills. The stereotype, however, is that they have the nerve to flout the laws both of the forest and of the state.

Prawn Seed Collectors

The second major socio-economic activity and its corresponding cosmology involves working as a tiger prawn seed collector, either from one's boat or by pulling a net on the banks of both the forest and the village to catch the delicate tiger prawn seeds. (Tiger prawn seeds are collected when they are inch-long and of hair-thin diameter.) This occupation became very popular in the 1970s; it pulled the poorest of the region out of stark poverty and has given women greater financial security. The income made through prawn seed collection is not, like that of the forest, shared between different team members, and is thus the individuals' to dispose of as they wish. Those who have the means fish from their boats by installing huge nets at the confluence of large rivers — either in the forest area (when permitted) or, as is most often the case, in the rivers not very far from the village. The more popular way of fishing prawn seed is practised by women who pull nets on the banks of the village islands or sail off (usually in groups of four to eight) to fish on the banks of forested islands. This mode of fishing consists of pulling a mosquito net fixed on a thin wooden frame behind oneself with one's body submerged in waist- to chest-deep water (see photos 9 and 10 on page 108). Those who practise this form of fishing, face the greatest threat from sharks, crocodiles and tigers.

The prawn seed collectors usually demarcate themselves from forest fishers, arguing that prawn seed collection is more akin to a 'business' and that committing themselves to the protection of the forest deity Bonbibi (as the forest workers do) might not serve any purpose. Unlike forest fishers, who can sell their crabs and fish to whomever they choose, the prawn seed collectors have to depend on the fluctuating prices commanded by the prawn dealers and businessmen to make a living. They therefore consider their job a 'lottery' — which can either 'lift them' or 'drown them'. This occupation is very popular as both women as well as men (and sometimes children who accompany their parents and pull their own nets) can take it up with very little prior investment (unlike poaching, which requires people to have rifles, cartridges, powerful torches, and connections) and because it can be carried out during one's free time. Even so, their livelihood provokes the anger of many. The forest officials as well as the forest fishers accuse the prawn seed collectors of poaching. Their odd hours of work, 'which know neither day nor night' (as their work is linked to the tides, it requires them to work at night too), as well as the entry of women and children into the forest, are considered by the forest fishers to be 'disturbing tigers' and defiling the forest, turning it into a riskier place. The landowners and service holders too are against this occupation as prawn businessmen who become rich in short periods of time increasingly threaten their money-lending activities.

Landowners

The third group comprises agriculturalists or, more specifically, landowners. They are usually the educated. They are also very often service holders working as school teachers. One result of the vast increase in the number of village primary schools in the 1960s and 1970s[6] has been the blending of many elements of the bhadralok model, including literary pursuits and political leftism, with the agrarian landlord's lifestyle (Ruud 1999a: 258). Some of the people belonging to this group are from 'up' places posted there by the WB state-regulated School Service Commission. The minimum salaries are four or five times higher than the earnings of the average fisher. It is this group that spends a substantial part of its salary in acquiring plots of land in the suburbs of Kolkata where they hope to settle when they retire. While still in the village many landowners hold the strings of political and economic power along with prawn businessmen and shopkeepers. They are also the ones who, on the whole, own the most land. Their houses, built high and with thick mud or brick walls, are often the target of armed robberies.

Gradually, more doctors (or 'quack-doctors' — to use a term with which they refer to themselves), shopkeepers, prawn businessmen, and dealers are starting to match the landowners' economic power; however, the landowners hold the moral high ground as possessors of education and 'sophisticated culture'. This group, part of the bhadralok, share the forest officials' concerns for wildlife and tigers. The essence of their bhadra identity is often revealed through their romanticised vision of nature. Bhadralok sensitivity to the Royal Bengal tiger and its association with both the regal and colonial images of hunting as well as its position as national animal, is often deployed to highlight the Sundarbans as a 'World Heritage Site' and thus provides them with some reassurance about living in not such a 'down' place after all.

Conclusion

The main division between these three groups of people is their stance on the forest and tigers. What is interesting is that the three groups are fluid as their positionality is often connected with age. Old people and young couples usually practise prawn seed collection, while young fathers and middle-aged men work in the forest. This is because, once young couples have made some money working as prawn seed collectors or labourers, or once their parents die, they start owning a small patch of land which they also cultivate or have enough resources to build a boat and work in the forest.

Notes

1. Ensign Prinsep, in 1822–23, surveyed the forests from the river Jamuna to the Hooghly, divided them into 'blocks' and numbered them. This was the beginning of the 'Sundarbans lots' (De 1990: 15).
2. 'Scheduled Caste', 'Scheduled Tribe' and 'Other Backward Caste' are terms given by the Government of India to classify groups of people that have been and still are on the whole economically and socially disadvantaged. This is in order for members of such groups to be eligible, under Articles 341 and 342 of the Indian Constitution, for positive affirmative action. These terms often replace the derogative traditional caste or tribe names. The words 'Untouchable' (used by the British), 'Harijan' ('children of God' — so named by Gandhi), and 'Dalit' (meaning 'oppressed' or 'broken' in self-recognition of their historical oppression) are rarely used. (For more on this, see the glossary.)
3. The slang meaning of *pōd* is 'arse'.
4. *Mach-kankra dhorar lok*, 'people who catch fish and crabs' for fish and crab collectors, *jangol kora lok*, 'people who *do* the forest' — this essentially refers to wood and honey collectors — and *black partyr lok*, 'people who do black' which refers to poachers and smugglers.
5. Dacoits are armed robbers notorious in rural Bengal. Operating in gangs, they defy local authorities to plunder, loot, maim, and sometimes even kill their victims. They have been known to rob entire villages. In the political history of Sundarbans villages, many landowners and political leaders traditionally depended on the militancy of lathiyals to intimidate opposition, rivals and rebel subjects.
6. Primary schools in WB grew from 14,700 in 1950–51 to 50,000 by 1980–81 (Acharya 1985: 1785).

III

Land and its Hierarchies

Garjontola, like many of the villages of the 'down' islands, stretches in a more or less horizontal line along the bund, which serves as pathway and perimeter separating Satjelia island from the Pathar river. Branching off in horizontal lines from the bund at intervals of about a kilometre, elevated mud tracks pass through the interior of the island, bridging one end to the other. Surrounded by a bund, and intersected by innumerable mud tracks — and also joined north to south and east to west by brick paths — this island has the appearance of being held together by a loosely spun flimsy net when viewed from the air. Houses, especially those of forest fishers and those who work in the prawn industry (collectors, dealers and businessmen) lie on the periphery of the island, scattered along the winding bund and exposed to the danger of embankments breaking, tidal bores and attacks by crocodiles and tigers. The houses of those who own land are neatly lined along the brick paths heading towards the safer interior of the island and the school. The brick paths, pride and joy of the islanders all over the Sundarbans, stand as the symbol of progress, status and political clout of the village, particularly its landed and connected social superiors. They start as big cemented blocks placed to serve as a jetty along the river bank and make their way to the houses of the village elite, who do not have to get their feet muddied like those who use the dusty, smelly and rickety bund-paths to get home. The greatest socio-economic divide in the Sundarbans, between landowner and fisher, is reflected not only in the kind of locality where one lives, but also in the distinctions between the geographies one uses. In this chapter, I will look at the symbolic import of land and agriculture, the contrasting spaces of land and forest and the significance of another social space: the *bhite* or homestead.

Agricultural land in the southern islands of the Sundarbans, very much as in the rest of WB, is at the centre of violent and hierarchal relationships. However, while land is seen as the greatest cause of acrimony amongst blood relatives, and the primary boundary between the affluent and the deprived, it does not necessarily lead to the kind of exploitation seen in other parts of South Asia (such as, neighbouring Bihar or Uttar Pradesh). This is partly because fortune in the 'down' islands is easily made or lost through natural calamities such as storms or the constant shifting of the course of rivers. When rivers shift course, they tear through bunds and reclaim land, leaving people suddenly landless and homeless. Shifts of fortune also arise from the introduction of new occupational activities, such as prawn seed collection and prawn farming, which enable the islanders to become relatively wealthy within a short time. The introduction of tiger prawn seed collection in the late 1970s and the proliferation of aquaculture farms to the north of the region greatly reduced the exploitation of the landless by the landed and gave some security to the poorest and most marginalised. Prawn seed collection is an interesting activity because, while lucrative, it is of low social status. The village elite therefore never practise it and rarely invest in it and, consequently, their economic status has become somewhat threatened by successful prawn dealers (more on the prawn industry in Chapter V). The other factor which has contributed to the relative lack of land-related exploitation is the history of the Gosaba islands, and the fact that they were, as briefly mentioned in Chapter I, bought by the Scotsman Hamilton who was keen on developing a co-operative society.

Being a well-endowed landlord or a 'service holder' (as referred to in the previous chapter) confers social status. This is the reason why those who come to the island to take up government jobs, such as school teaching, quickly invest in land. Even if a large part of their salaries gets diverted towards building a house or flat outside the Sundarbans, school teachers also buy land in the village and hire people to work it or lease it out for a share of the crops. The distinction between large landowners (and this naturally includes service holders), those who hold land and make a living off it, and those who work in the forest or rivers, is socially very clearly marked. Indeed, one of the markers of bhadralok status in the Sundarbans is one's access to the city, as it suggests not only wealth but also power. Wealth, because travelling from Garjontola one-way to Kolkata or its suburbs takes nearly a whole working day which is something the islanders cannot easily afford, and because it costs up to Rs 140, which is equivalent to roughly one-sixth of what a forest worker makes per month. Power, because of close ties to the metropolis or to city people such as NGO workers, doctors and forest officials living in or visiting the Sundarbans, means access to jobs, help in writing letters, advice in law cases, etc.

In Garjontola the other reason why there is less exploitation and disparity of wealth is because the gramer lok are predominantly from the geographically equivalent southern district of eastern Bengal and have cultural, caste and kin ties with each other; this somewhat inhibits them from marking their differences. This will become clear in the last section of this chapter where I will show how the islanders dealt with relatives who become richer. The only outsiders to Garjontola are the secondary school teachers and the temporarily visiting bee-keepers (more on them later in this chapter). Amongst the school teachers there are those *(i)* who are recruited to work as primary school teachers and clerks and who are from the more fortunate households of the village: both riverside as well as the connected interior, and there are those *(ii)* who come here on temporary deployment to work as secondary school teachers and who seldom have any prior links to the village, most of them being from other parts of WB. Because of the large size of their salaries, school teachers and clerks are the new landowners and, like the zamindars of the olden days, have very little engagement with the villagers' public life and usually leave the village once they retire. Certainly, the agrarian structure of Bengal more widely, has been characterised by the extra-economic coercion of landless labourers and marginal farmers (Cooper 1988). However, in the island of Satjelia, because the landless and marginal depend on the forest and on prawn seed collection, their land-based exploitation, even though very much a reality, is less important than in the other parts of WB or Bangladesh.

The symbolism of land in the Sundarbans' 'down' islands, where the forest is such an economic life-saver, lies in its alienation from the poor. In contrast to land, the realm of the forest is seen as favouring the deprived. If land, the fishers argue, ultimately leads to hierarchical relations, the dual quality of the forest, being 'equalising' as well as 'unifying', is seen as 'levelling' people. The relatively easy access to the forest is contrasted to the restricted access to land.

But, in a place where the uncertain environment means that one's holdings are not secure even in the 'safe' interior and where one can easily lose land, how are social relations between fishers and landowners negotiated? How is social status played out between these two economic groups in an area where most people are of similar caste backgrounds and part of the same genealogical tree? After giving a brief introduction to the history of land relations in the Sundarbans, especially that of the 'Hamilton islands' (i.e., Gosaba, Rangabelia and Satjelia), I will address how the location of one's homestead, one's choice of occupation, and the changing of surnames ultimately reflects the construction of the divide between the bhadralok and the gramer lok. Through laying out these differences, the purpose of this chapter is to explore the perceptions of the Sundarbans inhabitants regarding the locales of land and forest as symbolic entities that have an inherent impact on social relationships.

State and Local Politics of Land

The Left Front government came to office in WB in 1977. Upon coming to power, it was keen to implement the famous WB Land Reforms Act of 1955, which it subsequently further radicalised through the involvement of Gram Panchayat (village-level) bodies and the intro-duction of the Barga system. This system ensured that share-croppers got tenancy rights to the land they cultivated, while landlords only held the title deed. The specific land reforms *(i)* guaranteed that the rights of share-croppers were protected so that they got two-thirds of the produce (in effect they only get half) and could not be evicted by force; *(ii)* enabled the government to take possession of surplus land and to undertake its distribution among the landless; and *(iii)* provided housing sites to the homeless in the countryside (Siddiqui 1997: 42).[1] Thus, agriculture, in the Sundarbans as in the rest of WB, is dominated by small and marginal farmers, who work more than 68 per cent of the total cultivated area of the state. Besides, redistribution of powers and functions at the local level, and especially amongst the most deprived groups, is seen as necessary, at least in theory, for the land reforms to be fully effective. In 1992, the 'party' (a term commonly used to refer to the Left Front government, whose biggest party is the Communist Party of India-Marxist [CPIM]) further amended the Panchayat Act of 1973, which provided for the compulsory reservation of seats for members of the SC and ST communities in all the three tiers of local government so that they would now be proportionate to the percentage of the population of these communities in the three respective tiers. Similarly, provision was made for the compulsory reservation of at least one-third of the total seats for women candidates.

Local government bodies are elected at three levels: Zila Parishad at the district level, Panchayat Samiti at the Block level, and Gram

Panchayat at the village level (i.e., one Gram Panchayat for about ten villages). The region is composed of thirteen Blocks in the South 24 Parganas district and six Blocks in the North 24 Parganas district; each Block is represented at the Zila Parishad.[2] In terms of the region, the South 24 Parganas district headquarters (and the district magistrate) are in Kolkata (at Alipur), and this further accentuates, for the islanders, the feeling of the marginalisation of their region.

The island is composed of two regional (*anchal*) offices. The regional office has under its jurisdiction fifteen villages, of which Toofankhali is one. The Gram Panchayat, when I was there, was made up of nine Revolutionary Socialist Party (RSP) members, eight Trinamool Congress (TMC) members, and one (CPIM) member.[3] (This distribution of parties is different from that at the WB state level where the CPIM is dominant.) The members of the Gram Panchayat held jobs as cultivators, school teachers, doctors (mostly formally unqualified), kerosene dealers, tourist guides to the Sajnekhali sanctuary, or the wives of those who held such jobs. It is interesting to note that there was not a single elected leader who was a jungle worker or a prawn seed collector or dealer even though the prawn dealers and businessmen actively engaged in politics.

How does the Land Reforms Act of 1955 relate to the situation in Toofankali? The landed gentry, constituting 2 per cent of the population, own per household unit between 7 and 16 acres — still very much within the 25 acre ceiling imposed by the 1955 Act. Even though in Garjontola these people hold about 30 per cent of the total land, and even though the statistic for the landless is assumed to be 50 per cent for the whole of the Sundarbans, the number of landless households in Garjontola is not as high. The landless are often young couples who have broken off from the larger household unit and who work on other people's lands or in the forest.

Land is a constant cause of dispute not only within households and families but also between political parties. The panchayats in the rural areas have the de facto power of playing an adjudicatory role in land disputes. However, the affluent prefer resorting to the more costly judiciary courts rather than the interventions made by these popular institutions. Endemic political rivalries, especially between the CPIM and the RSP, endlessly block otherwise amicable settlements at the village level and so land disputes often lead to forcible harvesting or burning of fields of ripe standing crops and to violent murders.

The RSP, a party which has a very strong base in the Sundarbans, while a part of the WB Left Front government at state level, is the arch enemy of the government's ruling party, the CPIM, in the Sundarbans. In the rural sector the CPIM is well-known as the party of the middle peasantry (D. Basu 2001). In the Sundarbans, rivalries between the two parties are settled through setting ripe paddy on fire and digging breaches in bunds so that fields get submerged by salt water. In their intense fight for votes, both parties settled Bangladeshi Hindu migrants on private property in the southern islands of the Sundarbans in the 1970s and 1980s. These events have remained a source of hostility.

The Strange Legacy of the Hamilton Islands

It is important to note the special history of the Gosaba Block of islands, as briefly outlined in Chapter I. The three islands of the Gosaba Block, Satjelia, Gosaba and Rangabelia, were bought between 1911 and 1915 by Daniel Hamilton and settled between the second and the third decades of the twentieth century. Hamilton was the senior partner and chief executive officer of the important Mackinnon Mackenzie & PNO Shipping Company. He bought these islands in a bid to show the British government why and how it could implement the co-operative system in rural India. To fight against the indebtedness of the rural cultivators, Hamilton invited indentured labourers to the islands by leasing out land to them on condition that they not sell it. These people came from remote places such as northern Orissa, the highlands of Bihar, Midnapur and Khulna in Bengal. Bunds were erected, a distillation plant set up to convert salt river water into potable water, and public water tanks, dispensaries, schools, and granaries were built. Hamilton laid out his own set of rules for these islands: land could not be bought or sold; it had to be cultivated by its owner; and the inhabitants were not allowed to gamble, drink or maintain differences of religion or caste. Gosaba became the headquarters of Hamilton's estate and his three islands were together referred to as 'Hamilton abad'. Hamilton, like a true zamindar, started naming the villages which sprang up on these islands. Some places were named after his family members such as Emilybari, Luxbagan, Annpur, Jamespur.[4] Others were named after events — Rajat Jubilee (named after King George V's silver jubilee in 1935) — or after their specificities such as Pakhiralay (the abode of birds), Dayapur (the village of compassion), Arampur (the village of relaxation).

Hamilton, however, was a different kind of zamindar. He was Scottish and he based his banking system on the traditional Scottish system of banking. His motto was 'honest labour makes an honest man' and he held that 'credit worthiness' was determined by labour; he therefore decided to capitalise on labour and leased out 25 bighas of land and a loan of Rs 200 to each cultivator. Gradually, these programmes made the cultivators solvent. When the ex-moneylenders came chasing after them with legal documents in order to seize their new-found land and paddy, Hamilton set up his 'loan redemption scheme' in order to help the cultivators repay the moneylenders through long-term loans from the co-operative. He was so convinced that his system could sustain itself that, defying the British government, he printed his own one-rupee currency, which was widely circulated in the three islands. The islanders had to repay the Rs 200 initially lent to them by selling their products at the co-operative society. Each village had a co-operative bank, a paddy shell society, a rice mill, and a store for the sale of agricultural products. Directors of the village co-operative banks were called 'panchayat' and were responsible for the all-round development of the village; so finance, education, health, adjudication (except for serious offences) were all organised within the islands.

Alongside schools, Hamilton also built non-formal training centres with subjects such as agriculture, carpentry, fruit processing, book-keeping, dairy farming, and hygiene, so as to impart the 'Art of Independent Livelihood' to the islanders. To boost the economic development of the village, an agro-research, animal husbandry and cottage industry training institute was developed. Soon the thirty-three units became self-governing villages, which sent two representatives to the headquarters office in Gosaba twice a month. Hamilton was in close contact with Gandhi and Tagore. The latter even visited the place in December 1932 and with him Hamilton launched the 'Gosaba-Bolpur Co-operative Training Institute' whose mission was to train people to launch co-operative societies in India's rural areas.[5]

The main objective of education, believed Hamilton, was to 'build character' and make people 'trustworthy'. In his will Hamilton recommended that the villagers of his 'Hamilton abad' be exposed to a market economy only once they had become economically solvent.

Between 1913 and 1937, thirty-three village co-operative societies mushroomed. In fact, this experiment initially worked so well that Hamilton wrote in his *The Road to Independence* that 'India's road to independence (within the empire [*sic*]) runs through Gosaba with its sound Man Standard finance' (Bandyopadhyay and Matilal 2003: 240). In his speeches, he exhorted the government to follow his path and stressed how India's independence should be first economic rather than political.

Hamilton's utopian dream of recreating a co-operative society is one of the popular stories the islanders love to dwell on because it gives their islands a sense of history rooted in lofty ideals of social justice and equitable redistribution of wealth. It was this initial just distribution of land which had made these islands peaceful, explained the islanders.

Land, however, is seen as eventually hierarchising and corrupting. The islanders blamed the subsequent violence that broke out on these islands, and the present inequalities in land possession, on the bhadralok trustees of the Hamilton Trust. Not infused with the same zeal for social justice as Hamilton, it is alleged that after his death they usurped both the land and money he had left in his Trust for the islanders, before leaving the islands to return to Kolkata whence they had come. Afterwards, in the late 1950s, the government seized the Trust on the grounds that it had become a zamindari. The fact that the three islands of the Hamilton abad remained long bereft of any fresh water source is believed by the islanders to be the result of a curse cast by Hamilton's spirit on seeing the destruction of his dream of a co-operative society.

If the foundations of the three Gosaba islands are the ideals of a co-operative sharing society, the overall history of the Sundarbans is marred by violence — especially in relation to the state. After the state's annexation of the Hamilton islands in the 1950s, the other important occasion of land-related violence was, as mentioned earlier, the en masse settling of Bangladeshi Hindu migrants in the 1970s and 1980s by political parties. Landless Hindus from Bangladesh were settled on land that had been grabbed from richer landlords.[6] This became possible through semi-legal means with the implementation in 1978 of the 1975 WB Acquisition of Homestead Land Act. This provision shaped the discourse around land rights and legitimised the CPIM's and the RSP's grabbing of land from affluent landowners, who often were Congress party supporters.[7] The 1970s and 1980s were marked by extreme hostility between these three political parties at the local level as they became notorious for covertly organising the flooding of entire areas with salt river water. Once crop-lands were destroyed, the political party with the greatest clout 'gave' it (in return for their votes) to the landless, migrant poor. Very often, these colonies were once again flooded, this time by the Congress landlords, to literally 'flush out' the migrants. Now, large areas of cultivable land have become the prerogative of politicians or high-school teachers.

The brutal political situation is one of the main reasons why those who have the means — school teachers, doctors, politicians, NGO workers, and businessmen (especially ration shop owners, who work mainly as kerosene retailers and prawn seed fishery owners) — leave the place upon retirement. They buy plots of land far from the 'down' islands of the Sundarbans and as near as possible to Kolkata. While it has been argued that in WB, the growth in agricultural output has been driven by private interests (Harriss 1993), this is rarely the case in the lower islands of the Sundarbans because the service-holding landed gentry do not settle there nor do they invest in long-term development projects for the villages they live in. Due not only to the geographical and political insecurity of the area, but also the negative social status linked to living in the Sundarbans, their concerns for the Sundarbans are mainly restricted to having tube-wells installed or brick paths laid alongside their houses.

As I've mentioned earlier, along the 'up'/'down' division, the poor live near the river's edge or in 'colonies' established on reclaimed marshy land — such as Banikhali — and the rich along brick roads, near schools, dispensaries and NGO offices.[8] The government's reforms, despite their good intentions, have not on the whole de-creased the percentage of the landless in the Sundarbans; instead, as demonstrated in recent studies, inequality of land ownership holdings in the state of WB has increased overall (Bhaumik 1993: 64; Siddiqui 1997: 247; Harriss 2003; Hill 2003: 2–3). However, in the present-day Hamilton islands of the Sundarbans, these discrepancies are fewer and the landless can at times settle without too much dif-ficulty on the newly emerged lands which appear along certain parts of the island.[9]

There are no cottage or small-scale industries apart from the ones offered by the few NGOs that have the means to do so. The principal economic activities are agriculture and fishing. Fishing is carried out both for prawn seed and for crab and river or sea fish (by men).[10]

A large part of the fishing — both for prawn seed as well as for crab and fish — is done in the forest. Working in the forest is not only physically demanding but also dangerous, as tigers, crocodiles, venomous snakes, and sharks regularly attack and kill those who work there. The range officer of Sajnekhali for the WB Sundarbans estimates that there are 150 people killed by tigers and crocodiles each year. The estimate is the same on the Bangladesh side.[11] This is without mentioning the equal, if not greater, figure of people killed or maimed by snake- or shark-bite. The causes of violent mortality are not only wild animals, but also political party rows, armed robbers, failed abortion operations, diseases, suicides.

To summarise the facts and figures on key 'social indicators' in the Sundarbans: there are roughly 50 lakh people living in the entire WB Sundarbans today, of which roughly one-fifth live in the southern or 'down' islands. In the 1980s some 35,330 people worked in the forest annually, of which nearly 25,000 were fishers, 4,500 collected timber and firewood, 1,350 collected honey and 4,500 were involved in other activities (Chakrabarti 1986).

The 1971 census shows forty-eight of the state's fifty-nine listed SCs represented in the Sundarbans and 70 per cent of the STs or Adivasis of WB, numbering approximately 140,000 people, live in this region. Nearly half of the population of the Sundarbans belongs to SC and ST communities, as against 25.5 per cent for the whole of WB. In the Gosaba Block (Satjelia, Rangabelia and Gosaba) nearly 65 per cent of the population is SC, 8.5 per cent ST, nearly 20 per cent Muslim, and 5 per cent Christian (Banerjee 1998: 230).

But thinking along the lines of statistics often leads to bounded notions of identity. To go beyond essentialist conceptions, whether of class, caste or religion, greater attention has been given to locality and history as significant factors for understanding how the islanders see themselves and each other. The descriptions of 'self' and 'other' provided here are not necessarily grounded in age-old beliefs or predispositions but are also consequences of processes and interactions and particular events that are local and distinctive. What seems critical in relation to their view of themselves as fellow islanders of the Sundarbans and yet as distinct groups within this broader category, is balancing relationships with place, that is, forest or land on the one hand and the contingencies of work, religion and caste on the other.

Multiple Meanings of Jati and Dharmo

In a continent where caste and religion are important in the construction of social and economic hierarchies and often the markers
of divisions between people, what is the import of these categories
for the islanders? As outlined in Chapter I, the inhabitants of
Garjontola are for the most part of East Bengali origin and belong
to two of the lowest castes of Bengal, Pod and Namasudra. The
other communities they closely interact with are their immediate
neighbours, the Adivasis, and to a lesser extent the Midnapuris —
so named because their origins are in Midnapur (mainly OBCs) —
and Muslims from both the Sundarbans and areas in the North 24
Parganas outside the Sundarbans. The islanders maintain that the
divisions between these four communities are based on essential
physical, cultural and psychological traits. Each group plays up
stereotypes of other groups to denigrate them and attribute to
themselves positive stereotypes that establish their own superiority.
As we shall see, many of these revolve around each group's moment
of settling in the Sundarbans and subsequent possession of land.

The Adivasis — of Oraon and Munda origin — were brought to
the Sundarbans as indentured labourers from Hazaribagh and Santhal
Parganas for clearing the forest, erecting bunds, building the railway
system and the ports of Canning and Diamond Harbour (Pargiter
1934: 57).[12] They were brought in primarily because they fitted the
classificatory stereotype of the hard-working tribal, the alleged trait
that launched their entry into the colonial labour market.[13] Even if
the term 'tribal' is a 'fiction creation by government officers' (Mathur
1972: 460) or even if, as structural categories, 'tribe' and 'peasantry'
are hardly distinct from each other (Devalle 1992; Pathy 1984), the
socio-economic conditions of Adivasis are indisputably different
from those of the others. The fact that Adivasis drink liquor, eat food
considered 'impure' (such as pork), and are amongst the poorest,
means that for non-Adivasis, being 'tribal' conjures ideas of their
being traditionally 'primitive' and 'wild'. Adivasis in the Sundarbans
are spoken of in very condescending terms as having 'given up their
wild ways' after coming into contact with the other groups. Their
assumed distinctiveness as hard workers is still maintained in the
Sundarbans by the government's bestowal of jobs related to the upkeep
of bunds and embankments exclusively to them. The rationale

behind such recruitment is not to pursue the wider government policy of uplifting socially backward communities, but because of the Adivasis' alleged physical prowess and 'natural' closeness to nature and their historical role in the Sundarbans reclamation. Yet, even though the other communities point at the Adivasi older generations' slight but distinctly accented Bengali and their physical features, the Adivasis consider themselves to be part of the wider Sundarbans rural Bengali community and do not maintain any links with their Adivasi kin in Chotanagpur.

The younger generation of Adivasis cannot be distinguished from members of the other communities. In fact, Adivasis have a long history of cultural assimilation to the dominant communities in the Sundarbans. If they appear to consist of only 17 per cent of the population of the Sundarbans at the beginning of the twentieth century, this is because 60 per cent of them, even at that time, re- turned themselves as 'Hindu' on the census (O'Malley 1914: 69). The move in those days had been to try and assimilate within the mainstream. But today, partly due to the affirmative policy on equal opportunity in the public sector, 8.5 per cent of the population of the Sundarbans return themselves as Adivasis. Successful Adivasis who have become school teachers and clerks are pulled between, on the one hand, changing their names and marking a total break with the Sundarbans and their Adivasi origin and, on the other, highlighting the fact that they are Adivasis and openly disputing the trickery of the other communities that has deprived them of their land. They see themselves as 'honest' and 'strong' and often argue that their 'naturally truthful and courageous disposition' makes them especially suitable for the role of tiger-charmers.

The Midnapuris are considered of superior status not only because they are OBCs but also because they are, on the whole, the most educated and wealthy community in the Gosaba islands. The East Bengalis see them as aggressive and 'greedy' for land. Midnapuris, at least in the Gosaba subdivision, are more literate than the other groups, wield considerable political power in NGOs and government offices and are, along with some Muslims, part of the landed gentry. The population emigrated to the Hamilton islands in the 1940s, especially after the Bengal famine of 1943 when their region was one of the hardest hit. The Midnapuris are seen as arrogant because they are wealthy and because their OBC status makes them the socially dominant group. Their investment in plots of land in Midnapur or the suburbs of Kolkata is seen by the others as a lack of commitment to the Sundarbans. There are very few Midnapuri families in Satjelia. Most of them live in Gosaba and other islands which are 'up' in comparison to Satjelia. The Midnapuris believe that the recriminations against them are due to the envy of those who have not been as successful as them. They talk about their community's numerous freedom fighters (some of whom escaped imprisonment or hanging by settling in the Sundarbans) and about having produced the leaders and initiators of prominent revolutionary movements in Bengal; they see themselves as being the torch-bearers of civilisation in these 'down' islands of the Sundarbans.

The Muslims are generally seen, especially by the Midnapuris, as being hot-headed and belligerent and are usually blamed for the violence in the Sundarbans. This is so especially because, being landowners and prawn dealers, they previously were the political and economic rivals of the successful Midnapuris. The Sundarbans Muslims resent the fact that they are wrongly blamed for violence. They feel bitter about other communities dubbing them aggressive on account of their enterprise and courage. Indeed, they are both famous and infamous for their risk-taking — whether in forest-related occupations such as honey collecting and poaching or in new occupations such as prawn dealing. The recent history of Muslims in the Sundarbans is murky and something of a taboo subject. Too late in my fieldwork, I learned that in the 1950s and 1960s thousands were chased away from their homes and lands by the displaced Hindu refugees who had emigrated from East Pakistan (present-day Bangladesh). In Gosaba they are the rivals of the Midnapuris and the stereotypes spread about each group are more acrimonious as it is a richer island and so the stakes for control of political power are much higher. In Satjelia, where there are fewer of them and where they are principally forest workers, the only attribute used to distinguish them from others is that they are 'hardworking' and 'fearless'.

The Adivasis, Midnapuris and Muslims usually refer to the East Bengalis as 'people of East Bengal' (*purba banger lok*) or with the derogatory caste name Pod. East Bengalis are made fun of, especially by the Midnapuris, for eating their food 'raw' as the East Bengalis have a different way of cooking from the Midnapuris. East Bengalis retaliate by saying that Midnapuris eat their food 'charred' and joke about their dialect, the fact that 'they have two wives' and think nothing of it, and the architecture of their houses, which they see as conducive to incest. This is because generally Midnapuris live in joint families whereas East Bengalis tend to live separately. Tensions between East Bengalis and Midnapuris revolve around the fact that the latter, being socially and economically superior, 'accept' brides hypergamously from East Bengalis but refuse to give their own daughters to East Bengali grooms. There are some hypergamous marriages between wealthy East Bengalis and Midnapuris and between wealthy Adivasis and East Bengalis but inter-community marriages are rare and are being met with ever more social disapproval. Lovers from different communities elope to get married and go to live with relatives in other villages or settle in shacks along the railway lines on the outskirts of Kolkata.

East Bengalis take pride in the fact that their dialect is used in renown literary works of such famous Bengali writers as Sarat Chandra Chattopadhyay and Manik Bandhopadhyay, while the dialect of the Midnapuris is not. They also see themselves as enterprising and hardworking and think that they are better-looking than the others because of their generally slightly lighter skin. They blame their inferior position on the fact that they are not as 'shrewd and scheming' as the Midnapuris, and they naturally think themselves to be more cultured and 'educated' than them.

Much about the identity of the four groups revolves around their success or failure in the domain of landowning; the Midnapuris and Muslims are seen as being 'greedy for land'. These two groups are also seen as trying to safeguard their social superiority by keeping close ties with their richer counterparts in Midnapur, North 24 Parganas or the Kolkatan suburbia. The Adivasis, socially and economically the most inferior group, see themselves as those who have been deceived by the other groups into parting with their land. The East Bengalis are described by the other groups as people who use political clout to usurp land. The other islanders say derogatorily of them that they come in 'flocks' and that, if you give a small patch of land to one, the next day their whole village from Bangladesh will arrive. This, of course, is mainly due to the large immigration of Bangladeshi Hindu refugees to the Sundarbans (more on this in Chapter VI).

Jati

If people see themselves as being defined primarily by the geographical origins of their community and secondly by how far their community has succeeded in the Sundarbans (the index for this being land), the forest fishers often stress that such differences are trumped by the fact that they live in the same region. The landowners, on the other hand, because of the notoriety of the Sundarbans, try to disassociate themselves from this regional identification. In this section, I will simply highlight the use of the term 'jati' when the islanders talk of the four communities mentioned here. The Bengali jati, like the term 'caste', encompasses other collective identities such as religion, regional affiliation and gender. These different understandings of group identities highlight the tensions between the broad group of islanders who define themselves as 'educated' and therefore part of the bhadralok, and those who see themselves as forest workers or prawn seed collectors. So the islanders see differences between each other first along socio-economic lines. Yet, if education demarcates one as 'superior' to one's gramer lok kin, association with the forest, explained the forest fishers, 'levels' one, as the forest is seen as transforming all those who come into physical contact with it into 'one kind'.

Some of the forest workers have done well and have ensured a successful education for their children who are now working as school teachers on other islands. However, although their children are part of the 'bhadralok', these forest workers, so long as they work as such, have to share equally with their team members whatever they get from the forest. The relative ease with which different generations from one family, or at times individuals in the course of their life, change occupation, is a recurring trait of the inhabitants of Lower Bengal, that is, those of the southern part of both WB and Bangladesh. For example, Risley, a gazetteer writer of the nineteenth century, asserted that, though the majority of Paundra-Kshatriyas[14] — the respectable name many Pods took up for purposes of census classifications — are engaged in agriculture, they were also traders, goldsmiths, blacksmiths, tinsmiths, carpenters, and roof-thatchers. Some had 'risen to be zamindars, and some at the other end of the scale worked as nomadic cultivators on freshly cleared land in the Sundarbans, changing their location every two or three years according to the fortune of their crops' (1981, vol. 2: 176–77). O'Malley, another gazetteer writer remarked how the term *bhasa pod* (floating Pod) was the new name 'applied generally to such immigrants without reference to caste', tradition having it that they were washed over to the 24 Parganas from Hijili and other places in Midnapur in the cyclones of 1824 and 1834 (1914: 84).[15]

In the caste hierarchy of the four jatis mentioned, Midnapuris are at the top and Adivasis at the bottom, with Muslims and East Bengalis in-between. Although most of the inhabitants of Garjontola come from the same caste, they rarely refer to themselves by their traditional caste name of 'Pod' and find it offensive. One day, when, in the course of a conversation with a little gathering from Garjontola I was told that they were 'Pod', I asked who the Pod are. The story goes like this:

> Parasuram needed people to come and fight on his side. When he came and asked us Pods to volunteer our help and fight on his side, we got so scared that we crouched, hiding our faces in the upturned earth of our ploughed fields and sticking our buttocks up in the air. When Parasuram saw this he said, 'why, these are not people, they're just bums'. Since then, we've been stuck with our names and we don't really fancy it.[16]

They therefore prefer the term 'SC' which permits them to be disassociated from the negative connotations of being a gramer lok with a caste name which might betray one's lowly rural origins. Calling oneself SC not only permits relative caste anonymity, should anyone ever ask, it also enables one to obtain social and economic benefits such as stipends for school-going children and government jobs. Thus the main way in which the islanders improve their social status is less through the adoption of what Srinivas (1965) calls sanskritisation and the manipulation of the 'idiom of ritual pollution' (Lynch 1969: 13), and more through the adoption of fashionable urban first-names and high-caste surnames.[17]

In the Sundarbans more widely, upward mobility is not generally gained through the reinterpretation of what might have been the glorious past of individual jatis, nor are political groups in any way organised along caste or religious lines.[18] In fact, the ordering of social positions of the four groups mentioned earlier is often locally specific and linked to each group's successes on particular islands. Hence the island one comes from, whether one lives 'up' or 'down', whether one is landed or one works in the forest, whether one has family in Kolkata and its vicinity or not, are all markers of social status. One's connection to the city is the ultimate way of marking one's distinction. So, for example, while the four main groups are usually endogamous, one of the ways used to gain a higher social standing is by getting a bride or a groom from an 'up' island like Basanti or Sandeshkhali, and by, as much as possible, cutting off one's ties to one's rural roots. In the case of the 'down' islands of the Sundarbans, people try to assimilate to higher status groups by becoming a bhadralok through what Ruud has called 'modernisation' (1999a: 258) meaning in this context organising (whether Midnapuri, East Bengali or Adivasi Hindu)[19] the worship of the household goddesses of the Kolkata bhadralok — Durga, Saraswati and Lokkhi — or adhering to the tenets of what is seen as 'proper' Islam for the Muslims and the garnering of 'civilities' such as the knowledge of poetry and English, drama and Tagore songs.[20]

There are a number of reasons why most people in Garjontola do not care much about social hierarchies based on ritual purity and pollution. One reason is simply because they are nearly all SCs of one particular caste (Pod). Indeed, most of the families of Garjontola are related to each other through a common relative — Pareshbabu. In Garjontola people thus easily ask each other for services such as a haircut, a hand in ploughing land, digging ponds, house construction, fetching wood for fuel from the forest, repairing boats and even officiating as priests (*pujari*). The priest of the forest workers is not recruited from the Brahmin caste but from amongst those who have had the good fortune of knowing how to read; as for the other worships, those who have visited holy places as pilgrims are often asked for.

The worship of Bonbibi, by far the most widely practised, does not need a priest but only a person to read the *Bonbibi Johuranamah* — the booklet which recounts, first, Bonbibi's story and then that of the young woodcutter, Dukhe. (These stories are described in detail later in Chapter IV.) The person who has made the vow to Bonbibi (which might be for all kinds of reasons) needs to do the worship herself and the requirements are that she should start and end the reading of the booklet with other people reading the middle. During the usual three to four hours it takes to read the entire pamphlet, any person walking down a pathway and with some knowledge of how to read is solicited by those sitting around the Bonbibi shrines to relieve the reader by reading a few pages. (Very often, some of my neighbours would 'book' me in my role as school teacher, to read for an hour or so.) This obviously makes it possible for anyone to occupy the position of mediator between a divine power and humans. Other commonly practised forms of worship to deities such as Satyanarayan, Manasa, Shitala, Ganga also do not require a priest. Priests are solicited mainly by shopkeepers[21] to perform the rituals for the new financial year, by those who have rebuilt their houses, and by those (usually the landowners) who worship Saraswati, the goddess of learning. To make ends meet, those who become known as professional priests, usually resort to more lucrative economic activities such as land-owning, cultivation or prawn-dealing. In fact, they do not state 'priesthood' when asked what their occupation is; and their involvement in the material contingencies of economic life prevents them from becoming too particular with religious doctrine.

The other interesting reason given as to why in Garjontola most people do not care much about social hierarchies based on Hindu ideals of ritual purity and pollution relates to the fact that they work in the forest, with its 'equalising' ethos. This means not only that in itself the forest 'levels' hierarchical differences but also that people believe that they have to actively work at overcoming them. Being hierarchical could cost them their lives, they often asserted. This aspect of the forest's perceived influence on the 'equal' and 'equalising' social relationships expected of them is crucial and, to do justice to this, I shall devote the whole of the next chapter to it. Here, I simply want to highlight how the idea that the Sundarbans 'equalises' people is used to justify subtle social 'levelling' strategies undertaken all the time, such as stealing or sharing. People steal from richer relatives, ruin their successful neighbours' fishing ponds and kill their prize roosters. But, on the other hand, they also feel obliged to share with their poorer relatives or neighbours their best sari or a valued piece of clothing or tool, a newly received packet of sweets or fruits, a good haul of fish and crabs, or a hand at some task.

There is ambiguity over how one should live one's life — whether to follow the precepts of the forest or the increasingly popular dominating bhadralok ideology. In a bid to be part of this 'urban' middle class, many islanders change surnames with obvious rural-sounding origins. So, for example, the Hauli or Aulia insist that their name is a wrong pronunciation of Haldar, Middhe of Mridha, Bachar of Barman, and Boddi or Hakim, of Baidya. Similarly, the surnames Dāri, Mal, Malo, Majhi, which immediately connote one's traditional caste occupation as boatmen and fishers, are abandoned for the less obvious surnames Mondol, Mandal or Mondal (variant English spellings of the same Bengali name). This is the most common name of the 'down' islands of the Sundarbans; it is easily adopted as it can belong to any of the four different communities.

One of the previous inhabitants of Garjontola, who has become a teacher at the prestigious Ramakrishna mission of Narendrapur, changed his name from Mal to Pathak as he felt that the second name better 'suited the occupation'. *Mal* or *malo* connotes the caste of boatmen and fishers and is therefore a recognisable Scheduled Caste name whereas *pathak* literally means 'reader' and is a Brahmin name. The Muslims and Adivasis, too, change their names, the Muslims changing them to Sheikh or taking the surnames 'Morol', 'Laskar' while the Hindus are turning to such names as 'Mondol' and 'Naskar' to demarcate them from the Muslims. The Adivasis change obvious Adivasi names such as 'Munda' to 'Mondol'. Possessing an obvious traditional caste name is seen as bearing the residue of rusticity and ignorance. The islanders also see such names as reducing their chances of getting a 'service' job in the city. Therefore, one's caste and jati are subtly being masked and 'modernised' to suit the urban atmosphere where names which are 'rural-sounding' are distinct markers of inferiority and where one's claim to superior status can only be acquired through one's adherence to the subtle rules which govern the bhadralok sphere.

Dharmo

Social differences are linked not only to economic activity but also to religious practice. Indeed, district gazetteer writers of the late nineteenth and early twentieth century were baffled by the way people in Lower Bengal changed their religious practices when changing occupations.[22] Many Hindus who were originally fishers, for example, were returned as 'Muslim' when they became cultivators and Muslims listed themselves as belonging to the Hindu caste Namasudra in the 1891 and 1901 censuses when they turned to fishing. The religious differences between the Muslim Sheikhs and the Hindu Namasudras have always been loose and arbitrary (Nicholas 1969: 39–41). The Namasudras are the other important SC group in the Sundarbans (originally Untouchables and derogatorily called 'Chandal'). They are not only a cultivating caste but were known in the past for practising a variety of other occupations: shopkeepers, goldsmiths, carpenters, oilmen, as well as successful traders (Risley 1981: 188). Similarly, many semi-nomadic fishermen, presumably of the Pod and Namasudra castes, on becoming sedentarised and tax-paying cultivators categorised themselves as Sheikh in the censuses of the beginning of the century because they saw cultivation as linked to Islam (Eaton 1987: 10–11).

It is obvious that people in Lower Bengal have always been on the economic and social margins of Bengali society. They were brought to the region in order to reclaim forests and cultivate land and were initially cut off from their kin. Maybe to justify their lack of bhadralok practices of purity and pollution, the fishers sometimes said that their forefathers had abandoned these practices when they had arrived on the Sundarbans islands. They explained to me how, slowly, in a place where one's survival depended and still depends on one's neighbours' goodwill, they had grown to consider themselves as 'one' community — the people of the Sundarbans (*sundarbaner manush*) — where people from different communities all ate and worked together. They might have different culinary and religious practices, but when it came time to face the unpredictable rivers and wild animals of the Sundarbans, they were reminded of their common humanity. This was an explanation often provided for fishers' disengagement with the requirements of religion and caste. The other reason cited was Hamilton's ideal of a co-operative society where they had all been given equal access to land and expected to be 'neither slave nor master'.

In fact, the economic and religious practices and social orbit of share-croppers or labourers and fishers of Lower Bengal, whether Muslim or Hindu, have always been very similar.[22] Religious practice being very often linked to the occupation one practises, and occupation being something one can change, people shift religious practices when changing occupations. To match the example of Namasudras returning themselves as Muslim Sheikhs and vice versa, one could take the present-day religious transformation of those who become prawn seed collectors (more on this in Chapter V). Conversely, one of the marked distinctions between the bhadralok and the gramer lok on a religious level is the kind of deities each group worships. The deities of the bhadralok, like the bhadralok themselves, are seen as belonging to a superior order as these are 'proper Hindu deities' as opposed to the marginal or 'improper' ones on the border of Hinduism and Islam of those engaged in what are seen as 'menial' occupations linked to the forest or the river.

In this context I would like to draw attention to the fact that the negative stereotypes of Sundarbans Muslims as being 'aggressive' and 'rustic' are not extended to all Muslims. The inhabitants of riverside Garjontola look forward each spring to hosting urban Muslim bee-keepers for three months. The bee-keepers have been coming to the village since the early 1990s. They place between fifty and a hundred beehives in the garden patches of those islanders' homesteads which lie directly opposite the forest. Amongst those who live along the river, the few households who own a lot of land and aspire to be bhadralok refuse to sublet their gardens to them. However, most of those who work in the forest or as prawn seed collectors and live along the river are very happy to have them. The bee-keepers are, by Sundarbans islanders' standards, very educated, sophisticated and better-off and, being part of the bhadra urban middle class, have what are seen as the attributes of progress such as only one or two children, one wife and no beard. The bee-keepers are considered to be of a higher social status than the islanders. Their association with modern urbanity rather than with what are considered to be conservative country ways prompted the islanders to pay the same deference towards them as they did towards city people.

These men, called the 'honey-men' (*modhuwala*), never stay more than a couple of nights at a time and usually leave a junior assistant in charge of the hives. The fact that they are urban and better-off is obvious by the paraphernalia they sport, such as better quality clothes, watches, shoes, and plastic bags, and by their use of a more refined Bengali — and their many bhadralok complaints. The bee-keepers find it a terrible ordeal to live in the village, even when it is only for two days, and always complain about how, when they return to their own villages, their family members nag them about having become dark and thin. There are practically no facilities for tea or snacks, no electricity and no TV and, like any other visitor who visits these 'down' villages, they grumble about the lack of basic amenities. This reinforces the fishers' idea that they are living in a god-forsaken place and that the air, water and harsh conditions they are surrounded by make them cantankerous. 'Why,' the islanders would remark, 'even the suave and peaceful bee-keepers turn crabby when they stay here for more than two days.'

The residents of riverside Garjontola welcome the bee-keepers as this venture brings them cash, around 20 litres of honey, and much-appreciated entertainment and conversation. I even came across photos of the bee-keepers with the various family members of the household.[24] There are, surprisingly, no complaints about the bee-keepers' bees depleting the forest of its nectar supplies even though many of the bee-keepers' hosts occasionally depend on honey-collection from the forest. It is believed that the bee-keepers' bees, being smaller and more hard-working than the wild variety, lose no time first thing in the morning flying to the forest but, because these bees are 'foreign' or 'Italian', they are not very hardy and never really go very far inside and therefore do not threaten the forest honey-collectors' wild honey bees. The local bee-keepers stress that the forest is an abundant 'storehouse' and that there are enough flowers for both sets of bees. Meanwhile, the service holders and cultivators are bemused and completely ignore these close interactions between the bee-keepers and their riverine kin or neighbours.

The school teachers, regarding themselves as invested with the noble task of bringing bhadra knowledge and civility to the rustic gramer lok, are keen to mark their elite status by organising the celebration of Saraswati puja and the birthdays of Tagore and Netaji at the islands' primary and secondary schools.[25] They change the names of those Hindu students who have Muslim first names (such as Gazi or Ali for boys and Zorina, Fatima or Bonbibi for girls). I was told that it was because the gramer lok did not know better — they had, inadvertently 'wrongly' named their children and that it was up to the school teachers to give these students 'proper' names matching their religion, especially if these students were good enough to sit for public examinations. They felt that otherwise it would reflect badly on the village which would then be considered backward. When, however, I asked the grandparent of one of these children why she had named her granddaughter Zorina (a Muslim name), she laughed uneasily and said, 'So?' Perhaps thinking that I would judge her about 'not knowing better', she added,

> In the Sundarbans, especially us living in the 'downs', we all have to depend on the forest and on the protection of our forest deity Bonbibi; aren't we all her children? We just drink from different breasts, Muslims eat cows, we eat goats, but we have the same blood flowing through our veins as we have the same mother.

An important aspect of social life is that, if one is an inhabitant of the part of the Sundarbans linked to the forest, one is part of a 'collective' which has to adhere primarily to the 'cosmology of the forest' but it is important to note that this is also seen as 'Islamic' which, for the gramer lok, conjures up an ethos of 'egalitarianism'. The fact that the realm of the forest is seen as 'Islamic' takes on great significance in light of what Eaton has argued about cultivators categorising themselves as Muslims at the beginning of the century because they saw cultivation as linked to Islam, which was perceived as bringing about greater equality between people (1987: 10–11). This will be discussed in more detail in Chapter VI.

If local people appeared uneasy about discussing the Sundarbans' dark history of communal infighting, one can find signs of harmony between Hindus and Muslims at an individual level. Many people have 'elected' relatives amongst the other group. Quite by chance, when I was taken by one of my students to his family friend's house in another village, I discovered that the children of the house had both a Hindu and a Muslim name because their parents were 'of both religions'. I had not been given this information while we were on our way to this friend's place even though I had been briefed about the fact that my student's family friend was a singer by occupation. I soon learnt that theirs had not been a 'love' marriage. Tamal, the father of the children, narrated how he had gone to sing in a 'down' village. Enchanted by his voice, a middle-aged man had approached him with a marriage proposal for his daughter. This was because his daughter had a beautiful voice herself and wanted to marry someone from the 'singer jati' and not a fisherman like her father.

That the boy was a Muslim and the girl a Hindu had not deterred either family. When I pointed this out, Tamal explained that it is not uncommon to find Hindu–Muslim marriages throughout the Sundarbans and that these used to be much more prevalent in the earlier days — he said that his grandmother had been a Hindu as well. To facilitate the marriage ritual, in the case of these mixed marriages, the girl converts and the wedding is performed according to the rites of the groom's religion. However, the bounded and limiting constructs of 'Hinduism' and 'Islam', especially amongst the landed gentry, are all the time gaining greater currency and preventing such marriages.

Let us conclude with a scene from a compelling novel, *Padma River Boatman*, where a group of Hindu and Muslim islanders are sailing off for a distant island of the Sundarbans. In it, Kuber, the main protagonist, a Hindu fisher and boatman (these two occupations often go together), on seeing the two different cooking arrangements on the boat (one for Hindus, the other for Muslims), remarks to himself, 'Leave differences of religion and their petty rules to those who make their living by tilling the soil — why should boatmen be bound by such trivialities?'[26]

Politics of Homestead Location

In the Bengali cultural understanding of land and house, it is not so much having a roof over one's head that is important as having a *bhite* (homestead).[27] The bhite is the consecrated piece of land where one's house is built, or where one's parental house lies. It includes the courtyard and the adjoining non-cultivated land surrounding the house. Land is usually divided along horizontal strips from the bund, with a small kitchen garden patch in front, the homestead (usually consisting of a house and courtyard surrounded by thick mud walls for protection against tigers) and a pond behind the house and paddy fields beyond. Having a bhite is so important that in violent fights people often curse their opponents with losing it.[28] In the section that follows I will discuss the issues involved in the choice of the location of homesteads.

As mentioned earlier in this chapter, Garjontola is roughly divided between the wealthy western area and the poorer southern area along the river. The residential area where the landed gentry live is called 'Schoolpara' because the big houses (three of them brick) of the area accommodate most of the school teachers and because the brick path that strings these residences together leads to one of the two more important schools of the island. The habitations located here are those of the late Pareshbabu's family (who, with their 16 acres, were the richest household), the headmaster of Toofankhali High School, many of the school teachers, a couple of doctors, the school clerk, Tara the shop owner, the school matron — in other words, the socio-economic 'elite' of Garjontola.[29]

One of the first things that Badal, my host's cousin, told me was that in Garjontola they are all related. As I mentioned earlier, large numbers of Toofankhali islanders are related to Pareshbabu; therefore, his past is intimately linked to Garjontola's history. Pareshbabu arrived from East Bengal in the 1930s with nothing in his pockets and was known to have worked as a simple labourer on other people's fields. He had ended up the richest man of the village through an incredible combination of luck and shrewd moves. When he shot a tiger in the early 1950s, the Scottish nephew of the erstwhile estate manager, Sir Daniel Hamilton, gave him 3 acres of land as a reward and his claim to fame and fortune was clinched. Soon after, he made the right political connections and married each of his nine daughters to very successful young men. He now had roughly sixteen times more land than the average islander, owned a tractor, a tiller, a registered boat, and a two-floored brick house. His eldest daughter's marriage to Toofankhali High School's headmaster had mutually reinforced the two men's status.

Pareshbabu may have been the richest man in Garjontola but his blood relatives from the riverside had ceased the usual exchange of food, tools and visits when, after being targeted by dacoits, he had shifted homesteads. Deciding that his house on the river's edge was no longer safe, he moved nearer the interior of the island closer to the school. He then had the panchayat build a road to the school from the jetty so that he could reach both places easily from his house. Even though the new homestead was barely five minutes' walk from the old one, by shifting his homestead from the river's edge to the interior, Pareshbabu had moved 'up'. In due course, he had invested some of his money in a flat in Kolkata, and his village homestead, now situated amongst those who had done well for themselves, no longer saw any 'comings and goings' (*asha-jaowa*) from his kin living on the river's edge.

When I was still new to the village, Badal insisted on impressing upon me the fact that he had relatives living 'up' — in Kolkata and its suburbs. Over the months, I saw, however, that there were no 'comings and goings' between the rural and the city relatives and noted the silences about them, punctuated by the significant phrase about their 'blood having changed', affected as it must have been by their shift of homesteads and the air of Kolkata. So even though people are all related by blood, 'relatedness' is based on whether food is shared and visits exchanged. The location of one's homestead and the easy exchanges which are possible in relation to the geographical location of one's homestead are important not only to remain 'related' with one's kinsfolk but also in thinking through the terms along which kinship is understood.[30] To better grasp how relations with blood relatives are negotiated, and to introduce the widely practised custom of 'elected' relations, I will now show how Pareshbabu's poorer relatives became separated from his immediate family over his funeral ceremony (*shraddho*).

Pareshbabu died during the time I was conducting fieldwork. The funeral ceremony created some trouble since many of his Garjontola relatives refused to attend on the grounds that 'they had not been invited properly'; people from Schoolpara had been given preference over them in that the Schoolpara crowd had been invited by Pareshbabu's own son, Subhas, while they had been invited only by Nityo, a distant relative who worked for Pareshbabu. In fact, the acrimony turned out to be more about the fact that Pareshbabu's son had approached his neighbours, rather than his own blood kinsmen, to organise the actual ceremony. Badal said:

> They've become his relatives, those residing in well-off Schoolpara, just because they're rich, eh! We, as family, as his 'own crowd' (*mohal*) should have been the ones involved in the organisation of his funeral. We should have been asked to supervise the building of the marquee, do the shopping, cook, keep the accounts, organise for a singer and musicians to come.[31]

So those from Garjontola who felt that they hadn't been 'properly invited' had called a meeting and decided that they wouldn't go. Lokkhi, Badal's sister, complained:

> What do they think? That there is no rice in Garjontola? Well, they can stuff their faces in theirs, we're not going. What is important is to take part as family. Anyone can be called to eat!

The fact that the poorer blood relatives from Garjontola had not been invited to help organise the ceremony was taken as an indirect way of letting them know that their visits or 'comings and goings' to the homestead would not be welcome. They in turn were not ready to compromise their self-respect by attending such a meal, even though the banquet held the fascinating attraction of good food, colourful clothes and the chance of catching up with long-lost relatives and generally providing a break from the humdrum of everyday life. One of the greatest rift-causing factors between blood families is thus moving one's homestead 'up' and the often consequent subtle re-prioritising of people around invitation procedures, food sharing and access to homesteads.

Those whose homesteads are worst off are those whose houses are nearest the bund. Walking on the crest of the bund, which is anywhere between 2 m to 5 m above the ground, one sees the houses stretched on one side and the river on the other. Beyond the houses lie the ponds and the fields. Due to a gradual shift of the Pathar river bed, a long strip of land had emerged along the southern part of Garjontola. Even though these new sand bars are considered government property, it is common practice for the inhabitants of homesteads directly in front of them to use the sand bars as parking spots for their boats or as a latrine ground (hence the smelly bunds). The islanders also collect any honey or twigs fallen off the mangrove trees which sprout there. These newly emerged strips of land, as long as they remain 'un-bunded' and therefore submerged by the tide twice a day, are seen as being of no importance. Consequently, the islanders do not object to deprived relatives 'temporarily' settling along the bunds which are flanked by the new muddy sandbars.

Settling directly along a bund is dangerous (tigers swimming over; high tide waves washing over the top, flooding fields and drowning houses). People are generally not desperate enough to build a permanent hut there. No crops can be grown on these strips of saline land and they are anyway soon overgrown with mangrove shrubs. It is, however, not uncommon to come across the little makeshift huts of people who have been marginalised, built along the bunds adjoining the sandbars. These huts belong to old women who have been abandoned or who do not get along with their sons and daughters-in-law, women who are separated or widowed, or young women who are estranged from their husbands, either temporarily because their husband is working elsewhere as a labourer or because they do not get along with him any longer and have come back to their parental village.[32] In places, on a platform jutting out from the crest of a bund, a makeshift shack, called *khoti*, is built along an adjoining fishery by a prawn fishery owner. These serve to watch over the fishery at night and are used as a prawn seed transaction area during the day. They also become temporary living spaces for prawn dealers during the busy months. Along the bund there are also little grocery stores built by men who have gone through high school but found no 'service job' and now think that working in the forest is below their status as 'educated'.

To conclude, in contrast with living along the bund, living next to a brick road is a mark of success, just as living in an 'up' island is versus living in a 'down' one. The location of one's homestead corresponds to social status. People rebuild their houses every three to five years and change homestead locations when they feel threatened by their neighbours (including their wider families). Being well-off in the Sundarbans makes you susceptible to the envy or even wrath of your poorer relatives. Indeed, this, and not so much the pan-Indian belief in the 'evil eye' was very often the reason given to me by fishers and landowners alike as to why successful people never remain in the 'down' islands. As mentioned earlier, the successful have their fisheries poisoned, their ripe crops harvested and stolen or even at times set ablaze, their houses attacked by dacoits. As I learnt in time, these acts are seen as justified on the grounds that 'in the Sundarbans, we're in the same boat', so anyone doing better is seen as having done so on the back of others and thus becomes a 'legitimate' target of public offstage malevolence (à la weapons of the weak) with degenerations into episodic violent outbursts.

Land and its possession are seen as fundamentally 'alienating'. If in the three Hamilton islands, its history is based in the equity initiated by Hamilton's co-operative dream, in the rest of the Sundarbans, land is tarnished for the very hierarchical and divisive relationships it engenders — and even in the Hamilton islands land ultimately proves destructive, as the islanders tell it. What is of relevance is that divisions between people today are not so much based on distinctions of jati or religion as whether one owns a substantial amount of land versus whether one depends on the forest. Land symbolises hierarchy and exploitation and is seen as dividing families. In contrast, in the next chapter the forest will be highlighted as the domain of 'equality', a realm which unites every-one in a web of 'sharing'.

Notes

1. One of the more drastic land reforms in WB has been the provision of land and therefore the possibility, for the rural poor, of owning homesteads. There have been two pieces of legislation following the Land Reforms Act: *(i)* the WB Acquisition and Settlement of Homestead Land Act 1969; and *(ii)* the WB Acquisition of Homestead Land for Agricultural Labourers, Artisans and Fishermen Act 1975. This latter Act transferred homestead ownership (up to a limit of 1.08 acre and built before 26 June 1975) to the rural landless poor who had occupied someone else's land (Bhaumik 1993: 45–46).
2. South 24 Parganas: Canning I, Canning II, Joynagar I, Joynagar II, Mathurapur I, Mathurapur II, Kakdwip, Namkhana, Pathar Pratima, Sagar, Gosaba, Basanti, Kultali; North 24 Parganas: Sandeshkhali I, Sandeshkhali II, Haroa, Hingalganj, Minakhan, Hasnabad.
3. The RSP and the CPIM are both part of the Left Front government (in power since December 1977) but are violent opponents in the Sundarbans.
4. Emilybari got its name from Hamilton's aunt, Jamespur was named after Hamilton's nephew, Annpur was named after James' wife, and Luxbagan apparently after Hamilton's sister Lux.
5. The central government gave 1,50,000 to this institute in 1938, but Hamilton died the following year and the project never materialised.

6. The notorious examples of forceful settlements were in Jharkhali and Hetalbari.

7. For the whole of WB, until March 1996, it permitted about 273,000 landless persons to acquire homesteads (Siddiqui 1997: 232).

8. A marshland about 6 km away from Garjontola which had been dried only about a dozen years earlier.

9. Even though this latter kind of land (termed 'wasteland' in administrative jargon), as established by the WB Municipal Act 1993, enables municipal authorities to reclaim it for the promotion of social forestry (Siddiqui 1997: 234).

10. Strikingly, 98.5 per cent of the delta villages do not have access to fish preservation or processing units (Banerjee 1998: 247). There is not a single ice plant in Satjelia.

11. This information was corroborated by Tessa McGregor (personal communication July 2002), a geographer and biologist who worked in the Bangladesh side of the Sundarbans between 2000 and 2001.

12. I prefer the term 'Adivasi' to 'tribal' which has rightly been critiqued for being a category constructed as a consequence of the European perception of India to give administrative sanction to the colonial state (Devalle 1992).

    Hazaribagh and Santhal Parganas are in the Chotanagpur Plateau and part of the state of Jharkhand.

13. For an explanation of the basis on which the British classified their labourers, see Ghosh (1999: 33).

14. However, it seems that the Pods, like the other major Bengali cultivating castes, have long engaged in an upward status mobility effort, claiming the title Paundra-Kshatriya, which associates them mythically with the legendary Pundra of the *Mahabharata*.

15. From O'Malley's census report we learn that the vast majority of the inhabitants of the Sundarbans area, especially the districts of Khulna and the 24 Parganas, were Paundra-Kshatriyas (1914, Table XIII: 181). The Namasudras and the Paundra-Kshatriyas, along with the Adivasis, are considered the 'original settlers' of these two districts (O'Malley 1908: 65).

16. Parasuram wanted to wage a war against the Brahmins as they had not treated his mother with the respect due to a queen. He avenges her by exterminating them all. This story, however, seems to be a local and much changed version of the original story. In it, Parasuram is a Brahmin king who avenges his father's death by coming back to earth eighteen times to exterminate all Kshatriyas (the warrior caste) and rid the world of their oppression.

17. 'Idioms of ritual pollution' refers to the process by which lower castes seek upward mobility by emulating the rituals and practices of the upper or dominant castes. I use this term even though, as Fuller points out, it confuses rhetoric with actual practice as there is no agreed sanskritic Hinduism (1992: 24–28).

18. Like, for example, the Jatav who deny their Untouchable status (Lynch 1969: 69).

19. Even if calling Adivasis 'Hindus' is highly debatable, in the case of the Sundarbans the Adivasis would classify themselves as 'Hindus'.

20. Rabindranath Tagore (1861–1941) is the most well-known poet, writer, artist, and composer of Bengal. He founded an experimental school in a village he named Shantiniketan (literally, 'the abode of peace' in WB) based on the blending of Eastern and Western philosophies. In 1913 he was awarded the Nobel prize for literature.

21. With reference to the veneration of the goddess well-liked amongst the bhadralok, the more popular worship of the goddess Durga was not undertaken by individuals in the Sundarbans because of the cost involved. She has, however, now become the goddess celebrated by the shopkeepers of the markets of the 'down' islands of the Sundarbans. At her festival, three images of her are placed, one at each of the three markets of Satjelia island.

22. See examples given by Risley (1891, II: 176–77); O'Malley (1908: 65–68); Webster (1911: 39).

23. As observed by Niyogi (1997); Bouez (1992: 1–5); Dimock (1969: 23–24); Nicholas (1969); Mitra (1903, 1917, 1918); O'Malley (1914: 83–84, 1935).

24. As I came to understand it, a photo is considered a clear marker of who one associates with as well as proof of this association. Friends and elected kin often came to me to have their pictures taken together. At an election, each group of men, representative of different political parties, wanted me to take pictures 'for the record'.

25. 'Netaji' (meaning 'revered leader') is the affectionate name for the most prominent Bengali freedom fighter, Subhash Chandra Bose, who took up armed struggle against the British Raj.

26. See Manik Bandopadhyaya (1973: 94).

27. Indeed, the Bengali word for 'refugee' is *udbastu* — which means 'one without a homestead'.

28. *Bhitay ghughu charano* means to raze someone's homestead to the ground, to render a person homeless or to ruin them completely.

29. Incidentally, the school matron is the only Brahmin in Garjontola and came to the village in 1995 when she was appointed, in an ironical twist, to work as the janitor at the High School. Like the other school teachers, she had managed to procure a big enough sum to pay her way into getting the job, lived in a portion of Pareshbabu's homestead and made the students clean the classrooms.

30. I will take the conventional facts about north Indian kinship in general and Bengali kinship in particular to be common knowledge.

31. *Mohal*, a term which gained currency during the Permanent Settlement, means 'one's own place'. It comes from the word *mohalla* which means 'neighbourhood'. In the Sundarbans' context it denotes both a loose group of families all related by blood and also a geographical part, like a village mohalla or a forest mohalla.

32. As highlighted by Agarwal (2000) and Basu (1992), the Left Front's land reform efforts have been completely gender insensitive. These, for all the government's good intentions, have not helped change the gender imbalance within the rural areas by, for example, extending the registration process to widows or female-headed households.

IV

Is Salt Water Thicker
than Blood?

Soon after my arrival, I found myself plunged into a heated debate.
This was clearly not the first time that a discussion about what was
causing tigers to kill humans had occurred. It began simply enough
at the house of my hosts, Hori and Maloti Mondol. One of the
guests that evening was Mihir, a fifty-five-year-old neighbour and
a tiger-charmer who kept me enthralled with stories of the jungle
throughout my time in Garjontola. Tonight he was explaining his
technique of 'remote-controlling' tigers. Just as he was telling us about
'checking the *mal*' (forest earth/ground; see later in this chapter for
a more detailed explanation), he remembered an incident that had
occurred a few days earlier, when his hand had refused to settle on
the earth. By this he had understood that there was a tiger lurking
whose charms were stronger than his and that it was best to leave
the place. He also added that his charm was not working because
the group of youngsters he was accompanying were acting in a very
rowdy manner. Fearing for their lives, he told them to hurry back to
the boat, while he desperately went on flinging charms towards the
forest to keep the threatening tiger at bay. Then, realising that there
was nothing more he could do, he decided to return to the boat
himself. It was only then that he saw that his wife, Kusum, had not
gone back to the boat with the others but was courageously standing
beside him. He now demonstrated to us how he had grabbed her arm
and hurried back to the boat with her. Mihir concluded by saying that
the 'greed' of prawn seed collectors, the violence between 'different
parties', and the fact that there were too many people entering the
forest were causing tigers to feel disturbed and therefore annoyed
with humans. Because humans were taking the forest too much for
granted, the place was losing its sacred character, which ultimately
was ruining the effectiveness of charms.

At this point, Prodip, another neighbour intervened with a sneer,

Say instead that it's women! Ha, how can your charms take effect if you take your wife to the forest and think about her while reciting them?

Now Prodip Mondol is also a first cousin of Hori Mondol, my host. He officiates as priest and prefers to be called 'Thakur' (literally 'lord', a term of respect and usually a Brahmin caste name) and had of late become a 'proper' Vaishnavite — which in this case meant that he had become vegetarian.[1] The islanders often poked fun at him, saying he was lucky they did not tell his disciples that he ate fish when he proclaimed for all to hear that he was a vegetarian. People often got annoyed at the unsolicited displays of erudition he indulged in at the slightest opportunity and, as he was the youngest of his generation in the Dwarik household, I often saw his brothers and cousins mocking him. But he had won a small following amongst the islanders through acting as their officiating priest — and also through his colourful narratives about the kind of food he had been served at the various pilgrimage sites he had visited.[2] His accounts of his experiences at these sites were greatly enjoyed, especially one at a pilgrimage centre where he got the shock of his life by being 'surely mistaken for a Naga' and served what he took to be frogs, snakes, snails, and worms to eat.[3]

Back to the story of the tiger-charmer: 'Never!' retorted Mihir. 'The charms weren't working because the others were making such a din, it was only at the last minute that I rushed back with Kusum, and if I hadn't been present there would have been an "accident".' (The English term 'accident' is often used when a person is killed by a tiger.) The argument was becoming more heated. 'The extent of your ignorance about the laws of purity and impurity surprises me. You don't hesitate to take impure women into a sacred place and then you wonder why your charms do not work,' snapped Prodip. At which Mihir rose and said to his wife, 'Come, let's leave.' We all pleaded with him to stay, but he was adamant. 'You see,' said Prodip turning to me after Mihir's departure, 'first he takes women to a place where there are so many restrictions about purity and impurity, and then he does not even have the mental concentration to keep his mind off his wife while he is trying to make his charms work'.

Prodip then continued,

Previously, I used to worship Bonbibi, and even had visions of her: she was tall and plump, fair and very, very beautiful, had a compassionate expression, peaceful eyes like those of exquisite lotus blossoms. She did not teach me any charms but told me very softly that it was fine for me to enter the forest. I was so taken by her image that I made a clay statue of her the next day and worshipped her. I had this vision prior to setting off for the jungle to get wood to build my house. But, once my house had been built and I had married and had received a relatively large amount of land as dowry, I was afraid to return to the forest and decided to become a Vaishnav. In the forest, Bonbibi cannot be replaced by Krishna or Kali.

His dilemma was that he now owned land (contrary to the forest ethic) and also, he said, that 'forest deities are Muslim and Hindu deities are no good in the jungle.' 'But why have you stopped going there? If you say Krishna is the supreme god, then surely he has the power to rescue you from any tiger?' I asked.

No, the jungle is exclusively Ma Bonbibi's and she is sent by Allah, and they are Islamic, so if I want to go there I would have to betray Krishna, and so neither divinity would be happy.

After giving me an impressive list of the things he did, or refrained from doing (eating fish, for example — at which Maloti scoffed), as a Vaishnavite, he told me that he had become one because at least 'they know the Hindu gods from the Muslim ones'.

Prodip had the knack of getting on Maloti's nerves and by now she was already annoyed at the way he had upset Mihir and in her house too. Losing patience with his pompous self-aggrandisement as a man of religion, which I was diligently transcribing, she said

Purity and impurity has to do with the heart, not silly rules. Why, I call god's name when I am in the loo shitting, as it is the only moment of the day I have to myself.

'How disgusting, to think you would not have a better time and place to call god!', snorted Prodip. 'Well, shitting is a god-given necessity so I don't see the problem,' she answered back.

I then asked Prodip why he thought women were 'impure' and shouldn't be allowed into the forest. When he replied that it is because they menstruate, Maloti quipped, 'A god-given necessity!' A bit surprised that she was not showing more decorum, at least in front of the newly arrived guest (myself), and maybe to get back at her, Prodip then said that women are less pure because they underwent operations to stop getting pregnant. (Maloti had had herself sterilised and, being a health-worker, often enlisted women to undergo sterilisations.) Tiger charms would be ineffective because of the missing organ (as with Brahmin priests who can have no impairments if their ritual worship is to have any effect), he said. I remained silent but Maloti, not one to give up easily, said, 'What about your appendicitis? I presume its absence does not disturb you in the recitation of your *mantras* [sacred formulae recited during the worship offered to deities]?' Lost for a reply, and annoyed at this public snubbing, Prodip took his departure. After he had gone, Maloti told me that 'only a few nit-wits from some distant villages' believed him to be 'a proper Vaishnavite'.

> He does not adhere to half the rules he was listing; when worshipping, everything has to do with the heart, not ridiculous pantomime. Besides, in the forest, one has to adhere to a different set of rules.

The Realm of the Forest

What is considered of prime importance by the forest fishers is to remain free from the divisions of jati when one goes to the forest. This is the reason why arguments over whether women should be allowed in are in fact often the subject of heated discussion. Some of the forest workers do believe that the sacred forest will be defiled if women are allowed in. Others, like Mihir, believe that this is erroneous because, when one works in the forest, one has to overlook jati differences — and this includes, he explained, those of caste, religion, or, indeed, gender. Mihir, like many forest workers, argued that women could even become tiger-charmers, that he knew of some who had, and that it was those who believe in upholding these differences who had 'impure hearts' and therefore jeopardise the forest's 'purity'. When, out of curiosity, I asked to be taught some of the charms, I was told by Mihir that he would be ready to initiate me if I were ready to lead groups into the forest and give up crab-eating (seen as *makruh* or 'not recommended' in Islam). Later he explained how working in the forest did not give rise to the same kind of relations as those around land: 'Interactions around land are hierarchical and violent, as land is 'status'; it makes people greedy and divides families, but the forest equalises and unites.' (Prodip himself had clearly recognised this when he felt that the land he received as dowry transformed him into someone who could no longer enter the forest.)

That is why the little shelters erected in Bonbibi's honour are rarely located on a person's homestead but along tracks or pathways to protect, to 'show the way', to all who travel along those paths. The most important shrines though are located within the precinct of the forest, in small clearings along the banks of rivers. On the two main days of her yearly worship, in mid-January and mid-February, new images of Bonbibi are placed in little shrines by those who want to take up forest work in the coming year or by veterans of this line of work.[4] As night falls, the islanders sit in little groups and worship Bonbibi by reading aloud her story from the *Bonbibi Johuranamah*. In the evening her story is performed by islanders who have been practising their parts for weeks. They act and sing the story of this 'interstitial' being — mediator between Allah and humans, between village and forest, and between the world of humans and that of tigers.

According to the islanders, especially those who work in the forest, Bonbibi — the 'woman of the forest' — was sent by Allah to protect them against a greedy man-eating half Brahmin sage, half tiger-demon, Dokkhin Rai. The fact that Bonbibi was sent by Allah makes it difficult for the recent followers of Vaishnavism to worship her. Touched by the religious fervour of new converts, they are very keen to follow what they see as the precepts of conventional Hinduism, with its separation between pure and impure and its rational for differences of gender and religion. Emulating the 'up' islands, the islanders of the islands of Gosaba and Rangabelia organise big open-air fairs around the week of Krishna's birth. On one side there is usually a marquee where people can sit and listen to various groups of artists who sing all night in Krishna's honour, while on the other there are stalls of all kinds selling toys, snacks and hot and cold beverages.

The understanding or 'ethos' around the forest and Bonbibi is quite different. Her worshippers (unlike Prodip and the Vaishnavites) do not think of her in terms of 'Muslim' or 'Hindu' but as a 'forest super-power' who extends her protection over individuals of all communities equally. When I asked a Muslim man, who in his youth had been part of a Bonbibi theatre troupe, why he had stopped performing her play, he replied that it was because 'her play can only be acted when people of different jatis come together' and that, after some members of the troupe had left, the others felt that their group no longer represented enough communities. For fear of their group turning partisan, they had stopped altogether.

In fact, he had wanted to gather a few of the group back together and revive the performances but the *imam* had told them that, if they wanted to be 'proper' Muslims, they should cease enacting Bonbibi's story; so the man had stopped. Why was it crucial to be of different jatis when one wanted to enact Bonbibi's story? The man explained that anyone can lay claim to Bonbibi. In some parts, however, her Islamic links are veiled; in some islands nearer the mainland, she is increasingly called 'Bondevi' and worshipped with texts used for mainstream goddesses.[5] However, for those who live in the 'down' islands and work in the forest she remains an 'egalitarian' entity accessible to all. Not only must her shelters be placed on public roadsides but they should be open, either without a door or, if there are doors, they must always be locked. Her story should never be re-enacted by groups of people belonging to multiple jatis and 'la illah il Allah' should always be chanted at the end of her worship.

Bonbibi — adoptive mother of tigers and forest fishers

The forest fishers always invoke the story of Bonbibi as a prelude to the subject of their economic forays into the forest — as a sort of economic 'agreement' about the equitable sharing of food and resources between humans and tigers. The full story goes like this: Dokkhin Rai was a Brahmin sage who lived in the forest. One day, in a fit of greed, he decided to feed on humans. For this, he took the form of a tiger. This was possible for him as, through his ascetic powers, he could magically transform himself into anything he wanted. Due to his increasing greed, he gradually stopped sharing any of the forest resources with humans and legitimised killing them on the grounds that it was a 'tax' (*kawr*) for the products they usurped from what he had come to see as *his* forest. It was not long before his arrogance and greed knew no bounds and he proclaimed himself lord and master of the mangrove (*badabon*) and of all its beings: the 370 million spirits, demons, godlings (*bhoots, prets, dakinis, deo*), and tigers. He turned into a type of demon (*rakkhosh*) that preys on humans. All tigers and spirits became the subjects of Dokkhin Rai and, emboldened by him, they also started to terrorise and feed on humans. The trust that had existed between tigers and humans was now broken.

The story then continues with Allah deciding, out of compassion, for humans, to put a stop to the 'reign of terror' by lifting the 'exploitative tax' that Dokkhin Rai was extorting from the people of the 'land of the eighteen tides' (another name for the Sundarbans). For this task Allah chose Bonbibi, a young girl who lived in the forest. Her father, Ibrahim, following his second wife's wishes, had abandoned his first wife Gulalbibi in the forest while she was pregnant. Gulalbibi had given birth to twins, a girl and a boy but she had decided to keep only her son, Shah Jongoli, abandoning her daughter, Bonbibi, in the forest. A deer took pity on Bonbibi and became her surrogate mother. When she grew up, Bonbibi heard Allah calling her to free 'the land of the eighteen tides' from the exploitation of the Brahmin man-eating sage who took the form of a tiger. At the same time, Ibrahim came back to retrieve his wife and children, but Bonbibi called out to her brother and told him to accompany her to Medina to receive the blessings of Fatima, and then to go to Mecca to bring back some earth from there to take to the 'land of the eighteen tides'. As they arrived back, they called out Allah's name and mixed the holy earth of Mecca with the earth of the Sundarbans. Dokkhin Rai resented their intrusion and their invocation of Allah and decided to drive them away. But Rai's mother, Narayani, insisted that it is better for a woman to be fought by another woman and she took on Bonbibi herself. Seeing that she was losing the conflict, Narayani called Bonbibi 'friend' (*sai*). Bonbibi was so gratified by this that she accepted Narayani's 'friendship' and they stopped fighting.

In this part of the story there is a clear staging of a fight between the Hindu human/animal 'god' (or 'demon' depending on who you ask), Dokkhin Rai, and the Muslim messenger from Allah/'goddess', Bonbibi. This may simply be because the *Bonbibi Johuranamah* (the booklet that narrates their story) was written by a Muslim (on some booklets the author is mentioned as Abdur Rahim, on others, Mohammed Khater) towards the end of the 1800s; indeed, although in Bengali, it is written from back to front to emulate Arabic writing. Moreover, the charms against tigers that Bonbibi is supposed to pass on in dreams are also in Arabic. Dokkhin Rai is a Brahmin, a *muni* (sage) rather than a *pir* (Muslim holy man); his mother's name 'Narayani' is another name for the important Bengali Hindu goddess Durga. This fully inscribes him within the Hindu tradition. What is equally notable is that he stands for all that is wrong and brings about total chaos when he takes over the forest and incites tigers and spirits to kill people or to instil fear in their hearts. If Dokkhin Rai is the symbol of the benign sage turning into a blood-thirsty demon, the abandoned baby girl Bonbibi raised by a deer is, by contrast, chosen by Allah to be a mediator of peace, and becomes a powerful ally for humans.

The myth of Bonbibi is always followed by Dukhe's tale. Dukhe (from the word *dukkho*, meaning 'sadness') was a young boy who lived with his widowed mother grazing other people's animals. His village uncle Dhona (from *dhon* meaning 'wealth') lured him into joining his team to work in the forest as a honey collector. Dokkhin Rai's envious eyes fell upon Dukhe and he appeared to the uncle promising him seven boats full of honey and wax if he, Dokkhin Rai, could have Dukhe in return. After some hesitation, the uncle left Dukhe on the banks of Kedokhali island and sailed off. (Kedokhali is believed to be the only island that remained totally under the control of Dokkhin Rai after Bonbibi had established the forest as a kind of 'commons' to which all have equal access. 'Kedokhali' is translated by the islanders as 'the island where there are only tears'.) Just as Dukhe was about to be devoured by Dokkhin Rai, he called out to Bonbibi, who rescued him and sent her brother Shah Jongoli to give a lesson to Dokkhin Rai. In fear for his life, Dokkhin Rai runs off to his friend, the Gazi, who in the Bonbibi story was Dokkhin Rai's only friend and supporter. Gazi, who was a pir (Islamic holy man; see Chapter V), suggested that Dokkhin Rai must ask forgiveness by calling Bonbibi 'mother'. He then took him to Bonbibi and pled on Dokkhin Rai's behalf. Bonbibi, heeding the Gazi's intervention, accepted Dokkhin Rai as her 'son'.

However, this is not the end of the story. Dokkhin Rai then started to argue that, if humans were given a free reign, there would be no forest left. So, to be fair, and to ensure that Dokkhin Rai and his retinue of tigers and spirits end being a threat to humans, and humans stop being a threat to non-humans, Bonbibi elicited promises from Dukhe, Dokkhin Rai and the Gazi that they were all to treat each other as 'brothers'. She did this by forcing Dokkhin Rai and the Gazi to part with some of their wood and gold respectively and send Dukhe back to the village a rich man so that he no longer had to work in the forest.

Following the recitation of Dukhe's story, the islanders often explained that Bonbibi had left them the injunctions that they were to enter the forest only with a 'pure heart/mind' (*pobitro mon*) and 'empty hands' (*khali hate*). The islanders explained that they had to identify completely with Dukhe, whose unfailing belief in Bonbibi saved him, and consider the forest as being only for those who are poor and for those who have no intention of taking more than what they need to survive. This is the 'agreement' between non-humans and humans that permits them both to depend on the forest and yet respect the others' needs. This arrangement, they say, can last only as long as those who have enough resources of their own leave the forest and its wealth to those who are in need.

There has been much historically oriented discussion and speculation on the origins of this tale. The name Dokkhin Rai would mean literally, 'King of the South' (understood as referring to Lower Bengal).[6] Eaton, who documents the history of the Islamicisation of Bengal, believes that Dokkhin Rai was most probably a minor deified king of the Sundarbans (1987: 4). Eaton also points to another version of these stories, another 'agreement', this time between the explicitly Hindu Dokkhin Rai and the Muslim Boro Gazi Khan told in an epic poem called *Ray-Mangal,* composed by Krishnaram Das in 1686 (it thus predates that of Bonbibi by a couple of hundred years). Eaton believes that this story is a 'personified memory of the penetration of these same forests by Muslim pioneers', the Sufi holy men who, in the thirteenth century, brought agriculture and Islam to the region (1987: 4). In this version, although there is an initial hostile encounter between Dokkhin Rai and the Gazi, the conflict was ultimately resolved by a compromise: Dokkhin Rai, the 'tiger-god', would continue to exercise authority over the whole of Lower Bengal, yet people would show respect to Gazi Khan by worshipping his burial spot. Today, the two always appear together. Dokkhin Rai is marked by the symbol of a human head or as a half-man half-tiger and the Gazi's tomb by a little earthen mound (these are always present in the Bonbibi shrines).[7] Sometimes their full forms are shown. The story of Dokkhin Rai and the Gazi's initial distrust and subsequent friendship is especially popular in areas that were reclaimed earlier — the 'up' islands and the mainland.[8]

For the islanders, Dokkhin Rai represents the domination of class *and* caste (jati in the widest sense). He stands for hierarchy and the arrogance associated with possessing land and goods (i.e., wood). His absolute opposition to the forest 'ethos of equality' is shown by his declaring it to be 'his' private property. He thus suddenly changes from being a sage (one who refuses material possessions) to becoming a rich zamindar who is jealous of his property (forested land and wood). So, as well as being a Brahmin — someone of a superior caste —

Dokkhin Rai is also an exploitative landowner who is so greedy that he is 'keen to kill humans to feed his own greed' (this point will be elaborated below). This is the reason why the forest fishers place so much emphasis on the fact that they have to consider all jatis 'equal'. That is why, the islanders explained, Dokkhin Rai, the Gazi and Bonbibi should all be placed together in shrines: to show how different jatis and religions must come to an agreement when dealing with the forest.

But the logic goes beyond humans. Dokkhin Rai's exclusive claims over the forest and humans as 'his' food is contrasted with the fact that tigers and humans 'share the same food' because, as the forest fishers explained, both depend on the forest — tigers eat fish and crabs just like the islanders and, like them, tigers are 'greedy for wood'. These facts not only make tigers equal to humans but also 'tie' them to humans. Bonbibi herself called Dokkhin Rai, and thereby all tigers, 'brothers' to Dukhe by offering the products of the forest as food for them to share. (There is also a human–animal parallel in the fact that Bonbibi was suckled by a deer, whom she calls 'mother'.)

The reason why the Sundarbans forest fishers believe they are tied in a web of 'relatedness' with tigers is because they have the same symbolic mother in Bonbibi, because they divide the forest products between themselves and tigers, and because ultimately they share the same harsh environment, which turns them all into irritable beings. This idea is best illustrated through the discussions the islanders often have about the tigers from the Sundarbans in the Kolkata zoo. These tigers are said to have 'dried up' and have become 'like dogs' or 'mere shadows of their former selves' because they are cut off from the fresh food of the forest and the daily battle with the tough milieu of the Sundarbans. Correspondingly, the harsh life one lives in the 'down' islands of the Sundarbans, especially the life led by those who work in the forest, is believed to make people irritable and angry but also healthy and strong. Bonbibi, by eliciting an 'agreement' between Dukhe and Dokkhin Rai, that is, from those who work in the forest and tigers, works towards tempering the angry violence of their necessarily aggression-prone relationship around the sharing of 'forest food'. By defeating Dokkhin Rai's prerogative over the forest, Bonbibi is seen as ushering in 'Islamic egalitarianism' between different jatis — in this case, tigers and humans, and by extension, between humans, whether male or female and whether Hindu,

Muslim or Adivasi. Moreover, by treating the forest as a 'commons', she is seen as breaking with religious, jati and class distinctions.

The Tiger-Charmer: Managing Equality, Controlling Violence

The forest is seen by the forest fishers as a 'common food storehouse' that does not distinguish between those whom it feeds. In opposition to land and the restricted access to its fruits, the forest is seen as the realm where all are welcome to partake in its 'food' as long as this does not act to the detriment of those who need it most — whether tigers, deer, or small fishers and crab collectors. The importance of food and its sharing in the making and bonding of kin is of primary importance in the Bengali construction of sociality. As argued by Inden and Nicholas (1977), in Bengal, shared food is the basis of relationships that are both given as well as chosen and this is why it is important to note that what ties humans and non-humans in a symbolic web of kinship is the common forest and the shared food and environment it provides.[9]

How do the islanders perceive and practise kinship and relatedness in a world where they have to adhere to two differing ideologies — that of the forest versus that of the village? What is the position of tiger-charmers and how do they reconcile the dilemmas they face when they have to consider the forest as sacred and peaceful when it is actually violent and is also becoming, in their own words, 'polluted'? Or, how does one live according to the precepts of the forest when the harsh environment one inhabits endows one with a 'cantankerous' disposition, that is, arrogant, greedy and violent?

Those ascribed the biggest responsibility to ensure this 'agreement' between tigers and humans are the tiger-charmers. They have the toughest job of subtly negotiating between groups of humans and non-humans. The islanders believe that those who have been blessed with a vision of Bonbibi (and in some cases Dokkhin Rai) become tiger-charmers. Tiger-charmers are expected to be humble and peaceful so as to be in accordance with Bonbibi's wishes and yet also at times arrogant and violent so as to stand up to greedy Dokkhin Rai and those tigers who emulate him. It is tiger-charmers who decide in each specific situation the stance to adopt — whether meekness or defiance — to smooth potential disagreements between the two groups.

The tiger-charmer (*bauley*, also spelt *bawliya*, *bawali*) is considered to have the ability to control tigers. The word *bauley* traditionally stood for 'woodcutter', 'leader of a group working in the forest' or 'tiger-charmer'. Today, the islanders use it just to mean 'tiger-charmer'. Tiger-charmers have to follow 'Islamic rules' such as not entering the forest on Fridays (*jumma*: holy day for Muslims), refrain from eating crab or pork, or lending or borrowing money with interest charges.[10] Another rule is that tiger-charmers never announce themselves as tiger-charmers. Very surprised by this, I initially thought that the reason for such wariness was the long statist tradition (I mean both gazetteer writers as well as today's forest officials) of blaming them for the high number of tiger victims in the Sundarbans. Most forest-working teams refuse to venture into the forest without a tiger-charmer. The mockery made of tiger-charmers in old gazetteer literature was very much echoed in current forest officials' narratives about how 'these people' feed on the gullibility of islanders and how they are 'worthless and invariably the first ones to be killed'. However, I soon realised that tiger-charmers' reluctance to announce themselves as such had a deeper reason.

Most tiger-charmers work in the forest all year round. They work as crab collectors mainly in winter and as fishers in the monsoon season. Many also work as honey collectors in spring and from time to time, when the occasion presents itself, as woodcutters. They are not distinguished from the others when they go to the forest as fish or crab fishers; however, their presence is considered essential when going honey collecting or woodcutting. They are then supposed to 'feel' if it is sound to take people to the forest. They have the power to cancel a trip to the forest or to dissuade people from going there. The tiger-charmer is also believed to be able to control storms and cure ailments — especially spirit- and forest-related ones. However, at the village level, tiger-charmers do not hold important political or economic positions. They see their role as being a 'call', usually from Bonbibi, and therefore a sort of 'vocation'. The landed, such as the forest officials, see them as the epitome of backwardness and superstition. However, most of the riverside people count on the tiger-charmers' intervention to cure minor ailments and to exorcise them of 'fears' — usually those contracted by young people who visit the forest for the first time.

The tiger-charmers' power is called upon when forest working teams land from the boat to go into the forest and, again, when they have to depart. They are the first to alight from the boat and the last ones to climb back in. Thus, lurking tigers sometimes make off with the tiger-charmer even before he has time to utter his tiger-repelling charms. Once off the boat, his job is to crouch and 'check the earth' (*mal dekha*) by placing his hand on the earth — usually on a little mound — while reciting the names of the five pirs and the five bibis.[11] Once he has finished reciting his silent chants to pacify difficult non-humans — especially tigers and spirits — he ties a piece of earth to his body and keeps it there during the whole venture. Later, before leaving the forest, when all his team-mates are safely back in the boat, he has to crouch again on the forest earth and break the spell he had cast when he first alighted, so that animals can again go about their ways unhindered.

These precautions are explained as showing that one does not mean any harm to the animals. 'Checking the mal' also permits tiger-charmers to 'feel' if they have arrived at a 'correct' time. If they deem that the time is not right, they return to the boat, as one of the important precautions when setting off for the forest is to not disturb animals unduly. Just as it is bad form to arrive at people's houses during lunch or dinner, it is considered to be asking for trouble to enter the forest during the animals' dinner-time, which the islanders believe is at night. A 'correct' time to enter the forest is when tigers and other animals are resting, which is the morning and early afternoon. This is the reason why tiger-charmers usually refuse to go to the forest at night and resent poachers and prawn seed collectors, who are seen as not respecting wild animals' need for privacy when feeding (more on this later in this chapter).

The tiger-charmers have to strike a balance between the needs of non-humans and humans. If, when trying to place their hand down on the mal, their fingers start quivering and their hand refuses to settle gently on the earth (as in the story Mihir told), the tiger-charmer either has to leave or say stronger charms. If they leave, they return to the boat and row it to another part of the forest where they 'check the earth' again. The important aspect of this ritual is to show total deference. As one tiger-charmer explained:

> We crouch on the ground to ask for forgiveness from the forest and its inhabitants for barging in on them and upsetting their routine by the charms we use.

This act of submission is also explained as having to let tigers know that the intruders are 'beggars' who need to be fed because they have nothing left to eat back home.

Most of the tiger-charmers had taken up the task after receiving a vision of Bonbibi and mastering the charms she had taught them through dreams. The important thing, they said, was to remember that Bonbibi cares for the well-being of everyone and that, to ensure the forest animals' needs, humans are supposed to enter with a humble and generous disposition, which recognises, as Mongol explained, 'that the forest is the tiger's realm. I can't just come to your homestead and chase you off from your own house and eat up your food, can I? We're barging into his home, his place, shouldn't we be meek and ask his pardon?' Mihir elucidated,

> Before starting a charm I tell non-humans, especially tigers as they are those who have the biggest egos, 'Listen, lord, you will have to clear off from the path I have chosen, you go yours, let me go mine,' or 'Mother of mine, whether in water or in the jungle, clear my path, collect your tiger children to your bosom and show the way to your human children. Pleading your name, I say these words.[12]

'This kind of opening situates our acknowledgement of our position and does not leave anybody "discontented".' So tiger-charmers have to strike a subtle balance between having the required humility when entering non-human territory and retaining their co-workers' confidence through their reputation as being powerful.

As mentioned earlier, when tiger-charmers go as fishers or crab collectors to the forest, they rarely use strong charms and do not dismount from their boats to 'check the earth'. However, when they go on dangerous ventures such as honey and wood collection, they have to back up mild 'pleas' with strong 'magical formulae'. This is where the tiger-charmers' expertise is seen as essential and where their credibility is most at stake as they have to ensure that the whole team will return to the village safely. Anyone can invoke Bonbibi to come to their aid when they are crab collecting or fishing, say the islanders, because, not taking much, they do not risk much. The work of wood or honey collecting is risky, they say, because it can easily become 'stealing' from Dokkhin Rai. Also, the magical formulae used in these riskier ventures are strong and are believed to have the effect of completely upsetting the routines of tigers and the other forest beings. The most common charm consists of placing a folded leaf on the ground to symbolically hide any lurking tiger.[13] Another popular formula involves 'tying the towel': here the tiger is transformed into a pebble or a small shell and kept tightly tied inside a towel. These magical charms have the power to 'shut tigers' mouths', 'make them drowsy', 'force them to run away as if their bodies are on fire', 'make them ticklish and roll themselves on the ground', explained the islanders. These charms are therefore seen as violent.

The dilemmas faced by these professional mediators emerge very often in conversation. The islanders often argue with each other about the potency of charms in this day and age. One night, after performing some terrifying re-enactments of tigers that the islanders had insisted he do for my benefit, Bharat, who had worked all his life in the forest, said,

> Nothing really works against tigers, they've tried masks, electrified dummies, and guards holding guns, but nothing works. Your only protection is a total confidence in Ma Bonbibi; but this is impossible and when faced with a tiger you start doubting her, and your heart fills with fear. The solution then is to face up to the tiger and you have to show him that you are stronger by letting out a string of loud insults.

He then continued,

> Long ago, whilst a tiger-charmer and I were crab-catching we felt that 'the fakir' was around.[14] The tiger-charmer ran away. I was disgusted and speechless, but suddenly I decided to face the tiger and said in a loud angry voice 'OK you have come to take me but first let me give you a good beating.' This scared the four-legged fakir off.

Bharat was one of the few to speak of his own courage and I attributed this to his great age and the fact that he no longer had to fear tigers as he did not go to the forest any longer. I soon realised, however, that these were not the only reasons. The reason he could hold forth in such a vainglorious way was because, as he admitted, he had 'never taken the risk of being a tiger-charmer' himself. I wanted to know why he had never become one. He replied, 'Just as the tiger-charmer prepares a stick for the tiger, so too another stick is prepared for the tiger-charmer'. Becoming a tiger-charmer is a question of having the courage to become one, as the ultimate retribution is that, when you 'deal violence, you die in violence'. To acknowledge that one is a tiger-charmer in public is thus to invite the wrath of the non-humans, as this is seen as arrogance.

Thus, the main reason why they do not want to acknowledge the fact that they are tiger-charmers is the very nature of their work, an occupation, they say, which necessarily uses 'violence' against animals. This is why, once their day's work is complete, or once they move away from the spot where they have been working, tiger-charmers have to try to limit the damage done by breaking the effect of their charms with the corresponding counter-charm. That is also why many forest fishers are reluctant to become tiger-charmers or to accompany groups on honey and wood collection and also why, when going on the less dangerous jobs of crab collecting or fishing, professional tiger-charmers do not use these charms. Besides, the charms are seen as bothersome when undertaking these jobs because they are believed to have similar effects on crab and fish. 'How do you catch fish,' Mihir asked rhetorically, 'if they are going to swim away as if their bodies were on fire? Or crabs, if they are going to keep their mouths shut and not bite their feed?'

Practical Relations between Forest Fishers, Prawn Seed Collectors, Landowners

Relations, whether blood or 'elected', are very often elaborated around the fact that the Sundarbans is a harsh environment which makes people aggressive and tetchy as well as 'forthright'. The islanders point to the poor quality of land, the fact that paddy can only be mono-cropped, that it can be reclaimed at any time by the saline rivers and that their houses are always under threat of being submerged or blown away by the next tidal bore or cyclone. The islanders often say that having to deal with these calamities and the constant fear of their occurrence makes them violent with each other. They illustrate this by pointing to the general lawlessness, high number of murders, piracy and attacks by robbers in the region. The islanders believe that the constant interaction with the environment has the potential to transform them into 'violent beasts' — but also *matir manush*, 'people of the earth/earthen people' (meaning honest and plain-spoken).

To what extent is the rhetoric of being a matir manush based on the cosmology of the forest, which demands that fairness and honesty be a conscious way of life? The following anecdote is a good illustration: I was coming back from school and, seeing Mihir selling his crabs at one of the richer houses along the school road,

I stopped so that we could walk back home together, as we were neighbours. During his transaction, I had been surprised to note that he sold his crabs on credit. As we walked back, I asked why he had not insisted on getting paid by his customers. We both knew that the people living there had a ready supply of cash. He replied that he needed 'their goodwill' and explained that, with the kind of work he was doing, losing his temper could prove to be lethal. I assumed that this was a reflection of the typical patron/client scenario but, on seeing that he reacted the same way even with poorer clients, I was interested to learn more. I had also, on other occasions, seen Mihir feign anger with the school teachers; however, when he did so, he rarely actually said that they 'owed' him the money for the crabs he had brought them, preferring instead to stress that he needed to build a new roof, pay a doctor's bill, or organise a wedding, to retrieve his dues.

When I enquired why he used the language of the subservient instead of just demanding what he was owed, he explained that the products of the forest could not be exchanged, bartered or sold 'with anger or arrogance'. These were items *taken* from the forest — the forest goddess's 'storehouse'. They could be sold in the market or to specific wholesale crab and fish dealers and to individual islanders as long as there was no animosity and as long as the money made was to survive (i.e., not used to buy excess land or store gold). To insist on getting paid when another person wants the goods but cannot pay is tantamount to a repudiation of kinship or of amiable relations between neighbours. So the forest fishers believe that the economic morality of the forest has to be marked by 'production for use' rather than a 'production for exchange'. The danger, for a forest fisher, is when s/he is tempted to go in for the latter kind of production, because, while self-provisioning is legitimate, profit is not. Also, the ideology of having to 'share with tigers' may be seen as a kind of Sahlinsian 'generalised reciprocity'. This makes sense in light of the fact that those who refuse the 'relatedness' link with tigers and other wild animals are the very ones who poach from the forest or who indulge in Sahlins's 'negative reciprocity' (1974: 196).

Being a crab collector or a forest fisher does not allow one to make much money. For example, the economics of crab collection is as follows: crab collectors usually set off for the forest in teams of threes. The share is divided into four as the boat is considered as one person. The owner of the boat thus gets a greater amount but usually they take turns in using boats so that the extra amount evens out over the months. If a team wants to rent a boat then they usually pay Rs 250 for it. The price of obtaining government passes allowing them to enter the forest and registering the boat comes to about Rs 100 per month. Per month they need about Rs 300 worth of rice, pulses and vegetable, and 5 kg of crab-feed. (This is usually pieces of dried shark — early in the season. After the monsoon months, however, fresh skin-peeled frogs are used as crab-feed.) This amounts to a little less than Rs 220 per person per month in costs. As their overall income is around Rs 900–1,000 per month, once Rs 220 is deducted they are left with Rs 700 to 800.

Team work is very important for crab collectors (and forest fishers). While one rows the boat the other two have to tie the bait at the end of 10 to 12 feet-long strings attached at intervals of about 4 feet on a fine rope of about a kilometre long. Pieces of brick are also tied on to keep the cord close to the river bed. Once the bait has been tied onto the strings, the rope is gently unravelled into the shallow end of the canal, at a distance of about a metre from the bank. When the fishers have come to the end of the rope they wait a quarter of an hour before slowly rowing back to where they tied the end of the rope, while at the same time gently pulling the fine rope back into the boat. The crabs dangling from their feed (*thopa*) at the end of the twines are jerked into little three-cornered landing nets (*jalti*). The crabs are then placed at the bottom of the dinghy with some branches of the goran tree so that they do not tear off each others' claws, as that greatly diminishes their price.

The crabs are sold in three categories. The best are those over 400 g or the female crabs above 300 g laden with eggs which are considered very tasty. The category below this are the crabs weighing over 300 g and the third category are those over 200 g. The heaviest crabs have to be intact and are usually sold at a khoti for Rs 50–80 a kilogram. These are immediately shipped to Canning or Madhyamgram where they are auctioned and then packed before being sent off to the airport as export product. All the other crabs are sold between Rs 15 and 35 a kilo either house to house or at marketplaces to individuals. Each trip brings around 50 kg of crab. In the fishing season, the forest fishers can get very lucky. In one day they can sometimes catch up to 250 kg of crab and fish. But when that happens, they immediately leave the forest and return home to distribute the fish or sell it at a very cheap price.

Once a team had been gone for barely four days when they returned with 250 kg of *ari* fish (a kind of oily sea fish). They sold the fish for an average of Rs 16 per kilo and made Rs 4,000 in one go. But this is rare, and the fishers often encounter forest officials or dacoits who help themselves to some of their best fish and crabs on the grounds that these are government property. Fishers and crab collectors are also fined if they are found in the banned core area of the forest or if they have fresh wood in their dinghy (the fine is Rs 10 per log). The LIC (life insurance) is now compulsory and their family is supposed to get Rs 45,000 if any *accident* happens (except being hit by a storm!). They see their work as honest and this is why they are so careful to abide by the rules both of the state (they rarely go without passes) and the ideology of the forest (returning home as soon as they deem having caught enough fish or crabs).

While crab collectors and fishers recognise that they are under an obligation to 'practise calm behaviour', wood collectors are under no such compulsion and often legitimise angry outbursts against the bhadralok on the grounds that they are helping to fight injustice. One day, whilst Subhas, a wood-cutter, was unloading wood he had collected from the jungle, Nemai, a school teacher, asked him the price. 'Rs 40 a maun [unit of measuring wood roughly equal to forty kilograms],' replied Subhas. 'How expensive!' remarked Nemai. 'Now wait here, let's get our accounts right,' said Subhas angrily.

> How many maun do you think there are on this dinghy and how many days' work do you think this represents? We've been battling with the forest and its dangers while you've been sitting cool in a school paid by our taxes; now just who do you think is trying to make a fool out of the other?

Telling me how Nemai just walked away, his head hanging low, muttering crossly to himself, Subhas explained:

> I showed I was irritated just to give him a lesson. Not many people have the guts to tell them the truth to their face because they act as moneylenders and because they think they are refined. Yet it is known that they are the biggest thieves and have no qualms about stealing from the government, like by ensuring that the brick roads pass in front of their houses or by taking bribes before hiring a new teacher.

People who work in the forest are 'better' than those who work the land because the forest is a *pobitro jayga*, a 'pure/sacred place', the forest workers explain. It is such a 'pure' place that food, whether cooked or collected from the forest (such as crab or fruit), tastes divine because it is untainted by violence and untouched by the polluted soil of the village. The islanders often talk about the 'special healing nature' of the Sundarbans forest earth; this was made especially evident when, as we were getting off a launch, a local forest official told me to remove my shoes so as to better feel the 'earth connection'. He explained how the jungle soil has intrinsic cooling qualities beneficial for the well-being of the body. Echoing what the islanders often said, he told me that not only did the forest act as a 'purifier' and healer of mind and body ailments but also that it is imperative that one enters the forest with 'pure' disposition (here echoing the tiger-charmers). Those who did not would meet their death in the forest, become the target of wild animals or be killed by roots or branches of trees.[15]

So it is not just the tiger-charmers who have to enter the forest with a 'pure heart'. To have a 'pure heart' one has to respect some very specific rules such as keeping quiet in the forest, not defecating, urinating or spitting directly on jungle land or in the river, nor throwing bidi butts or burnt pieces of wood either in the river or in the forest, nor washing the soot off utensils nor combing hair, nor dropping one's axe nor inadvertently make any mark on a tree.[16] The islanders also have to eat up any cooked food which might be remaining at home before leaving for the jungle, or finish up cooked food in the boat before alighting on the forest territory — as a symbol of penury.[17] Entering the forest on certain days such as on the new moon or the full moon, or before 7 a.m. or after 4 p.m. is seen as 'disturbing' animals. There are also a large number of other tedious rules such as not going to the forest if called from behind, if one has had nightmares or is ill and, most importantly, if one is quarrelling with a family member or neighbour.

Tiger-charmers have more stringent rules. After finishing work, they have the moral responsibility of 'cutting off' the effects of charms so that the animals 'can go about freely again'. They have to accept Islamic injunctions and refrain from eating pork as this is *haram* (forbidden) and crab, prawn or turtle meat as these are makruh (not recommended), thus paying respect to the fact that Bonbibi was sent by Allah. Tiger-charmers are supposed to be calm and upright and are not supposed to lose their temper, become violent, lie or steal. There are also a whole set of rules for those left back home — they are not supposed to close doors, fight, soap or oil their bodies and hair, wash or wring clothes or towels, put vermillion in the parting of their hair and on their foreheads, attend a fair or ceremony, or eat meat when their husbands are in the forest. Thus, they act out of companionship with the forest workers and adopt the symbols of widowhood to highlight their complete submission to Bonbibi's or to Allah's power over life and death.

This is why, after a good catch of fish or a very lucky collection of honey, the forest workers think it is inappropriate to remain in the forest even if the season or the tides are propitious for gathering more. Just as Bonbibi was sent by Allah to curb Dokkhin Rai's uncontrolled greed for human flesh, it is now for humans to show the same kind of restraint and to abide by the laws of the forest left by Bonbibi. But entering the forest with a 'pure heart' requires more than limiting what one takes: it also means curbing greedy wishes or deceitful motives (i.e., the urge to hunt/poach). Animals are Bonbibi's 'elected' kin. Because a deer saved her life by suckling her, Bonbibi is believed to consider the deer of the forest as mother. Similarly, as she has adopted Dokkhin Rai — the sage-cum-tiger — as her 'son', both directly and by becoming his mother Narayani's 'friend', she is related to tigers too. But Bonbibi is not only connected to non-humans. She also adopted Dukhe, a poor Sundarbans islander, as her son. Through the adoption of Dukhe she has adopted all those who depend on the forest. Tigers and forest fishers, linked by the same mother Bonbibi, are thus 'brothers' and 'equal', as it is believed that the forest in its 'purity' does not distinguish between the different kinds of beings that depend on it. 'This is why, before entering the jungle, we place ourselves entirely in Bonbibi's hands, vouchsafing to her that we are entering the jungle not of our own free will but forced by our economic situation,' said Sukumar Mridha, echoing what many others told me.

Some of us have been lucky to have received visions of Bonbibi and we try to respect her injunctions: not going into the forest on Fridays, on a full moon or a new moon day, never killing deer or tigers, and reciting the formulae she teaches us in dreams. She knows that actually *we do not have the choice* and that if we go there it is because we are forced by our stomachs and the hungry mouths at home. This is why we jeer at those who have good situations yet go prawn seed collecting along the banks of these rivers full of hungry crocodiles or go to the jungle to poach deer or fell big tree logs in foolish acts of bravado when their actual reason is greed. Ultimately, the only ones who are safe are the crab and fish collectors, as they are satisfied with little (and do not deplete *the storehouse of Bonbibi*) and, as they do not alight onto the soil of the jungle, they do not threaten the animals.

Entering the forest, like pilgrimage sites (one of the forest deities' place of worship — the Gazi's — is called *pithasthan* [pilgrimage place]), can be seen as a sort of 'liminal phenomenon' that brings people who are in its realm to partake of a sense of community feeling (or 'communitas') with each other (Turner 1974: 166). As such, the forest serves inherently to isolate one from one's socio-cultural environment, bringing people into 'a form of institutionalised or symbolic anti-structure' (ibid.: 182). One of the important philosophical dilemmas of forest fishers, and especially of tiger-charmers, is trying to find a compromise between living a life ruled by the demands of the cosmology of the forest versus one ruled by those of rural Bengali sociality.

The Forest and its 'Levelling' Effect

In contrast to relationships organised around land, where befriending the powerful and well-connected (those living 'up', i.e., politicians and bureaucrats) brings one success, the forest fishers believe that the forest has a common law for all. Bonbibi established regulatory laws for the 'proper management of the forest commons,' explained Mihir, and the forest is thus to be shared equitably between all. Thus, humans and animals 'understand' each other because both know the laws bequeathed by Bonbibi. Many stories were narrated to show how dealings between non-humans were 'fair'. A popular 'true' story was about how a villager had caught a glimpse of a group of monkeys' sense of justice:

> A young monkey was playing tricks on another monkey and at one point started pulling his tail and beating him. The other monkeys, seeing this, caught the offending monkey and buried him in the bank of the river with just his head sticking out. The tide started rising and the monkey was soon gasping for breath. After some time, the other monkeys thought the naughty monkey had been punished enough and let him go.

Dealings here were considered 'fair' because the monkey was punished and the punishment meted out was seen as appropriate and just. When I asked how this is different from humans' sense of justice, Prodip explained that humans are malicious and would have hurt the offending person longer than was necessary, perhaps even, in their anger, killing the offender.

It is because forest animals have such a heightened sense of justice, or are so 'pure', that the islanders think it improper to bring back any wild animal, fruit or vegetable from the forest to the village. One of my newly-wed neighbours, Saira, a young woman married to one of Mihir's sons, described the taste of forest fruit as 'ambrosia', better than anything she had ever tasted. When I asked her to tell her father-in-law and husband to bring back some so that I could taste them, she replied, 'But they'd turn bitter'. She then pointed at a coconut tree behind the house and said:

> One of my brothers-in-law tried. He was so delighted by the coconut he had tasted in the forest that he brought back one of the nuts and planted it but, having grown up in our village soil, the kernels are small and tasteless.

'Why do you think that is so?' I asked.

> Well, you see, the village earth is so poor that jungle trees find it difficult to adapt to it; we've been overworking the land and she's now old and overused. However, there's another reason everything tastes so much better there, even the food cooked with little oil and spices, and that is because everything there is so pure. The village is 'polluted' by fights, divisions and hierarchies and this makes the forest fruit turn bitter, the forest animal unhappy, and us people unhealthy.

The forest soil is much richer and the fruits and vegetables much tastier because it is 'holy land', since it is mixed with a clump of earth from Mecca, I was often told. 'Where the village is tainted because of violence and divisions, the forest is pure and sacred, just like its earth and honest animals', said Mihir.

The forest fishers therefore rarely bring back vegetables or fruits from the forest; nor do they track, kill or bring back any wild animals. Besides the risk of incurring Bonbibi's wrath, they said, these animals, being 'pure', have the power to curse human beings. Bhim told me that his uncle once brought back an otter from the jungle and put it in the pond for the children to play with. They looked after it well and kept it a few days but finally released it back into the river because it seemed to grow unhappy and weak. However, the separation between the forest and the village is not completely water-tight. Some of the forest animals are seen to be happy to 'settle' in the village for some time — female tigers come in winter to give birth, when the paddy crops are ripe and high, to protect the cubs from the prowling male tigers of the forest. Bimal had saved a hen by mending its wing during a trip working in the forest and when he was about to return to the village, the hen flew back to his boat and refused to leave him. Since then he had kept her with him, letting her sleep next to his cot at night. He said that, though she was tiny, she was the most courageous hen he had ever seen. She used to fly right into the face of danger and attacked kites that came near the chicks, and always saw to it that all the chicks were fed equally. He therefore provided her feed in a special plate.[18]

I had heard that possessing land compromises one's chances in the forest and that the more land and property one owned, the less one's chances of coming back from the jungle safely. But somehow I had always thought that this was a mere figure of speech, a set of metaphors the islanders had to be heard using for fear of reprisals, especially by lurking non-humans who take offence when they are spoken about trivially. I had been told that it is very dangerous if those working in the jungle fight or have misunderstandings with their neighbours and family members, particularly their husbands or wives. I knew about the importance for those working in the forest of having the goodwill of the whole village and the assurance of the care and affection of their loved ones if they want to return safely from the jungle. What surprised me was to see how closely these injunctions were followed in choosing how one dealt with one's kin and neighbours — such as delaying the payment one receives for one's crabs, refusing to get into rows with one's neighbours, being a pauper or at least not possessing anything of importance like land or gold. It also means being generous and always being ready to give away anything one brings from the forest lest someone's covetous eye falls on it and cause misfortune and, of course, remembering not to be greedy.

This rule was also extended to me one day. My hostess Maloti, fearing that I might endanger myself through my foolhardy wish to accompany Mihir to the forest even after she thought I had 'seen and known enough', challenged me. 'Wasn't Mihir telling you the other day how you have to enter the forest with a pure heart and empty hands?' I said that I understood Mihir to have meant 'without either devious motives or firearms' and that I had neither. Maloti then explained that this could also be extended to not writing more about, nor taking more photos of, the forest than was necessary. 'Don't tempt the tiger,' she said in an attempt to close the chapter on my desire for future trips to the forest.

Briefly, to conclude, whereas land is symbolically linked to hierarchy, divisions and violence, the forest is seen by the forest fishers as a space which brings everyone to an equal level. The forest, the zone of peace and equality where all enter as 'children of the same mother', is 'pure'. This is why, on a practical level, people who work in the forest are required never to engage in hierarchical or divisive behaviour even when in the village. However, living so rigorously along the lines set by Bonbibi is very impractical. How does one adhere to the rules of staying 'pure-hearted' and 'empty handed'? How does one negotiate between being part of the 'violent' Sundarbans people because of the harsh geography and yet 'peaceful', 'forthright' and 'pure' by being a forest fisher? In the next section I will illustrate how understandings of land and forest and the corresponding expected behaviour are major causes of dilemma. If the forest is the sphere where all 'sharing' humans and non-humans are 'equal', how do people resolve their disputes and find a common plane of interaction between conflicting rhetoric around marriage, society and social relations?

The 'Comings and Goings' of Relatives

One hot afternoon, after a particularly ferocious fight with Hori, her elder brother, my neighbour Arati declared loudly that she could not suffer her blood family any longer and that she would shift homesteads. Her shrill voice cursing her brothers, cousins and neighbours early each morning, had already made her infamous. Arati was in her early thirties. She had married of her own volition when she was about twenty and refused to live with her in-laws because of their resentment of their son marrying her. She had resolved the initial problem of finding a homestead by calling upon her school friend and distant cousin, the young Ratan, who was the upcoming RSP leader of their portion of the village, to find her and her husband a spot at Banikhali. Banikhali was a previously marshy place which the RSP had distributed to those who were landless (many of whom were Bangladeshi Hindu refugees) and who had the appropriate

Party connections; it lay at quite a distance from either Arati's or her husband's villages.

A few years later Arati's husband left for the Andaman Islands in search of work. Arati sold off their piece of land in Banikhali and came back to live on her parents' homestead. Arati was then expecting their second child. All through her time at her mother's house Arati had never depended on her parents economically. Neither did she rely on her elder brother Hori, who lived separately with his wife and sons. She had made ends meet by pulling the net along the river bank for tiger prawn seed (though she would not have been able to do that had her mother and sister-in-law not taken care of her two sons). When Arati's father died in 1997, her mother and two brothers had refused to give her any land. Her brothers argued that she had received enough for her dowry (which she alleged was not true as hers was a 'love' as opposed to an 'arranged' marriage) and that, if they gave her a portion of land, they would have to give their other four sisters allotments too, which was physically impossible as the whole of the land amounted to a bare 2 acres. Besides, Hori, the elder brother, having moved out of his parents' homestead, could not lay any claim to his widowed mother's land and only owned half an acre.

This example illustrates the way couples easily shift homesteads. Arati and her husband had first built a small hut in Banikhali. With the departure of her husband for the Andamans, and the birth of her second child, she needed someone to look after them while she made ends meet. When her husband, after a couple of years, returned with some money, they built a hut for themselves on her parents' homestead. Her husband worked in the forest while she continued being a prawn seed collector. In exchange for baby-sitting her sons, she gave her mother and sister-in-law some of the prawns and small fish which got caught in her prawn seed collecting net. Now that the children were going to school and she and her husband had enough money put aside, she wanted a piece of the parental land on which to build a separate hut. When her mother and brothers refused, she decided to settle along the bund.

As discussed earlier, building one's house immediately along the bund meant being on the margin not only of village geography but also of its sociality. This is why, initially, Arati's brothers and cousins tried to prevent her from settling there. She remained adamant and found the place suitable for the following reasons: it was next to the house of her friend and prawn seed collecting companion Miti. Miti was the wife of her neighbour, Sasadhar, and Arati also had a soft spot for his mother as she had been the only one to accept her marriage to her husband, who was a forest fisher. Besides, she was assured by her cousin, Ratan, that she would not face Party pressure to decamp. So Arati and her husband built their house along the bund. One end of the house rested on the bund and the other on stilts planted on the bank of the river. Her elder brother Hori was furious, not so much because she had deprived him of his chance of laying claim to that piece of land (which anyway would have been of no immediate use to him) but because he saw it both as an affront on him and an unsafe spot for his two nephews of whom he was very fond. He, however, soon gave up trying to talk her into coming back because he realised that having her continue living on their homestead would lead to more fights, and his wife had had enough. He was happy that his two nephews felt comfortable enough to come over and share meals or sleep over at his house.

The ease with which Arati and her husband moved homesteads and huts is very representative of how the islanders move whenever they feel that the tension with their blood family members is becoming too much to bear. Also, because she worked as a prawn seed collector, she was wealthier than her landowning female cousins. Having cash at their disposal is progressively enabling riverside women to refuse the exploitation they constantly face, especially in peasant families, and this is the reason why many of them decide to live on their own. What, however, is interesting is that, when I pointed this out, I was told, half in jest, that it is because in the Sundarbans people have such cantankerous natures that they cannot bear to live together. It was also used to account for the way the islanders are continually aligning and realigning themselves into various socio-political groups and constantly openly fighting with each other; having to 'wrestle with tigers and crocodiles each day' and living in this salt environment makes one irritable and angry and always up for a fight.

I happened to be fishing one day as Arati passed by me to get to her younger brother's house for one of their routine exchange of tools, food and information. I told her how much I had enjoyed the prawn she had caught during her latest fishing expedition which she had given to her elder brother's family (with whom I was living). 'Caught such a lot', she replied, 'that I distributed them all over the place.' Curious to learn more about her web of food transactions, I asked her who else had been the beneficiaries of her generosity.

'My mother and younger brother, my cousins and Sasadhar, our neighbour.' She must have noticed my extreme surprise as she hastily added, 'But I didn't step over the threshold of his homestead, I didn't have to lose my face, I sent Tukai.' I said in disbelief, 'But you claim that he's been poisoning your roosters, and the other day you wished him terrible things: that he drown, that his house burn down, his eldest son die . . .'[19] 'He's a real monster, and we're not on talking terms but I sent Tukai, I didn't go there myself,' she insisted. (Tukai is her little seven-year-old son.) 'But the prawn were sent by you, weren't they? What is the point of giving something to somebody you always fight with?' I asked, puzzled. 'I'm friends with his wife and mother who supported my marriage, they're both always kind to me, the prawn was for them. Sasadhar is like my brother, a mean, double-faced, lying bastard. But he borrowed some money from me which he needs to return. I can't afford to completely sever all ties with him as otherwise I will not see my money again. You see, we also need to have the goodwill of those who live around us,' she concluded as she left.

Being of the same age as well as neighbours, Sasadhar and Arati had played and fought together as children but what shocked me was the violence with which they, like the rest of the islanders, still fought with each other, as well as how generous they were with each other. I asked why she fought so often. She laughed out loud and said,

> But haven't you noticed that here it is a pastime we all engage in? We are 'people of the low-tide lands' (*bhatir desher lok*), always in contact with salt air and water; we are bad-tempered, just like our tigers. Stay here for a while and then see if this place doesn't affect your bhadra placidness; I can assure you that you too will be fighting like the rest of us.

Yet, a lot of the stories they told about each other highlighted the immense web of gratitude in which they seemed to be inextricably enmeshed. Sasadhar's mother had supported Arati's 'love' marriage; Sasadhar's wife used to go fishing with her and they had become close friends; during cyclones they had taken refuge in each other's houses and had begged food from each other during harsher times. Similarly, a few days after her terrible rows with her brothers, they were talking and exchanging food with each other again. Fighting, said Arati, is an evil they all have to put up with because they live in the Sundarbans but the important thing was to try and repair relations as soon as possible through the exchange of food and small talk.

Can Salt Water be Thicker than Blood?

The other very prevalent kind of 'relatedness' is 'making each other kin'. This 'kin-making' very much resembles the descriptions of 'fictive' kinship in the anthropological literature, for example, by Lambert (2000) or of 'ceremonial' relations (Bhowmick 1976: 74). I prefer to use the term 'elected' rather than 'fictive' or 'ceremonial' because I feel that these terms do not appropriately reflect both the degree to which such relationships are assimilated to blood ones, and the element of affect on which they are held to be based. Such ties include those not only between same-aged people who call each other 'friend', but also relationships between people of the opposite sex (who then refer to each other as 'brother' or 'sister') and of different ages.[20] One can have such a relation with a woman of one's mother's age or classificatory group who is then literally described as one's 'flower mother' (*ful-ma*, because they would 'tie' themselves to each other through an exchange of flowers). This is also possible with a man of the same category as one's father, a 'godfather' (*dharom bap*) or with people of the age of one's children and referred to as 'goddaughter' (*dharom meye*) or 'godson' (*dharom-chele*). The terms of appellation are similar to those used for blood kin and very often the relation is solemnised through rites.

For the ritual solemnisation of such relations, an auspicious date is picked and both families invite close blood kin, neighbours and previously 'elected' relatives.[21] A festive meal is cooked, a new set of clothes exchanged and then, asking 'the sun and moon to be witnesses' (sometimes Bonbibi or Gangadevi are invoked in place of the sun and moon), they establish that, from that day on, the other person is a *mother, father, daughter, son,* or *friend.* Performing this ceremony means that the two families are now required to invite each other to all their social and religious ceremonies and to come to each other's succour in times of need. On a daily basis it means being able to eat, visit and stay at each others' houses. Once two people are 'united' in this way, the relation their families share with each other is lived out in the idioms of blood. For Hindus, this consists of respecting the rules of consanguinity, one being that neither family can marry into the other. This bond often stretches over generations and at least one representative from the descendants of such families is present at social ceremonies.

As I started seeing it, these relationships are at the centre of new networks of social interactions and play a vital role in the exchange of food and information between islanders. As such 'relatives' are often from different villages, the islanders draw on them when cross-checking important information such as the credentials of a 'suitable' bride or groom for the marriage of a younger relative, or for information on political connections and parties, or again to find out the price of something, whether it be land, potatoes or fishing nets. These relations are also very useful when food or temporary shelter is required, for instance, when one is caught in a thunder storm or stranded on an island because one has missed the boat, or needs rest after having walked several kilometres.

How are these relations embedded in the wider relations of blood, jati, religion or class? Elected relations sometimes meet the disapproval of blood family members who do not necessarily see the need to 'increase relatives'. Those blood relatives who are not ready to share with these new relatives grow distant and break off all interaction with their own kin. During the house-to-house survey I conducted, those I questioned were rarely indifferent to this custom. Some of them deplored it, saying that it was neither practical nor very cheap to entertain even more relatives than the ones one was saddled with through blood and marriage.[22] The complaints people have against their 'elected' relatives are generally of the same order as those levelled against blood kin — that they are selfish. However, the riverside people also pointed out that it is the landowners who are the staunchest critics of this system even though they themselves have many such 'friends', especially city-living ones. They say that this is because landowners are self-centred and hierarchical and do not have the same understanding of the Sundarbans environment as themselves. When I pointed out that, at Pareshbabu's funeral, his family had invited their Adivasi and Muslim friends, they replied that their relationships to these people were not bound in the 'sun and moon' or in Bonbibi as were their own 'elected relations' but were just 'relations of convenience' without a 'mirroring of hearts'.

There are many reasons why people enter 'elected' kinship. As in Midnapur (Bhowmick 1976), a small number of people entered into such relations with the belief that it would cure their child. Sickly children are sometimes paired to a healthy child (in some rare cases with the child of an inferior caste) and 'polluted' food exchanged (*etho* — food considered polluted because it was touched or tasted by someone else) so that the good fortune of the healthy child is passed on to the sickly child.[23] It is believed that such a pairing 'unites' the two children by blood and thus annihilates the negative effects of the 'evil eye' on the sickly child.[24] The other reason is to show recognition for a favour. Here relations are initiated with those (usually doctors and veterinarians) who have managed in extremis to save one's child or one's milk cow from death. These naturally have the tendency to lead to unequal, exploitative and resentful patron–client type relationships and the islanders mention in this respect having been cheated or not treated as 'one's own'.[25]

Another small proportion of these relations are entered into because of a particular event where one person has saved another from some grave danger or misfortune. Nirapada, for example, had made friends with two courageous men who had come to the rescue one night when he and his wife had been collecting prawn seeds from the river and were caught in a violent storm during which their boat capsized. They would have drowned had these two strangers not risked their lives in coming to help them. Another time, a young woman narrated how a very honest man had 'saved' her. Her father, entrusting her with quite a large sum of money, had sent her to the market to engage in a transaction. On the way, she had stopped by a tree to pee and only realised once she reached the market that she had lost the money (which had been tied to her waist and which had fallen off when she had stopped). Very worried, she retraced her steps and along the way met a man who, on hearing about her misfortune, returned her purse, which he had found. As he had been 'her saviour', she called him her 'godfather' and, as a mark of appreciation for his honesty, her family honoured him and organised a ceremony to mark their newly established kinship to him.

One day while I was travelling through Bangladesh, Zeeshan, a random travelling companion, asked if we could stop on our way as he wanted to introduce me to his 'friend'. After we left his friend's place I was curious to know how the friend-making ceremony had been conducted and how 'food' circulated between the two families as Zeeshan was Muslim and his friend Hindu. Zeeshan explained how the ceremony was conducted 'according to *shonatan dharmo* [Hindu precepts]'.

> We chose our two sons, Robi Chandra Mondol and Zubaer Mondol Robin. After they had bathed and dressed in new clothes we asked them to take an oath that they would never cheat each other, nor take offence and be ready to forgive each other so that the relationship between our two families kept going.

'Why according to "shonatan dharmo"?' I was interested to know.

Because my friend is Hindu and I wanted to mark the friendship so I decided it should be done in his religion. We cleaned the place with a wet cloth [dipped in a bucket of water mixed with some fresh earth and cow-dung — women generally clean their houses every morning with this mixture, it is called '*lep deowa*'], lit some incense sticks and decorated the place with flowers to purify and beautify the place. Some of us use the Koran-sharif, others use the Gita, but what we use is irrelevant, the main thing is to have witnesses. We had five witnesses; cooked mutton, rice, dal and everyone ate together. Each family invited people from their side and we all dined as if we were one. Now, when one of us has a celebration of some sort, he invites the other. We also know that if one of us faces a problem the other will come to help.

'What about food? What do you do during Qurbani Eid — do you also give him some meat?' I asked inquisitively. 'I usually slaughter a goat and distribute it amongst my relatives but for Qurbani I bring my friend a really large fish I fish out of my pond. Sometimes I've also brought them meat but I make sure I buy it from the market so that it is killed in the Hindu way'.

As most Hindus in Bengal, irrespective of caste, eat fish and meat (except pork and beef) I was interested to learn why he did not give him any of his Qurbani meat, especially as he told me he could not afford to sacrifice cows and only did goats, and so I asked, 'Why, do you think they would mind if you gave them some of your meat?' 'I don't think they would mind per se. But other Hindus might not like it and object or think I am giving them beef — something I would never do — and so I don't want to impose it on them. I prefer giving them fish or meat bought from a Hindu at the marketplace — its just trouble-free.'

As conversations with older people on the subject deepened, they suggested that this 'elected' kin-making custom is a kind of guarantee against the harsh life they lead, where staying alive is 'a lottery'. This custom is widely practised because, as Shukuri, a woman in her late sixties explained, when they had arrived to clear these lands, the threat of snakes and tigers had loomed large over their everyday lives and having neighbours with whom one could recreate the security of blood families had been necessary. Many of the young women who came as brides while the island was still being cleared needed substitute mothers to teach them about life in this new area.

Indeed, men were often related by blood as younger relatives kept coming to settle from their home villages; the women, however, were not necessarily related and found themselves in a world where these elected bonds were precious as they ensured social and emotional well-being. Many women never travelled back to their paternal houses because of the expense and the risk involved in crossing the border without passport or visa to East Pakistan and later Bangladesh. In the harsh lonely surroundings of these recent settlements, it was one's newfound godfather and godmother who provided both the economic ties one needed and the emotional support of 'home'.

The majority of people entered into such relationships because of what they call a 'mirroring of hearts'. This 'mirroring of hearts', the islanders explained, highlights similarities of two people's lives, such as two men working together, women with children of the same age and gender. These relationships are struck especially when one is young and are popular amongst adolescents, especially those of the same age and gender, and are often talked of in affective terms. When wanting to know more about a 'sharing', 'mirroring' or an 'understanding of hearts' I was often told stories of love and separation.[26]

One day, on enquiring where one of my middle-aged neighbours, Bhuban, had been over the last two weeks, I was told that he had gone to his sister's place for her father's funerary rites. When I asked which branch of the family she belonged to, Bhuban replied that it is 'the branch of his heart'. He then told me the story of how they had met and grown to be so fond of each other. They had studied together at college and did politics together. He wasn't well off, whereas she, Paro, being one of the professor's daughters, was rich. She had been impressed by one of his political speeches and often brought him food from home and left it in his room without letting him know it was from her. Then some friends started to make fun of their relationship and he got scared that his reputation might get tarnished. So one day he dragged Paro to the principal's office. Dramatically, after stating how they were in the modern setting of the college, he requested that the principal substitute his presence for that of the sun and moon and called on his authority to witness and bless their 'relatedness of siblings'. The principal was relieved but Paro was disconsolate, as her passion was now made impossible for all time. She decided never to marry. Paro's family, who had thought Bhuban had designs on their daughter, started thinking well of him in his status of 'brother' and now regularly invited him over to their place. He participated so much in the general life of the family that Paro's brothers would often solicit his help in family matters and eventually even asked him, after they had found a suitable boy, to convince Paro to marry.

Had he ever regretted not getting married to her? Pangs of remorse had overwhelmed him all through his college years and he had always felt the pain of separation. Bhuban then turned to me and asked what alternative he could have had. The girl's people lived somewhere 'up' and had all the trappings of the rich, whereas his parents lived on the river's edge and barely managed to pay his college fees. Had she become his wife, she would have had to adjust to a harsh life and he had feared it would have spoilt her love for him. So he had preferred sacrificing his newly emerging feelings of 'love' for 'affection'. He now reasoned that, by becoming her 'friend/brother', he had also insured that their love for each other remain 'true'. Why 'brotherly friendship?' I had asked Bhuban. Just 'friends' elicits ambiguity as there is a possibility of a sexual relationship, whereas the ideal of brotherly love is based on 'selfless care and affection'.

As Lambert demonstrates in her study of Rajasthan, this kind of relatedness is usually described as superior to and purer than reproductive kinship because 'it does not originate in the pollution of sexual intercourse' (2000: 79). Had they got married, her family might have had difficulty in accepting him or their marital state. But, by giving up an affinal relation for an elected 'brotherly friendship' he had ensured that their relationship be one of equals (as opposed to the hierarchical one shared by spouses). This had permitted him to strike a subtle compromise between their interpersonal relationship and that of their two larger families. The proof of her family having accepted him as a trustworthy family member lay in the fact that he had been called on to tell her to get married (as an elder brother would) and now, thirty years later, they were both able to come visit each other when either of them was ill, and to partake in all the ceremonies their two families organised.

The basis of these relationships is the sharing of food and affective sentiments. In equally distributing forest products, just as in Zeeshan's story, it is around food and partaking in food that the tension revolves and is resolved. The combination of nurturance, shared environment and sentiment are all seen as forms of acknowledged 'elected' relatedness, and as operating irrespective of one's genealogical tie or of class, caste or religion. The extent to which this 'elected kin-making' defies the differences of both jati and religion is noteworthy. The establishment of such relations, with the expectation that its protagonists will partake in shared meals, death pollution and similar periods of mourning for blood as well as 'elected' kin is common throughout the Sundarbans.

Understanding the 'situatedness' of persons in the world and their relationships is the aim of the 'anthropology of the person' suggested by Ingold. Ingold disputes the idea that social life is the aggregate of interactions among individuals in frequent mutual contact, to suggest instead that social life is not a 'pattern of interactions' but an 'unfolding of relationships' (1990: 222). In the Sundarbans, the renewed meal-sharing and gift exchange between 'elected' relations are an example of this 'unfolding of relationships'. This is helped by the fact that there are very few differences in Bengal between the dietary restrictions of a Brahmin and those of other Hindu castes. Differences arise when communities eat pork (usually STs, certain SCs and Christians) or beef (Muslims and Christians) or when individuals, for some reason or another, prefer to not eat certain commonly eaten food (such as crab as in the case of tiger-charmers). However, on occasions when 'elected' relatives are invited, people make sure that they do not cook or offer taboo food. The proper managing of the sensibilities of 'friends' and 'elected relatives', just as for blood relatives, is all about being attentive to their wishes.

Notes

1. Vaishnavism, a branch of Hinduism, entails the worship of Vishnu as the supreme deity, as well as his incarnations, Krishna or Rama. It was popularised in sixteenth-century Bengal by Chaitanya. Vaishnavism, characterised by an emphasis on *bhakti* (devotion) and simple worship of Krishna and Radha (Krishna's consort) has, since its inception, appealed to the masses. Modern Vaishnavism, partly due to the Hindutva ideology which is trying to unify different schools of Hinduism, is increasingly finding popular resurgence in rural Bengal, especially among the low castes.
2. He said that it was while on a pilgrimage that he realised that Vaishnavism was the 'true religion' (*sanatan dharma*).
3. A Naga is someone from the state of Nagaland in the north-east of India. They are notorious for their taste for lizards, dogs and other animals consumed by South-east Asians but not by South Asians. The veracity of this story is highly doubtful but it is the space it allows for a totally non-Brahminical dietary menu that seems of import in the narration of this story.

4. See photo of Bonbibi's worship (Illustration 3 and 4 on pages 104 and 105).
5. Recent discussions with Projit Mukharji have revealed that in a similar bid to 'Hinduise' local deities Baban Gazi is now being called 'Bamun' (i.e., 'Brahmin') Gazi.
6. It has been suggested to me by Professors Chris Fuller and Johnny Parry that Dokkhin Rai might be a reference to Shiva and/or Yama, the god of death, who is believed to reside in the symbolic south. However appealing this symbolic connection, the islanders themselves never made it. I leave them the last word.
7. Also mentioned in Bhattacharyya (1947: 49). See Illustration 1 on page 105.
8. This worship, though considered a marginal cult, is common on the outskirts of Kolkata.
9. Many studies have pointed out the importance of commensality in the constitution of kinship in South Asia (Lambert 2000; Raheja and Gold 1994; Uberoi 1994; Trawick 1990; Parry 1979; Östör et al. 1982; Fruzzetti 1982; Inden and Nicholas 1977; Vatuk 1972).
10. O'Malley highlights how the jungle-goers only worked six days each week, as one day was set apart for 'the worship of the sylvan deity presiding over that particular forest' (1908: 193–94). When I asked islanders why there was an injunction against entering the forest on Fridays they replied that it was because Bonbibi 'goes to Medina to pray' or that she 'goes to perform the haj'. When the forest workers go for crab or honey collecting trips of ten days they usually spend Fridays in the boat without getting off it.
11. These are *i)* Ali Madhab, *ii)* Moklesh Fakir, *iii)* Jalal Fakir, *iv)* Mongolesh Shah, and *v)* Moniruddin Fakir; the names of the five bibis: *i)* Bonbibi, *ii)* Fulbibi, *iii)* Gulalbibi, *iv)* Dulalbibi, and *v)* Fatemabibi.
12. In Bengali: *shono probhu, amar poth amay chere dite hobe, tumi tomar pothe jao, ami amar pothe jayi* (the first line), and *mago, jole male, amar oi poth chere dao, bagh shontan buke tene ei manobi shontaner poth dekhiye dao, ma tomar name dohai ei katha bolchi* (the second line).
13. This was called *atali muri* and usually undertaken with a leaf from the gol tree.
14. Tigers are never called by their name 'bagh' but always, especially by the crab collectors, reverentially referred to as '*phokir*' for 'fakir' because like fakirs they too are believed to use magic and attack with counter spells; they were also referred to as 'bawro beral' literally 'big cat'.
15. The numerous kinds of pneumatophoric roots of Sundarbans mangroves are real death traps. Some are like stilts all around trees and others stick out of the ground like spears; these are believed to have an agency of their own and stories abound about how certain people trip and get impaled on them.
16. These obligations have some resonances with Muslims' obligations to stay pure between 'udhu' (ablutions) before one starts namaz until its completion; it also has parallels with purity rituals before setting off on Hajj. In the

forest, when one needs to urinate or defecate, s/he does so in the river or after having placed some leaves and branches over the soil so that impure matter does not touch the soil directly.

   Bidi is a thin and cheap Indian cigarette made of tobacco wrapped in a tendu leaf.

17. Refusing to eat is the principal way of expressing resentment throughout Bengal, so I wondered if such a refusal implied that the person was lacking much needed peace. Someone suggested that having a cooked meal waiting meant that you were not that badly off and that venturing into the forest in this circumstance was greedy. Delaying or refusing to eat showed your self-sufficiency and therefore your 'arrogance'. It was also suggested that if you were hungry you would invariably be tempted to take more than your fair share from the forest. Which is why one comes across poultry in the forest.

18. As part of Bonbibi's worship, people often release chicks or young hen in the forest.

19. The three most terrible curses inflicted on a person in the Sundarbans.

20. *Bondhu* for male friends and *sai* for female friends. It is important to note that *sai* is a loaded word and its import is often highlighted in reference to Bonbibi's story and her 'friendship' to Narayani.

21. Makar Sankranti occurs mid-January. It is also the main day on which Bonbibi is worshipped, the other day being mid-February.

22. A woman told me that her mother had 'paired' her with a dog as they were too poor to add yet another set of relatives to their already impoverished family.

23. Very often that of an Adivasi. Though the Adivasis, the first to have been brought to the Sundarbans to reclaim forested land, had initially been allowed to settle and cultivate that land, they were either evicted or resettled on the same land as sharecroppers (Bhaumik 1993: 31). Many also had their land wrested from them by the arrival of affluent cultivating communities (Das 1968: 14).

24. 'Jealousy and envy lie behind the evil eye as well . . . the harm is caused, often unconsciously, by the gaze of envious people. All kinds of trouble can be brought by the evil eye, and any display of good health, splendour or success is likely to attract it' (Fuller 1992: 238).

25. Bhowmick not only discusses how such relations played a very important role in breaking social distinctions in Midnapuri social life but also gives numerous examples of how these inter-caste (even of Brahmins or other upper castes with Untouchables) and inter-religious (mainly Hindu–Muslim) relationships operated (1976: 74–76; 145–58 and 119; 145 respectively). He also devotes an entire chapter to the subject under the heading 'Minimising Group Distances' (ibid.: 141–58).

26. Giddens (1992: 38) distinguishes 'passionate love' which, he says, is a universal phenomenon, from 'romantic love', which is culturally specific. 'Mirroring of hearts' fits his sense of 'romantic love' as introducing the element of narrative into an individual's life.

1. Bonbibi, the Gazis and Dokkhin Rai

Bonbibi with Dukhe on her lap, the Gazis and Dokkhin Rai (who is represented as half-tiger, half-man) photographed here whilst still in the process of being decorated and painted.

2. Carrying Bonbibi to her shelter

A procession through tiger prawn fisheries carrying images of Bonbibi to her shelter.

3. Preparing for Bonbibi's worship

Preparing the shelter where the statues of Bonbibi, Dukhe, Shah Jongoli and Dokkhin Rai are going to be placed and worshipped. Instead of pooling money and buying one big Bonbibi, the tradition here is for each forest fisher to bring their own image of Bonbibi. They are then all placed side-by-side in one common shrine and worshipped together.

4. Bonbibi, Shah Jongoli and Dokkhin Rai

A picture of the consecrated images. Bonbibi is holding Dukhe's hand while Shah Jongoli chases Dokkhin Rai away (also notice a small Gazi in the right corner of the picture and the Gazi's mounds in front of the statue of Bonbibi and Dukhe).

5. Islanders worship Bonbibi

Islanders assembled on the roadside in front of a Bonbibi Shrine during her worship.

6. Walking along a bund

One can see the river eating into the bund on one side and a big fishery on the other.

7. Crossing the Matla river at low tide at Canning

8. Bamboo bridge across a canal showing low tide

9. Woman prawn seed collector with her net

10. Women collecting tiger prawn seeds along the bank of the Pathar river

V

Roughing it with Kali:
Braving Crocodiles, Relatives
and the *Bhadralok*

With the one jati that Hindus and Muslims will form, Narayan will come
as an avatar to settle the sadness of this Kolijug.[1]

This is what Arati said at the end of a long answer to my
question about why she had not been invited to her nephew's
wedding. She explained how in 1995 one of her neighbours —
Gora — had come back with a woman whom he had presented
to his family and neighbours as his wife Amina. Some of the
village matobbors[2] had objected that Gora, being a Hindu, should
be married with the woman, as she was Muslim. Gora decided to
ignore these objections and stay on in Garjontola with his wife. It was
not long before one section of Garjontola split into two factions —
one group calling for the groom's family and the couple to be
ostracised, while the other group, much smaller, vehemently dis-
agreeing. Eventually, the groom's family was reintegrated into the
village fold but the differences between the two groups, one that
had supported this union, and the other which had first demanded
ostracism and later wanted compensation to be paid for this breach
of societal rules, had remained. This was why, Arati explained, she,
her mother and younger brother had not been invited to her nephew's
wedding; they had supported the wedding whereas the rest of their
family had not. She ended her long story with the observation that
political parties fighting for power had used Gora's marriage to carve
out potential electorates, and that the only redemption for the times
we live in, was for 'Hindus and Muslims to form one jati'.

Following through this story will lead to a complex unravelling of
the Garjontola islanders' relationships with one another, especially in
connection to the relatively new occupation of prawn seed collection.
Arati's motivation for upholding this marriage was actually another
bid (after her failed attempt at reclaiming land from her elder brother)
to assert herself. Similarly, the explanation as to why two sections of
riverside Garjontola had fought over this Hindu–Muslim marriage

stemmed not so much from a socio-moral issue as to whether two jatis should intermarry, as from conflicts between two prawn khoti owners.[3] The anecdote of this Hindu–Muslim marriage and its effect in the realm of kinship will be used as a foil to highlight issues of gender, especially in relation to the three main socio-economic occupations the islanders practise.

A Hindu–Muslim Marriage and its Aftermath

Let us return to the story of the marriage and trace through its complexities. After some ado and many heated exchanges, those who had initially opposed Gora's union agreed six months later to let Gora and his wife stay in their part of Garjontola — but on condition that he, his wife and his family be ostracised from riverside Garjontola sociality. They argued that the groom's entire family should be ostracised since they had accepted the marriage, which was proof of the fact that they had 'preferred' a woman from the Muslim jati to one from their own jati. They therefore should go and live with the Muslims. Opposing this, the other group, composed of a cluster of families including Arati and her husband, had refused to sever ties with the couple and the groom's family, and had in turn themselves been excluded by those who led the ostracising. They were left out of social and religious gatherings but the exclusion did not involve any segregation on an economic level. Arati, for example, still fished with the other women of the village and her husband was still part of his team of forest workers. In any case, these divisions were followed only within the precinct of the village and so feuding families were reunited when relatives from other villages hosted weddings or funeral ceremonies.

After a couple of months, however, Gora's father, growing very annoyed at being constantly excluded from his neighbours' festivities, went to see the leaders of the ostracising campaign and told them that he had had enough and that he considered this snubbing of his family to be very unfair as Gora's decision to marry had been taken independently of him. He insisted that his family be reintegrated into the larger group. They accepted on condition that his offending son and wife be driven out of the house and that he organise a *Narayan sinni* and feed the five sections of Garjontola.[4]

As mentioned earlier, Garjontola consists of 975 people and about 209 households. These 209 households are divided into five geographical 'parts' (referred to by this English term) which are also connected to the arrival of the five main families of the village and their moments of settling in Garjontola. The division into parts had come about because, most people being related to each other, it was a way devised by the islanders to limit expenses. Thus, for a ceremony like a wedding or a feast given in honour of the recently deceased, a family will invite only those who live in their own part, along with a few very close blood and 'elected' relatives from elsewhere. As this system was followed in all the parts, no extended family relative was supposed to be offended about not being invited. The lines of division between these parts were more or less geographical. There was also an imperative to invite, whatever one's occupation, caste or financial capacity, all the members of one's part. Thus, inviting the five parts of Garjontola to the Narayan sinni would have meant inviting more than a thousand people, which would have bankrupted Gora's father. So, after some arguments, the village heads agreed that, following the usual custom, it would be enough for Gora's father to invite just his part of Garjontola. Gora's father organised the Narayan sinni and invited the sixty-odd hearths or nuclear families of his part (which would have consisted of about 276 people had everyone attended but usually only one representative from each family is sent, to limit costs). Gora and his wife went to live at the far end of his father's fields, and his parents were reabsorbed into the larger village fold.

But this expiatory worship and food distribution did not put an end to the feud between the two warring groups. The dissenters refused to attend the ceremony and then, a few months later, undertook the responsibility of organising the second marriage of one of their members' (Jayanta) daughters. This further complicated matters. Jayanta's daughter Ritu, already a married woman living in another village, had decided, six months after her marriage, to come back to her natal Garjontola, to marry Gora's paternal uncle's son, who was her childhood neighbour and sweetheart. Arati's group, who had felt slighted by the way Gora's father's had sought the approval of the ostracising group's heads, leaped on the occasion to reaffirm their group's difference and themselves organised Ritu's second wedding. The leaders who had opposed Gora's resettlement in the village naturally boycotted this wedding.

I had gradually come to know, from private conversations with Arati and Maloti, the details of how the sixty hearths of the part of Garjontola I lived in were theoretically supposed to be divided into two groups for all religious and social matters. But I was surprised that no one else had mentioned this ostracism, and I was keen to know more about it. What further surprised me was that many islanders from the other parts of Garjontola did not even know about it and that many people of the same part said that this was just another family fight and that they had not 'ostracised' Gora but had simply ignored him because they had not been invited to his wedding. Some said it had to do with 'party politics'. Others explained that it was all about prawn seed collection and an ongoing feud between prawn businessmen. These reasons were interlinked. But whatever the islanders' reasons for excluding or ignoring Gora, within six months most people had simply stopped taking the injunction seriously. Realignments had occurred with people from both groups participating in each others' social gatherings without bothering to ask the leaders of the ostracising campaign for their consent, and new alliances and divisions had been established.

In this row, Arati's elder brother Hori and his wife Maloti had supported their cousin Badal who was at the forefront of the ostracising group. Arati's mother and younger brother had, like her, supported Gora's marriage. It was when I asked her about her absence from her nephew's wedding that Arati had told me this story. We had both been sitting on the top of the bund watching the celebrations in honour of god Hori. This is a relatively recent cult started by some of the riverside islanders of Garjontola to counter the popularity of goddess Saraswati's annual worship organised by the school teachers at the high school. I was curious to learn, as Arati had not been invited to her nephew's wedding, and had also been segregated from their part of the village by her cousin Badal, if her presence that afternoon was in defiance of her cousin or, on the contrary, a way of tacitly showing him that she wanted to be 'part' of them again. I was also curious to know from Arati why she had supported the two non-normative weddings and why she had concluded her long story with a reference to how the sadness afflicting this damned age (*kolijug*) could be dispelled by a newfound unity between Hindus and Muslims.

She explained that the real motives for her row with Badal lay elsewhere. He had become a khoti owner, a prawn businessman, and had wanted her to sell him her prawn seeds. Arati, however, preferred selling them in the rival village Lahiripur and to Gora's wife Amina's father who was also a khoti owner. The real reason why Badal had made such a show of disapproving Gora's marriage to Amina was, she claimed, mainly because Amina's father was the preferred prawn dealer of many Garjontola prawn seed collectors. Amina's father, said Arati, always paid up front and was honest. Being of the same family as her, Badal had offered much lower rates for her prawn seeds and only paid at the end of the season. Now, with Amina settling in the village, her father would have greater reason to visit Garjontola and establish links with other prawn seed collectors, which Badal resented. In Arati's view, Badal had started this whole to-do about Gora's marriage because he resented the fact that Amina's father was doing better than him. She also pointed out that Badal himself had no qualms in taking his own prawn seeds to Bangladesh because he felt that he got a better deal trading with Muslims than he could with West Bengali Hindu counterparts. Another reason for her antipathy to Badal was that he had recently started campaigning for the Bharatiya Janata Party (BJP) and Arati was a staunch RSP supporter. By posing as the moral guardian of the village through his objection to the Hindu–Muslim marriage, and by being one of the initiators of the yearly Hori procession, Badal had tried to exploit the islanders' aspirations to a better social status. At the same time, he had been hoping to wrest some political power from the RSP, partly because Badal had felt that the RSP-leaning Prawn Collective Union leader was 'useless' and that he could gain political advantage.

When I asked Badal himself about the division of their part, he blamed it on prawn fishing, which, he said, made his cousin Arati and the other prawn seed collectors 'greedy' and was threatening 'village life' because people, especially women, were 'becoming too rich and stubborn'. Even though he himself was a prawn dealer, he had loved living on the considerable acres of land his grandfather had owned. It was because he had lost the land that he had become a prawn businessman. Badal was somewhat peeved that his command to cease all social interactions with Gora's family and their allies had been so widely ignored. He had organised the Hori procession with some of his BJP party members to redress his image. But, as it had been attended by a ridiculously small number of people, it had been a failure. Badal's potential career as a BJP leader was being nipped in the bud. Arati was showing her open defiance of him by persisting in selling her prawn seeds to Amina's father, by supporting, in his words, 'improper marriages' and by living on the bund like the marginalised.

What in the meantime had started to annoy Arati was that Hori, her elder brother, had allied himself with Badal and had used Badal's injunction of ostracism in order to keep her out of his family gatherings. Even though this did not stop her or her children from being regular visitors to his house, nor stop her children from eating with their cousins, neither Arati nor her husband were ever invited to share celebratory meals. Arati, however, felt that she could now take things in her own hands. She had made money as a prawn seed collector and felt strong enough to speak her grievance about her brother's refusal to share some of the parental land. When she realised that Hori would not part with the land, she had tried to get Badal's support by finally agreeing to sell him her prawn seed. But, as Badal had done nothing about the land, Arati had resumed dealing with the khoti owners of Lahiripur, especially with Amina's father.

Badal, in turn, had finally relented and told her that she and her family could reintegrate with their part and group if, as Gora's father had done, they also organised an expiatory Narayan sinni for the whole part. Arati had been keen that they do so (or at least so she said). However, when she broke the news to her husband, he violently objected to the idea and categorically refused. Furious, he said that he would support a hundred other Hindu–Muslim marriages if need be but would not rub shoulders with 'that self-appointed guardian of our part who is no saint himself'.[5] If she organised a Narayan sinni and invited the leaders of the ostracising group, he threatened that he would also organise a Narayan sinni and invite the dissenters. That afternoon when the Hori celebrations were happening was a few days after this row. In defiance of her husband, Arati had decided to attend. Annoyed, he had taken the day off and had travelled with their two sons to visit some of his 'elected' kin on another island.

Arati's husband's support for Gora's marriage and his vehement opposition to his wife's wish to reintegrate into their village part was, as he in turn late explained to me, for two reasons. One was because he was the 'elected' brother of one of Amina's brothers and felt that he owed it to Amina's family to support her since they had backed his wedding (whose issues were described in the previous chapter). Second, he argued, he did not see why the heads of his part of the village had kicked up such a commotion about this marriage. His refusal to organise the propitiating worship also had to do with his personal feelings towards his in-laws. He did not like Badal but got along with Hori and Maloti and was in return very much appreciated by them. Their sons, his teenaged nephews, often appealed for small sums of money from him and he was always ready to oblige Maloti and his other sister-in-law living in the village when they requested him to accom-pany them to the forest. He felt he had nothing to lose by being ex-cluded from his in-laws' social celebrations because he continued to enjoy good everyday relations with the ones he cared for; his wife should not involve him but deal with them directly if she wanted to be reintegrated.

There was also a strategic reason for his refusal to ceremonially re-enter his in-laws' fold: he thought it was best to keep his distance from them as he did not really believe Arati would be successful in reclaiming her brother's land. The final reason he put forward was of a political nature. It had been a BJP group that had mounted the campaign and he was an RSP supporter. In yet another conversation he told me how, as a forest worker, he had a responsibility not to be co-opted into 'divisive' ways of thinking, which would surely result from getting entangled in family affairs. His wife could do what she wanted with them but, as a forest fisher, he had to remain a cool person (*thanda manush*) as opposed to hot-headed. The main pre-requisite for remaining 'cool' was to avoid owning land, engaging in politics or family rows.

In the background of Arati's dilemma was her attempt to figure out how she could get a piece of her brother's land and thus build a hut on a proper homestead. This would give her social status as well as enable her to take part in her blood families' weddings and mortuary rites. Arati's predicament overall thus shows the tension between three very distinct worldviews — one supported by her husband, that of a forest worker, the other by her cousin, that of a landowner, and the third by her own role as a prawn seed collector — and thus different expectations of behaviour. These conflicting expectations were often the cause of family feuds. Prawn seed collectors, who were not under the same interdictions as forest fishers, and because they were making money which was theirs to keep, were gradually asserting themselves against hierarchies of gender and economy.

Women and Prawn Seed Collection: Practicalities and Dilemmas

The rivers and canals of the WB Sundarbans occupy a key place in relation to the fishery resources of the state. The prawn fisheries of the area have been earning considerable amounts of foreign exchange for India and tiger prawns in particular have been called the 'living dollars' of the Sundarbans (Nandi and Misra 1987: 1). Around 10,000 hectares of the Sundarbans have been converted into prawn fisheries (Anon. 1993). But, while fisheries are mostly located in the northern region of the Sundarbans, their success depends on prawn seeds collected from rivers in the southern islands (experiments to hatch tiger prawn seeds artificially on a large scale have only now started to become partly successful).

Because it can be undertaken throughout the year, prawn seed collection was very popular. It had become, within twenty years, one of the most stable sources of revenue for the Sundarbans islanders, especially women. A couple of hours of net-pulling easily allowed a woman to make more money than the wage she would have made from working a full day in someone's fields. In the southern islands of the Sundarbans, prawn seed collection picked up in the late 1970s and became widely practised, especially after the disastrous cyclones of 1981 and 1988. The 1988 cyclone, as mentioned earlier, resulted in many rivers breaking the bunds of the southern islands, leaving agricultural land completely infertile for the next three years and a loss of crops worth Rs 83 crore. Once land was flooded by the region's saline rivers, people usually resorted to working in the forest collecting crabs, fish, honey, and wood — and now prawn seeds.

Prawn seed collection also expanded very rapidly because the late 1970s and 1980s was a time when the government came down heavily on those who did not possess forest passes, which were relatively expensive and thus a luxury few islanders could afford. The officials were known for their ruthlessness in extorting fines even from the bereaved relatives of tiger victims who had ventured without passes into the forest. Thus, prawn seed collection quickly gained popularity because it could be practised along the banks of one's island during one's leisure time and required a very modest investment (a mosquito net mounted on a thin wooden frame), it was easily available and sold for significant sums, and it was legal and not yet tainted with the stigma it subsequently came to bear. Prawn seed collectors were and are predominantly (but not exclusively) from families where the men work in the forest as honey or crab collectors, fishers or woodcutters and live along the river's edge and come from the same socio-religious background.

In the Sundarbans, prawn seed collection thus enabled the poorest, and especially women, to gain economic stability. As the islanders often pointed out, the introduction of prawn seed collection saw the most marginalised islanders starting to eat two square meals a day. However, it also came to be greatly criticised because of its negative effect not only on the ecology of the region but also on sociality. Prawn seed collectors were condemned for being 'greedy' and 'violent' and posing a threat to the 'ethics' of the environment and village life. These criticisms are still levelled, on the one hand, by those who regularly work in the forest, such as crab, honey and wood collectors, and, on the other hand, by local environmentalists, NGO activists and the educated elite. However, this unlikely alliance should not disguise the very different perspectives at stake. The disapproval expressed by forest workers is rooted in local ideas of the forest ethic and its rules. The criticisms levelled by the second group, mainly the village elite, spring less from concern for safeguarding the global commons of the Sundarbans than from an urban, middle-class understanding of gender and morality.[6] They described how prawn seed collection is an activity purely moti-vated by 'greed'and how it threatens the firmly established hierarchies between different socio-occupational groups such as landowners, forest workers and prawn seed collectors. The prawn seed collectors themselves, and especially poorer women, see these condemnations as thinly veiled attacks on them, and their bid to economic autonomy and social respectability.

While studies have argued that globalisation has been detrimental to women due to growing structural gender inequalities (Panini 1995: 57; Arora 1999; Centre for Women's Development Studies [CWDS] 2000; Dalal 1995; Dewan 1999, in Ganguly-Scrase 2003: 545), the view held by many women, especially those from a lower middle-class background, is that it has given them greater opportunities to challenge preexisting patriarchal norms and has rendered them more empowered compared to an earlier generation of women (Ganguly-Scrase 2003: 545). Ganguly-Scrase locates these debates in terms of two major contrasting approaches in the subcontinent to studies of the impact of the liberalising process of globalisation on women. There are the studies which focus on the poor and highlight their growing gender inequalities, and those that explore feminine desire and subjectivity, focusing mainly on studies amongst the upper and middle classes. 'While the former studies focus exclusively on feminization of poverty and exploitation of labor, the latter's concern is the realm of culture' and therefore 'overlook the experiences of people who do not neatly fit into the extreme ends of the social spectrum' (Ganguly-Scrase 2003: 545). One might also argue that what is left out of the picture is how the experience of globalisation amongst poor women can also be a study of 'feminine desire and subjectivity'.

Kali

So how was the experience of globalisation of the riverside women of the southern islands of the Sundarbans? Even though the down islands of the Sundarbans are yet to be supplied with electricity, the Sundarbans islanders have already had their own 'general break with all sorts of pasts' — Appadurai's criterion of a world in which modernity is decisively 'at large' (1996: 3). Appadurai examines the 'general break' or 'rupture' that 'takes media and migration as the two interconnected diacritics which effect on the *work of imagination* — the constitutive feature of modern subjectivity' (ibid.). Newspapers and the TV are rare but the Sundarbans islanders have migrated all through the last century and still do so in search of work. Radio and word-of-mouth are used to keep informed about what is happening in the world and to argue about how that in turn affects them.

What about Bonbibi? How is she perceived by this relatively young and often ex-migrant working group? One has to know in this context that Bonbibi's image is prominently visible in the many shrines attached to the different WB government forest offices. The government staff explanation was that Bonbibi's image was there for the benefit of the forest workers (who came to undertake the formalities required to get passes) and the tourists. The staff members of these offices were usually not from the Sundarbans; their protective deities are not Bonbibi but more mainstream goddesses such as Kali or Tara (another form of Kali). Hence their somewhat condescending argument that they promote Bonbibi's image as a comfort to the forest workers and the tourist appeal of her symbolic role in upholding the sharing of forest-products between humans and tigers. The forest workers do indeed offer coins and respect to these government shrines before setting off for the forest after having paid their dues and collected their permits from the officials.

However, Bonbibi's presence on government terrain points to an interesting paradox. Those seen as believing in her powers were discredited as being superstitious fools (forest workers) or seekers of exotic practices (tourists) by forest officials. Bonbibi's forest-working worshippers were sometimes made the butt of jokes by the very same forest officials who preferred relying on Kali. This distinction between Bonbibi and Kali thus constituted another marker of difference between the inhabitants of the Sundarbans and forest officials. While the former were seen as 'superstitious', rural and backward because they worshipped a local goddess, the latter (who were nearly all Hindu) saw themselves as sophisticated, urbane and progressive because they worshipped Kali. Besides, Kali is well-inscribed within the Hindu pantheon (as opposed to Bonbibi, whose Islamic origins are increasingly seen as problematic) and therefore, in their eyes, more suited to their status of forest official — considered a few notches above that of a Bonbibi worshipping forest worker.

However, while forest-workers — usually male and middle-aged — continued to have great devotion to Bonbibi, more and more prawn seed collectors were calling upon the powers of Kali to protect them. Although the Sundarbans prawn seed collectors — both men and women — were becoming increasingly more reticent about worshipping Bonbibi, they did not turn to the relatively common and affordable worship of goddesses such as Lokkhi (the Bengali equivalent of Lakshmi, the goddess of wealth) or Saraswati (the goddess of learning) or the more bhadralok goddess Durga. The prawn seed collectors took up the relatively expensive worship — because it is more elaborate and needs animal sacrifice — of goddess Kali. It is highly significant that in the Sundarbans, as in many other parts of rural WB, Kali is also famous for being the deity of choice of those who are involved in violent professions. Deities in the Sundarbans (like elsewhere in South Asia) are generally seen as the patrons of particular occupational activities. As an islander explained,

> You know, gods are like government ministers, they have different departments divided between them and Bonbibi has been ascribed the forest. So just as we have to flatter relevant government officials, forest workers have to flatter Bonbibi, school teachers Saraswati, and prawn seed collectors, like those engaged in violent jobs such as highway robbers, policemen, taxi-drivers or poachers, Kali.

Kali's growing popularity amongst the prawn seed collectors (and here I refer mainly to a Hindu population), is explained on the grounds that their occupation is both bloody and risky and therefore seen as necessitating a violent cosmic deity. This highlights important consequences. How did forest-working men perceive the entry of women into the forest? To what extent is the adoption of Kali — a goddess notoriously linked to violent and predominantly male occupations — by net-pulling female prawn seed collectors, an attempt to redefine the place of women in contemporary Sundarbans, both on economic as well as on social levels?

In relation to the widespread belief about the sacred nature of the forest, I was curious to know more about why some people argued that it had lost some of its purity because women were now entering it. I put the following question to Sukumar, a forest fisher who also worked as a poacher on the side: 'What about women? What are Bonbibi's recommendations for them?' 'The same as for us men, they have to be pure [in its meaning of both *suchi*, i.e., "clean", and possessing "genuine intentions"].' This reminded Sukumar of a story 'of a terrific woman' who was head of a team. He was soon telling us how, when he had gone catching crabs with a couple of friends in the core area, they had been caught by the forest guards. To enter into the formalities that such a meeting entails, their little boat was tied to the forest guards' launch. The range officer was having his lunch so the guards told them they would have to wait. There was another boat which had also been caught, and which had been tied along the opposite side of the launch.

> All of a sudden, I noticed that their leader was a woman, and what a woman! She looked like the director of a team acting in a well-rehearsed play. She seemed to be holding her men in total control, silently, with her steely gaze commanding one to put the sails up, the other to ready the engine, the third to fetch and hand out the rifles. . . . I was watching, mesmerized, and felt that my hands were obeying her silent directive: 'Untie my boat' and as if in a trance I untied the ropes that were holding her boat to the launch.

'Whoooff, even if she had ordered me to climb in with them I think I would have obeyed, I was spellbound. Abruptly however, her deafening war cry, loud above the roar of the engine, pulled me back to reality.' Sukumar paused.

> The range officer ran out and when he saw their boat speeding away he ordered her to stop and his men to fire. Rifle slung over her shoulders, standing tall on the deck of her boat, she shouted back, 'Careful now, you are service holders, your lives are surrounded by the compassion of

concerned people, we 'do black' [i.e., are poachers], our lives have no value, we are reckless. Now think twice before you come closer, because if you do, my rifle will cry out loud and clear.

'Imagine, what a courageous woman', said Sukumar still totally in awe. 'They were from Midnapur, a friend later told me, wood poachers, poor people like us [though I am not so sure about this], nice people, they had offered us tea and biscuits, maybe to ensure our silence,' he said. 'But how did you plan getting out of this [vis-à-vis both the ranger and Bonbibi]?' I asked. 'Well, when the ranger asked me, I said they would have killed me if I had not complied and, as far as Bonbibi is concerned, cutting a reasonable amount of trees is not bad for the jungle, it helps it to breathe and to get new undergrowth.'

'And what about the lie?' I asked, to which he replied, 'What does it mean to be self-righteous if it means giving somebody else away? Bonbibi does not want us to be heartless after all.' 'But you know these "black parties" are rich, why waste your pity on them?' I continued. 'But service holders are richer, plus they have the security and respectability attached to their occupation,' he continued. 'Tell me sincerely, how much of the fines they extract from us actually go to the government?'

Forest officers often linked prawn seed collectors and poachers, saying that the two groups helped each other. The connection was made in a rather surprising context by one forest officer, who was describing how he did not believe in charms but that, in 'calling Mother with an open fervent heart, against the dangers of the jungle, the two most important weapons are devotion and courage'. 'Bonbibi?' I had asked. 'No, Tarama [another name for Kali],' he replied. But he also added in the same breath that the only time he was attacked by a tiger was when he went to pee in the jungle. He made no explicit connection but I found it strange that he mentioned the reason why he had alighted, as the forest boats usually have toilets. He also said that he often entered the jungle unarmed because he believed that, if he had no intention of hurting 'wildlife', then wildlife would not hurt him. It was then that he remarked,

Forest life is now polluted, you cannot speak the truth any longer. The islanders were so poor, ten-fifteen years ago they were very poor. Now prawn money has made them richer but they have not been able to use that money properly. They do not send their kids to school, they steal the solar lamps installed along some jetties by the government and do not respect the fact that the forest is government property. Ten years ago WB had the second highest revenue collected from forest products but this has now come down because illegal wood poaching has increased and government licensed felling has been reduced.

In the setting of the Sundarbans prawn industry, Kali did not entirely conform to her more mainstream portrayal. She was stripped of the motherly qualities attributed to her in urban middle-class homes and her usual portrayal of the magnanimous and compassionate mother, ever-ready to forgive her errant children — an image made famous by the great Bengali poet and composer of songs Ramprasad Sen and mystic Sri Ramakrishna Paramahamsa — stood in stark contrast to the stories of gore and greed which were narrated about her in the Sundarbans.[7] Here, popular stories of Kali focus on her association with those practising illegal and/or violent occupations invoking her destructive power and fickle, greedy and blood-thirsty nature. Depicted as the *enfant terrible* of the Hindu pantheon of gods and goddesses she was sometimes linked to Dokkhin Rai in his cruel form of the man-eating monster of the Sundarbans.[8]

On a practical level, her worship, being expensive, is undertaken by prawn khoti owners, their dealers and agents, as well as the prawn seed collectors. This is in contrast to the worship of the forest deity Bonbibi, undertaken by individual forest workers or by small family units even if they usually work in teams. As I saw it, Kali's image permits the Sundarbans prawn seed collectors to reject the *bhadramahila* (literally, civilised/cultured woman) ideal of womanhood marked by urban and upper-caste/class ideals of female docility steeped in 'tradition' and 'spirituality' as popularised by Indian nationalism (Chatterjee 1993) while allowing them to feel as if they were more urban, 'civilised' or modern because they worship her. The choice of Kali in her violent and blood-thirsty form offered a social redefinition of what it meant to be a village woman with clout and economic status and offered a possibility of 'civility' (modern as opposed to traditional)through association with a goddess who was at once firmly installed within the Hindu pantheon and yet also permitted enough room for 'deviance'.

Kali is seen by the prawn seed collectors as offering a space to claim a sense of urban civility because she does not have the dubious Islamic origins of Bonbibi. She is the goddess usually worshipped by the forest guards, people who represent both the upwardly mobile and the larger exterior world of which a few of the prawn collectors had been part, as migrants. Moreover, Kali is deemed more 'powerful'. Her inherent violence, in sharp contrast to Bonbibi's peaceful disposition was believed to offer greater potency in dealings with life-threatening dangers such as crocodiles and tigers, as well as the risky contingencies of the prawn industry. By choosing Kali, the Sundarbans' women prawn seed collectors refused their relegation to the margins; she permitted them, as one of them pithily expressed, to be part of 'the cut-throat world of global business'.

If Kali is seen as fitting with the necessarily violent, risky and bloody nature of their occupation, she is also seen as befitting an occupation inscribed within 'modernity'. Prawn seed collecting thus located within a contemporary temporality as well as a spatiality which extends beyond their village (their prawns reach the plates of people belonging to the distant lands of Japan and the USA), allowed the collectors to consider their occupation — and their chosen deity — to be 'modern'. Kali made sense both because she was violent enough to be subversive and yet also urban enough to be 'global'. It was because she was both inside and outside the confines of their village world that Kali made sense. And because the prawn seed collectors saw themselves as situated within a greater 'global' experience, however remote that 'globality' appeared to be from the material and social realities of their daily lives.

The 'Blue Revolution' in the Poverty-Stricken Land of the 'Living Dollars'

The commercialisation of prawn seed, and hence its aquaculture, occurred around the world in the 1960s and 1970s. In the early 1980s, major improvements in hatchery production and feed-processing techniques allowed rapid advances in prawn farming techniques, making it possible to produce dramatically increased yields. Drawing parallels with the 'Green Revolution' in agriculture, which contributed to the growth of large-scale export-oriented agribusiness enterprises in the global south but which were also subject to widespread criticism for their environmental and social impacts, Quarto et al. have called the massive growth of the prawn aquaculture industry the 'Blue Revolution'. It has become a global industry that has an annual farm-gate value of over $40 crore, and an annual retail value of over $200 crore (Rosenberry in Quarto et al. 1996: 1). However, if the Green Revolution primarily benefited individual farmers, this revolution, especially where it concerns brackish water prawn cultivation, has been seen by environmental activists as spelling ecological, economic and social doom for the communities of the global south.

The economic and ecological reasons for the condemnation of the prawn industry are clear enough and briefly elaborated in the following paragraphs. If over 85 per cent of worldwide farmed prawn production takes place in Asia, the near totality of the product is exported, two-thirds of it mainly serving consumers in Japan and the USA, with the rest being dispatched to Europe, Canada, Hong Kong, and Singapore. Spurred on by governments eager for increased export dollars, prawn aquaculture development has been aided by generous support and incentives from international lending institutions, including the World Bank, Asian Development Bank, Inter-American Development Bank, and others.[9]

The World Bank participated actively in launching the prawn (or 'shrimp') industry in Asia. Out of an investment of US$16.85 crore in 1992 for Indian agriculture and fisheries, the World Bank allocated US$42.5 crore for aquaculture development. A substantial part of this sum seems to be destined for intensification and expansion of shrimp ponds (Barraclough and Finger-Stich 1995: 15–16). However, as argued by Quarto et al., the global economic figures and the allure of quick investment returns disguise the fact that prawn aquaculture is a 'boom and bust' industry where the spread of deadly infectious viruses in prawns has episodically caused hundreds of lakhs of dollars worth of losses (1996: 1). The prawn aquaculture industry is extremely vulnerable and investments are continually at risk.

If the economic scene is unstable, the environmental harm caused by prawn seed collection and prawn aquaculture farming is even worse. It has caused severe environmental degradation, especially in mangrove regions. The tiger prawn seeds constitute only 0.25–0.27 per cent of the total catch; the rest of the 'by-catch' is discarded. According to Sarkar and Bhattacharya, this wastage as well as the techniques involved in collecting prawn seeds constitute several ecological and occupational hazards: *(i)* immense damage to the mangrove biota leading to severe fish stock depletion and thus threatening the equilibrium of marine ecosystem food webs; *(ii)* the uprooting of the mangrove seed and salt-marsh vegetation which sets off soil erosion due to the constant dragging of nets along the coast and tidal creeks; *(iii)* a decrease in the quality of water triggered off by mud erosion in the catchment areas; and, *(iv)* skin infections, waterborne illnesses, infertility and many other diseases which afflict especially women collectors due to their constant contact with the salt river water (2003: 260). Once fisheries, especially those made for the cultivation of the brackish water tiger prawn species we are dealing with here, are abandoned, they become wastelands, unfit for any other resource-extractive purposes.

The islanders, both prawn seed collectors and non-prawn seed collectors, were aware of these detrimental environmental consequences — and these were already tangible: prawn seed quantities had markedly decreased, the sea level in the area had risen to an estimated rate of 3.14 cm a year over the past two decades (the global average is of 2 mm a year). Informed by NGO activists such as Tushar Kanjilal, the islanders know of scientists' predictions that in the next fifty years, if the sea level rises by just one metre, 1,000 sq kms of the Sundarbans will be inundated (Bhaumik 2003: 1). Also, since the first settlements in 1765, the population of the Indian Sundarbans has risen by 200 per cent. Prawn seed collection thus understandably heads the list of environmental concerns the authorities feel they need to address.

While the environmental threat caused by prawn seed collection and farming is very real (Bhaumik 2003; Kanjilal 2000; Sarkar and Bhattacharya 2003; Vidal 2003), those who denounce the prawn business — NGO activists, the rural elite, common islanders, even prawn seed collectors — put the issues in moral terms, a morality that goes beyond environmental degradation to speak of the associated so-called 'social degradation' of those involved with prawn seed collection. Since the beginning, this occupation has been marked by violence. This is not just a factual observation noted globally (see the examples given in numerous reports) but is very much an all-encompassing reality in the Sundarbans.[10]

The greatest violence and hatred is expressed between landowners and prawn fishers. When breaches in bunds or embankments cause land to be temporarily submerged by salt water, the easy option is to convert one's flooded paddy fields into prawn fisheries. However, by law, this requires permission from the landlords of the adjoining lands, especially if they want to reserve their lands for agricultural purposes since, once a field is converted into a necessarily salt-water fishery, it contaminates the soil surrounding it. As permission is not readily given, those who want to start fisheries sometimes resort to opening breaches in the bunds and embankments that keep riverine salt water out. Once an area is flooded, it becomes difficult to refuse converting it into a fishery. Landowners who want to keep their land for paddy production sometimes resort to poisoning neighbouring fisheries. Equally, as prawn seeds are fragile and suffer very high mortality rates, it is not difficult to accuse one's neighbour of having poisoned one's fisheries. This dynamic gives rise to endless and often murderous fights between landlords who want to keep their fields for paddy production and those (usually very small holders) who want to convert theirs into fisheries. Also, the resentment of erstwhile landowners seeing prawn dealers become rich in such short lapses of time often pushes them into bullying landless labourers who turned to prawn seed collecting into returning to work their fields.

In Bangladesh and WB the growth of an export-oriented brackish water prawn aquaculture industry started in the 1960s and centred on Khulna and Cox's Bazar in Bangladesh and in Midnapur in West Bengal. The industry picked up very rapidly and by the late 1970s prawn seed collection had become very popular in the Sundarbans. This development represented a major shift from the traditional fishing sector as practised essentially by Hindu caste groups and by men. Prawn seed collection, in contrast, was started in Bangladesh by Muslim communities who were increasingly disadvantaged as landless labourers and marginal farmers. It soon spread as it was relatively free from the social hierarchies linked to agriculture and could be practised in one's own free time and with very little investment. Moreover, initially at least, it was devoid of stigma.

The islanders narrated how in the beginning it was a craze, nearly everybody took up prawn seed collection as it was such an easy way to make cash — prawn was then dubbed the 'living dollars of the Sundarbans'. Thus, the wives of school teachers and important politicians were, like their poorer counterparts, known to have hitched up their saris and spent entire days wading in rivers pulling behind them the fine net used to collect tiger prawn seed. The threat of crocodiles in those earlier times was remote and dealers paid well. Another very important factor for the popularity of the occupation was that the price of a prawn seed did not depend on one's gender or contacts and it was fixed primarily by the laws of the global market economy. However, the fact that this occupation was started first in Bangladesh and mainly by Muslims, and that it became, both in Bangladesh and in West Bengal, popularised especially amongst the very poor, is of relevance to understand why the occupation came to take on the negative moral connotations it has today.

What also seems of note is that initially prawn seed collectors made money relatively quickly, thus bringing about the wrath of those who considered themselves too *bhadra* or 'civilised' to practise prawn seed collection. The antipathy of the village elite towards the prawn seed collectors has to be understood primarily as a struggle for control of the economy. They resent the fact that share-croppers and wage labourers refuse to work their fields for a pittance, and that they now prefer to borrow money from prawn dealers rather than them, the landowners. Prawn dealers are very often forest workers (sometimes ex-poachers) or prawn seed collectors who 'have made it' and have become rich. They are usually people of the same social background as forest workers and prawn seed collectors and live, like them, along the river's edge.

The prawn seed collectors often boast about how they were their own masters and how easily one could become prawn dealers (albeit this is usually practised by men) through hard work and luck. In contrast to the forest workers and to school teachers — both groups seen to be dependent on the state for forest passes and salaries respectively — the prawn seed collectors took great pride in not being subject to the patronage of the state or of landowners. They strove to gain social status by keeping very much informed about world news and by highlighting the fact that they were part of the global economy and therefore held a more prestigious occupation than a mere landowning cultivator. Even if being a prawn seed collector meant being subject to exploitation by both local as well as international market forces, the prawn seed collectors saw it as better than being the landless labourers of the local landowner. However, if the two sectors, agriculture and prawn, vied for economic status, social status was still very much the prerogative of the landed gentry. It is in this context that we have to understand the critique levelled at the morality of prawn seed collectors, the discourses of their 'greed' and 'violence' developed to prevent their access to social respectability.

Historically, there seems to have always been friction between cultivators and fishers in Bengal. When the British established the Permanent Settlement in 1793, they left *jalkar* rights — rights relating to the produce of the water — open for the zamindars to increase their income.[11] This system increased the dominance of the zamindar landlords even if they usually leased their jalkar rights to middlemen who, in turn, hired fishers. Fisheries thus became private properties that could be bought and sold. What is interesting is that the rights to a body of water and that to the land which surrounded it were usually vested in two different persons. When rivers shifted their course, the rights of jalkar followed the river so that if it flowed over a cultivator's land, the cultivator lost access to that land and did not gain any compensatory rights to fish even though his land lay beneath water (Pokrant et al. 2001: 97). However, in contrast to these private fisheries, fishing in the public navigable rivers was allowed and went untaxed. These were defined as the property of the state and the public had the right to fish where rivers were not leased out to individuals (ibid.: 96–97).

Over the nineteenth century, the colonial state created a system based on rentier capital and in the process undermined the long-standing customary rights of the fishers. In 1859, the Board of Revenue, in an endeavour to build up revenue, leased out portions of navigable rivers, especially the Hooghly and Ganga, to leaseholders (ibid.: 99). But by 1868, in the wake of legal disputes, the Government of Bengal abandoned the policy of auctioning parts of navigable rivers in deference to the views of the Legal Remembrance and the Advocate General who, in following English law on the subject, were of the opinion that the rights to fisheries in tidal rivers were vested in the Crown, in its capacity of trustee, for the benefit of the public and that exclusive rights of fishery could thus not be granted to private individuals or to certain classes of persons to the exclusion of the public (ibid.: 99–100, quoting *Indian Law Reports*, 11, Calcutta, 434). However, customary rights kept clashing with capitalist interests. The zamindars pressurised the Government of Bengal through the British Indian Association (BIA) to ensure their jalkar rights. Eventually, the chief secretary of the Government of Bengal established that fish, even though in public rivers, did not become the property of the person who had the fishing right as they were *ferae naturae* and therefore belonged to the state.[12] By the end of the nineteenth century, the customary rights of fishers were nearly non-existent.

It is thus not impossible to imagine why, in Pabna in 1873, the *polo* (fish trap) became a badge of insurgency that was used in peasant mobilisation against zamindars (Guha 1983: 127–28, 229, in Pokrant et al. 2001: 109). In short, the zamindars, in collusion with the colonial state, by redefining fishing rights along a system based on rentier capital similar to that of agricultural production, undermined the long-standing customary rights of Bengali fishers. This brought about the total collapse of an industry of prime importance to the economy of Bengal and greatly impoverished rural Bengal. The life of fishers has been given voice in a powerful Bengali novel, *A River Called Titash* (1956) by Adwaita Mallabarman, himself a man from the fisher community of Malos. This novel, as well as the novel mentioned earlier, *Padma River Boatman,* both written in the first half of the twentieth century, gives us poignant 'thick descriptions' of the marginalisation faced by this community. These authors bring to light the harshness and precariousness of fishers' lives, the relative equality in the kind of gender relations they shared, the interactions they had with the agricultural and trading communities, and their perception of the natural world and the terrible economic poverty fishers had sunk into by the early 1900s. It appears from these novels that among fisher communities there was not the gender and caste segregation which existed and lives on in landowning castes and classes. The other interesting aspect in these books, which matches what I found, is that both river and sea fish are considered as 'commons' property and 'collectable' by the poorest. Fishing was practised by fisher castes, castes that were generally landless (which, in the rural Bengali hierarchy of social relations denotes being one of the lowest socio-economic communities).

History seemed to repeat itself when, in December 1996, the Supreme Court of India ordered the closure of all semi-intensive and intensive prawn farms within 500 m of the high tide line, banned prawn farms from all public lands, and required farms that closed down to compensate their workers with six years' wages in a move to protect the environment and prevent the dislocation of local people (Primavera 1998: 1). None of these stipulations were put into effect.

Prawn seed collection is the first link in the long chain of activities between the catching of the almost invisible hair-like prawn seed to its final dispatch onto the global market. The development of hatchery-produced tiger prawn seed is highly inadequate in West Bengal, making the aquaculture farms of this region largely dependent on the supply from the natural resources of the Sundarbans. In this context, it is important to focus on the activities around the collection, counting, buying and selling of the prawn seeds.

Collecting

There are two main ways in which the islanders go about prawn seed collection. One is by boat which involves fixing a fine triangular net in the river, pulling up its conical-shaped end every half hour, and pouring the contents into a container on the boat. The second method, by far the more popular, consists of pulling along a 3 or 4 feet-wide by 5 to 6 feet-long rectangular-shaped mosquito net mounted on a wooden frame, wading in waist- to shoulder-deep water, along the bank of a river. These two methods, in WB, are practised roughly along gendered lines for economic and practical reasons — usually women and children fish by pulling nets whereas men (sometimes with their wives) fish from their boats. Pulling nets along the banks of their villages enables women and children to remain close to their locality so that women can easily go back to their household chores and children to their classes or games. Those fishing from their boats often spend the whole night on the river. Net-pulling is also undertaken along the banks of the forested islands, even though it is illegal, especially as it yields a greater catch. This is usually undertaken by a group of intrepid young women or groups of men and women of all ages. They row their boats to the large river intersections, settle on a bank, and pull their nets for six to seven hours.

Pulling along the river banks of villages is risky as the rivers, es-pecially after the efforts of the government in the 1980s to establish crocodile hatcheries, are now infested with crocodiles, the largest of which grow to a length of 23 feet or 7 m. Pulling along the banks of the forest islands is even more dangerous as there, apart from the crocodiles, one also risks being attacked by tigers, sharks and venomous snakes. Each year, the number of crocodile victims — mostly women — keeps increasing. As mentioned earlier, the estimate by the then Sundarbans range officer of 150 people killed per year by tigers and crocodiles is plausible. However, Pranabes Sanyal, chief conservator of forest (wildlife), WB Forest Department, claimed that the number of tiger victims in 1996 fell to a single person and that this was because 30 per cent of ex-fishermen, woodcutters and honey collectors had shifted to prawn seed collection (1987: 1). If tigers have been taking fewer victims in recent years, casualties caused by crocodiles have sharply increased.

Counting, Buying and Selling

When the collectors return to dry land, the prawn seeds are counted. This procedure entails hours of sitting along the village paths, while separating each individual greyish inch-long live tiger prawn seed of hair-thin diameter from the haul, using a white bivalve shell. The counting of prawn seeds is a long-drawn-out process which often erupts in fights, as sometimes dead tiger prawn seedlings (which turn reddish) or non–tiger prawn seedlings (differences are apparent only to the trained eye) are passed off as the real thing. The counting is usually supervised by two parties: the collectors, who try to count as quickly as possible, and the prawn seed dealers working for the khoti owners, who tell them to slow down. The dealers walk down the village bunds with aluminium pots in the hope of coming across collectors who have returned from fishing, and buy prawn seed from them. The prices vary greatly, and change not only in relation to seasons — the peak months being August to October — but from village to village, and often even within a lapse of hours, depending on how good or bad the catch of the day has been in each particular village.

In the monsoon months, when prawn seeds proliferate, women catch around 1,000/day and men in boats around 3,000. During this time the price for 1,000 prawn seeds goes down as low as Rs 50. During the leanest months, January and February, when the catch falls to 200–300 per person/day, the rate goes up to Rs 400 for 1,000 seeds. However, even during the monsoon months, people can be lucky and make a good sum and vice versa during the lean months. There is thus no guarantee of the amount of money a person might make and this is considered to be yet another factor contributing to the riskiness of this occupation. If much of it is a lottery, there are, however, some factors based on experience and many prawn seed collectors can guess the probability of getting prawn seeds not only according to the season but also in relation to the lunar cycle (whether it is full moon or new moon), the wind velocity and the wave amplitude. The dealers usually negotiate their prices with the collectors. The collectors can, to a certain extent, be choosy with dealers but they are also under pressure to sell off their seeds as soon as they possibly can to prevent their dying.

Dispatching the Prawn Seeds en Route to the Fisheries

Four to seven men usually work as dealers and agents for khoti owners. When dealers are not out on the bund to buy prawn seed, the prawn seed collectors come to the khoti. The most important items in these little shacks are the notebooks belonging to each dealer with lists carefully drawn up of the number of seedlings bought, the names of each collector, and the time and dates, so that collectors, dealers and khoti owners know fairly accurately the number of seedlings they have bought and placed in their little fisheries. They sell these off to the bigger fishery owners not by counting the seedlings all over again but by letting businessmen count the seedlings from any one of their pots picked at random.

Khotis for prawn seed transactions are relatively new in Garjontola. Three or four men form a partnership by pooling around Rs 5,000 each. Each day, they entrust in theory about Rs 500 to 1,000 to the four to seven dealers working for them — which means that fortnightly the khoti partners dispense an amount between Rs 30,000 and a lakh. However, in practice, this is not normally the case. Due to demands of kinship ties and the risks of the prawn industry, the businessmen or khoti partners rarely have such large amounts of money at their disposal and so offer to pay the prawn seed collectors the bulk of their earnings along with interest at the end of the three months' prawn season. However, it is up to the prawn seed collectors to agree to this deal or sell their prawn seeds to other dealers. Either way is perilous for the collectors: in the first instance they risk losing a good amount of their money if the season has been bad; in the second instance, they risk alienating a known dealer and thus having to travel to another village to sell the easily perishable prawn seed.

'Nothing but a Lottery'

The violence and risk linked to this industry are manifested at all stages. During collection, prawn seed collectors — especially women, given that they are the ones pulling the nets — face the risk of being attacked and killed by crocodiles, sharks, tigers, and snakes. Counting the prawn seed gives rise to endless charges of cheating. Pressure groups of all kinds try to establish their hegemony over the prawn seed collectors' wares. With the passing of prawn dealing from the management of outsiders to insiders, the fight for control has become more intense. In some places, prawn dealing has been taken up by party activists who have chased away previous prawn transactors. Many such small fisheries of transition are starting up in the villages of the southern islands of the Sundarbans so that by the time the prawn seeds reach the larger mainland fisheries they are bigger and can be sold at a higher price. All these factors cause the price of prawn seed to decrease. The risks entailed are also very high, the dealers have to take measures against the fisheries' exposure to the hazards of the weather: excessive rain causes the fishery chambers to flood.[13] Likewise, if the ratio of food or lime and phosphate is not right or if the sun heats up the fisheries, the prawn seeds die and a good part of the season's collection is lost. Sarkar and Bhattacharya report that there is a mortality rate of 15–20 per cent of the prawn seeds at this stage (2003: 262).

The prawn industry is big money. Let me give an example: during high season for two of the villages of Satjelia island — each with 3,000 inhabitants — one night's catch produces around Rs 1,50,000 for the village of Toofankhali and around 5,00,000 for the adjoining village Lahiripur. However, this economy is subject to extreme fluctuations. The prawn transacting boats that take the prawn seeds to bigger fisheries or the fully grown prawns to Kolkata or Bangladesh are regularly attacked and their crews beaten up by pirates, with vast amounts of cash and prawn seed looted. The boats are also heavily fined by the Border Security Force (BSF) when they illegally cross the border to sell the prawn seeds in Bangladesh, a frequent practice as the Bangladeshi dealers pay a higher price for them than do the dealers from West Bengal. Even the fisheries where the seeds were grown into full size tiger prawns were known as hotbeds of violence where different fishery owners vying with each other for better markets poisoned each others' fisheries. These were usually owned by four or five partners who employed around forty-five labourers. These fisheries dotted the landscape for two-thirds of the bus route to the Sundarbans. Above these vast expanses of water contained in squares, platforms were built atop bamboo poles where men holding rifles could be seen keeping a close guard day and night. In all these regions, rice fields are increasingly being converted into prawn fisheries, displacing old hierarchies and installing new ones in their place.

Yet another reason for the negative connotations of the prawn industry is its utter unpredictability, at all stages, for those who engage in it. The islanders often talked of the prawn industry as being 'nothing but a lottery'. Whether one is a collector, a dealer or a fishery owner, to engage in the prawn industry is a 'risky' business. People either make or lose millions and just as they are susceptible to gain in economic and political power, gain the chance to migrate towards the city and thus access higher social status, they can just as easily lose their life to tigers or crocodiles or their possessions to a storm or a retributive attack.

If the prawn dealers, agents and businessmen are unapologetic about their occupation, the collectors, usually women, frequently highlighted to me the moral dilemmas surrounding their work. I pointed out earlier the moral perspective on the negative effect this occupation is assumed to be having on village life. This criticism is levelled on two accounts. The first of these is made by many islanders, especially those who work in the forest and who are always quick to point out the way in which prawn seed collection contravenes the 'ethos of the forest' and is therefore cursed by Bonbibi. In fact, many forest workers with family members engaged in prawn seed collection usually blame tiger attacks on them. They argue that the prawn seed collectors have 'de-sacralised' the forest, transforming it into 'a big marketplace' where people unscrupulously disturb animals by walking in and out at all times of the day and night.

The idea that the forest is a sacred place is especially upheld by the crab and honey collectors and the woodcutters through the imposition of minutely elaborated rules pertaining to the forest. The imperative for them is to follow such rules when entering into the forest to prove their goodwill to the forest deity Bonbibi. Because the prawn seed collectors could not or did not want to respect these rules (as they did not consider themselves forest workers) they were branded as being greedy and with having no 'real' understanding or respect of the forest. The other criticism, levelled by the village elite, was that prawn seed collection had to be condemned as it made women 'uncontrollable' and the poor in general 'arrogant' by challenging the understood hierarchies of gender and society. Let me illustrate this point with an example. One Friday, the day of the weekly market, I was sipping tea at Toofankhali's marketplace Hatkhola with a socially mixed group of islanders of all ages who were discussing the recent killing of a prawn seed collector by a crocodile. One of the men, a school teacher, seated on one of the two benches which surrounded the shop, turned to me and said, 'Do you know the main reason for all these prawn seed collectors' deaths? It is greed. So many of these villagers running at the break of dawn to the river with their nets to pull in dollars. The American and the Japanese taste for tiger prawn is spoiling our traditional way of life.'

Later, on our way back home, Arati asked in a sarcastic tone, 'Do you know what he actually meant by 'traditional way of life'? He meant being able to exploit us on his fields for a few rupees. Prawn has saved us, they are the living dollars of the Sundarbans, and the dollar will any day win against the landed gentry and their ruthless exploitation.'

Many prawn seed collectors were amongst the biggest critics of the occupation as they genuinely believed that by entering the forest they brought upon themselves the wrath of the forest deity Bonbibi and that those who practised this occupation were ultimately doomed because they flouted the rules of the forest. Others highlighted how numerous poor parents were making their children pull nets instead of sending them to school. Countering these critiques, prawn seed collectors retorted that it was unfortunate they were stigmatised but that many did not have the money to send their children to school. 'It was sad that people died but what are the options for making a living in the Sundarbans, especially for the landless and for widowed or divorced women?' they asked. The islanders often spoke of a time before prawn seed collection, when life was tough and where they could not satisfy their hunger. With prawn seed collection things had changed, those who had been quick to pick up this occupation were now in a better position to afford schooling and food for their children.

What caused the prawn seed collectors great concern was the dwindling number of prawn seed. Going against the village elite, such as the landowners and school teachers who are lobbying to have the occupation banned, the prawn seed collectors want government regulations imposed and a greater protection of the prawn industry.[14] This is for two reasons. Apart from the economic guarantee of knowing that their wares will not decrease fourfold in value from one day to the next and the ecological threat of seeing prawn seed disappear, they want prawn seed collection to be recognised as a legitimate occupation (as opposed to being seen as a quick money-making occupation with no future) so that it might gain social approbation. The negative image of prawn seed collection is reinforced in innumerable ways. The increase of tiger and crocodile victims is often blamed on prawn seed collectors and yet they are not seen as victims. When the islanders narrate to outsiders the difficulties of living in the Sundarbans, it is essentially honey collectors and woodcutters who are cited as the most vulnerable groups. What is strange is that even though prawn seed collectors, and therefore women, are now, as a group, the most affected lot, and despite the fact that crocodiles and sharks are producing far more victims than are tigers, prawn seed collectors do not evoke the sympathy the honey collectors or woodcutters do.

Roughing it with Kali

The discrepancy of status between the glamorous tiger versus the common crocodile or shark is directly transferred to the inequality of status between the perceived pious and industrious forest workers versus the immoral and greedy women prawn seed collectors. The motives for this are both the local ethos of the forest with its associated laws and the discrepancy between the status of men and women. Why a person finds death in the clutches of a tiger is often attributed by the islanders to their possessing one of the following traits: violence, greed or arrogance. These are believed to be the characteristics of tigers and thus, if one has the misfortune to display them, one is seen as making a mockery of the tiger and thus unwittingly becomes its target. Those who work in the forest generally accept that becoming a honey collector or a woodcutter means internalising the ominous adage 'to work in the forest is to tempt the tiger' (*mohal kora mane bagh chesta kora*), along with the courage this necessitates.

By contrast, the forest workers see the prawn seed collectors as entering the forest without having internalised this threat. They consider the prawn seed collectors to be 'careless' not only about their own lives but about the jungle at large, thus putting all the other forest workers' lives at stake. As a crab collector explained, there are two main protocols that need to be remembered when entering the forest; first, that the presiding deity of the forest is Ma Bonbibi and, second, that the Sundarbans are the 'storehouse of Ma Bonbibi' (*ma bonbibir khamar — khamar* means storehouse/granary, usually a place where crops are stored). All who enter the forest must do so in a spirit of 'brotherhood' and consider the fruits of the forest as being for the poorest. The forest is often spoken about as a sort of 'commons'; those who work there are obliged to share equally anything they bring back from the forest. In contrast, the forest workers argue, the prawn seed collectors believe in 'grab and be gone' and do not have the same ethos of sharing as them.

In complete contrast to the forest workers who need to respect elaborate rules in relation to the forest, the prawn seed collectors are seen as uncouth and thieving, and as 'ill-mannered looters of the forest' as one tiger-charmer called them. They do not respect any of the forest rules and fish at odd times of the day and often at night, as they have to accord their timings with the changing tides. As most of them are women, they have to look after children, send them off to school, comb their hair, etc. Anita, a veteran prawn seed collector, explained:

> There are so many forest rules, which ones should we keep and which ones can we safely dispose of? As it is difficult to decide, and as we work more often along the banks of rivers flowing along villages rather than the ones flowing through the forest, we prefer foregoing of these rules.

Moreover, although there are specific interdictions against defiling the territory of the tiger, there aren't any such elaborations with regards to crocodiles or sharks. Neither are the rivers, when flowing outside the forest, considered 'sacred'.

Ganga, the river goddess, the patron of the boatmen and the sea fishers, might have had the potential to become the patron of the prawn seed collectors. She is, after all, seen as a 'theiving' goddess, always grabbing land and homestead. Yet, Ganga is also seen as too 'local'. One of the popular jokes about Ganga highlights her disreputable petty greed. It goes like this: Once, a boat taking passengers to the market met with a huge storm. It started rocking so dangerously that one scared woman cried out in terror, 'Ma Ganga, please let me cross safely and I shall organise a ritual feast (*bhog*) in your honour next year.' The weather continued to be rough and the woman now implored her adding that she would organise this ritual feast each month; she soon extended her mark of devotion to each week and this carried on and on until it became every day. The woman invited all her co-passengers to be witness to her promise. Finally the river calmed down and the boat reached the shore. On alighting from the boat the woman turned to the river and said, 'So, Ma Ganga, you tried to con me through fright, eh? But I appealed to your greed and tricked you!'[15]

The narration of this story and the laughter induced by ridiculing Ganga's greed contrasted sharply with the stories the men recount of the forest where spirits and tigers must be appeased through strict rules highlighting their subservience. Prawn seed collectors who spend their days wading in river water did not choose Ganga as their deity, notwithstanding the fact that she is seen to be just as greedy and occasionally as violent as Kali. The rejection of Ganga as the preferred deity of prawn seed collectors because she was 'local' led me to look at prawn seed collection and its social content from the women's perspectives. As one of my female prawn-seed-collecting neighbours explained,

> Ganga is neither strong nor violent enough, besides, she isn't a "world deity" (*biswa debi*). Who knows about her? Whereas Kali, with her reputation of being a cut-throat goddess, is just perfect for us.

It isn't as if all the prawn seed collectors worship Kali; on the contrary, she is much less worshipped than Bonbibi. Ganga too is worshipped, but as a minor deity, and mainly by those who own boats. Kali, however, is increasingly gaining popularity amongst prawn seed collectors on the grounds that she is powerful. Forest workers are seen by a surprising number of women prawn seed collectors as a generally superstitious lot, whereas the women see themselves as pragmatic and they often express serious doubts about Bonbibi's potency. For prawn seed collectors, Kali is the goddess that they propitiate and worship.

The reason why Kali, a goddess not previously worshipped by this community, is rapidly replacing Bonbibi is also because she is seen as 'contemporary' or 'modern' (*adhunik*). When I asked how, I was told that she was 'modern' because she was favoured by the police and taxi-drivers — representatives of contemporary suave and urban professionals (at least for the islanders). This was also why the poachers had adopted her as their deity of choice. Kali, in the Sundarbans, is seen as a goddess favouring 'black parties', that is, those engaged in illegal activities such as poaching and pirating. Once, in the early days of my fieldwork, while discussing the forest with a man who was a poacher, I learnt that he did not worship Bonbibi because he 'believed in firearms' and used them against wild animals (i.e., Bonbibi's animals) and that 'Ma Kali was therefore more appropriate'. He then explained that even though the deity of the forest was Bonbibi, he did not worship her because 'She refuses to protect firearm users, she assures her full protection only if you enter the forest with bare hands. When you are a poacher,' he went on to drive the point in,

> you refuse to acknowledge the animals as Bonbibi's, you not only take the jungle for granted, but actually greedily plunder it. How in these circumstances can you imagine that Bonbibi will come to your rescue? She's good to fish and crab parties, but for us black parties it's different, with our firearms we bear more resemblance to dacoits and policemen than to crab catchers.

The islanders often narrate how she had appeared to lure them into shady deals. She is greedy for human blood and offers people ponds full of gold and fish in return for one of their children. It was told in a story how Kali appeared to a poor woman and offered her some pots of gold which were under her house if she gave her two sons to Kali. The next day the floor cracked and the woman saw the glittering pots. But she built a small wall around the crack, put flowers and a lamp and each night prayed to Kali, saying, 'Please Ma, I have made you a place for you to keep your possessions, but you keep them to yourself, I have no need for them.' The islanders narrated how the poor woman nearly went mad in fright as she frantically searched for another place to live in. Another common story tells of an instance when some islanders went fishing in the middle of the night and saw big pots containing wads of bank notes below the surface of the water. Usually in those situations, it was reported, one of the older and wiser persons would say, 'today mother is grazing her money, let us leave her to do it in peace' and they would leave. Kali arouses greed.

In contrast, there is a Bonbibi shrine in many forest office grounds — the government's 'use' of her thus signifying her as a 'legal' deity. So in some ways Bonbibi is 'tamed' while the prawn seed collectors see themselves needing a goddess who can deal with the 'illegal', who is perhaps 'illegal' herself. Kali offers the perfect compromise as she is both a 'mainstream' goddess, hence giving them status as 'modern' people, as well as a goddess linked to the unlawful dacoits of olden days and the poachers of today. The condemnation, both from the local point of view highlighting how their occupation goes against the 'ethos of the forest' as well as the global condemnation that their occupation is causing the near annihilation of the Sundarbans ecology, has relegated the prawn seed collectors to the margins of occupational respectability. This is why Kali is seen as offering the possibility of both a redemption in the context of modernity and progressiveness as well as a space to 'express their power'.

This popularity of Kali with people who see their occupation as violent and/or marginal may be compared to the growing attractiveness of deities such as Kataragama, Kali and Huniyam/Suniyam in Sri Lanka. Locally, these deities were traditionally linked to immorality, black magic and even considered not as gods but as demons. However, in Sri Lanka's tumultuous and war-torn present, they were considered the most appropriate deities to combat the stresses of modern life because, having overcome demons (*asuras*) themselves, they were seen as being the most resourceful in overcoming obstacles. Unlike Vishnu, seen here as the unequivocally moral deity, Kataragama, for example, is seen as 'willing to do *anything*' (author's stress) to help his devoted adherent and has hence become the god of the politicians, businessmen and big-time crooks in the city of Colombo (Gombrich and Obeyesekere 1988: 185). Similarly, in the Tamil-dominated eastern coastal fishing villages of Sri Lanka where the ravages of war have left the population terrorised and deeply scarred, it is Kali who is increasingly being worshipped because she is seen as the most responsive and powerful deity. Identified by these Sri Lankan fisher communities as 'rough like the sea', she is seen as the only deity having the power to 'change the position' of those experiencing the immediate vulnerability to a violent annihilation and to return to safety those family members who have disappeared (Lawrence 2003: 107). This is not to suggest a common pan–South Asian understanding of Kali. What I am reiterating is how gods and goddesses are given new operative capacities which are perceived as better helping people to deal with the contingencies of changing lifestyles.

Appadurai has argued in 'Grassroots Globalization and the Research Imagination' that 'in the public sphere of many societies there is concern that policy debates occurring around world trade, copyright, environment, science, and technology set the stage for life-and-death decisions for ordinary farmers, vendors, slum-dwellers, merchants and urban populations'. And that running through these debates is the sense 'that social exclusion is ever more tied to epistemological exclusion and concern that the discourses of expertise that are setting the rules for global transactions, even in the progressive parts of the international system, have left ordinary people outside and behind' (Appadurai 2001: 2). Appadurai argues that there is a growing divorce between debates around these issues amongst academics from those that are held by the poor and their advocates. He, however, finds some glimmer of hope in the series of social forms that have emerged to contest these developments and to create forms of knowledge transfer and social mobilisation that proceed independently of the actions of corporate capital and the nation-state system. These social forms, he says, 'can be characterised as "globalisation from below"'. What I find interesting is how in this case the prawn seed collectors themselves came up with their own 'strategies' to deal with globalisation; even if this strategy involved the undertaking of the worship of a deity, albeit a 'global' one.

Sweat and Blood: The Smell of Tiger Prawn

Once, while we were sitting on the bund with some women prawn seed collectors, Arati began telling me about how a young woman called Kalpana had met her death the previous year. Kalpana collected prawn seed to meet the needs of her small family. She went out each morning at the break of dawn with Arati, Shobita and Nonibala, her three friends, and pulled the net for four to five hours along the riverbanks of her village, Annpur. On the morning of her death she had pulled the net for three hours before being caught by a crocodile. As the crocodile caught her thigh and dragged her into the deeper waters of the river, Kalpana screamed out in terror and started beating the animal with her net. Her three friends ran to help her. One of them jumped in after her, trying to retrieve her from the murky waters, while the others shouted for help. What follows is keeping as close to Nonibala's narrative as possible. Kalpana's frantic gesticulations, cries and loud splashes as she fought with the crocodile pierced through the heavy white mist. After what seemed a horrendously long time they were replaced by the cracking of her net or bones or both. Nonibala was standing there in frozen torpor and then she swooned. When she sat up and desperately scanned the river for signs of life all she saw were bubbles and ripples disappearing into the stilling beige-brown surface of the river. She then noticed the trail of a slowly dulling bright red moving away from her while a soft cloying wetness, the limp end of a sari, washed itself around her legs. It felt as if a sudden soundless shard stabbed her through the heart, leaving her immobilised and speechless, as she realised her friend had been dragged away to the river's depths by a crocodile.

The islanders of Annpur came rushing to the riverbank immediately. The news spread fast. This was the fourth person in the locale to meet her death through these water monsters. Some other women had survived losing a limb to sharks. In fear, and to respect the dead woman's memory, the collectors stopped work the following days. The islanders agreed that the rivers were getting riskier and that they should refrain from collecting prawns by net pulling, especially during the upcoming monsoon months at the peak of the prawn seed collecting season. But within a few days these resolutions were forgotten: the men returned to work in the forest as crab collectors and fishers collectors and the women to pull their nets along the river's banks. During the winter months, which followed the reaping of paddy, there was little need for cash. But, during the summer and monsoon months, not only were there greater quantities of prawn seed but also more need for money.

'In the case of tiger victims, people make a big hue and cry but what about crocodile victims? There are no big stories for us, no explanation,' exclaimed Nonibala. She continued, 'Dokkhin Rai, according to some people, is someone one can at least pray to and plead with, but crocodiles are dumb creatures.'

As I explained earlier, the islanders do often provide arguments about why people are killed by tigers: there are rules in the forest and the islanders often explain that, if one only respected them, one would remain safe as tigers would refrain from attacking. Going to the jungle, they explain, is to know that the forest is Bonbibi's storehouse as well as a protected part of the global environment. But the rivers, when flowing along the inhabited islands, are not as symbolically demarcated as the forest and as those rivers flowing through the forest; besides they do not have stringent laws associated with them. The few rules pertaining to rivers are essentially upheld only by boatmen. The prawn seed collectors argue that prawn seed collection is seen in such a negative light because these are hatchlings collected for cash, not as food. So unfortunately, if traditionally river fish have always been a 'commons' property, prawn seeds are not, or at least are not seen as such. Prawn seed collectors are spoken of as being 'greedy' as they are seen as not knowing when to stop pulling the net because they always hope to make 'even more money'. 'But what is wrong in that?' suddenly asked Arati at the end of a conversation on the subject.

> Am I not paying for these prawns with the sweat of my brow? It's not as if I'm staying indoors and supervising my workers and yelling at them while my money multiplies in banks. Here I'm working my limbs off. Have you smelt tiger prawn, don't you think they smell of sweat and blood? It is ours. How dare people say we are greedy and have no self-respect just because we want to earn and make a decent living? Do you now understand why we need Kali on our side?

This outburst leads one to reflect on the paradoxical appropriation of Kali — she has been adopted by the prawn seed collectors both because of her connection to urban and middle-class professions and because of the context of growing Hindutva, and on the other hand because she is devoid of all the rules Bonbibi's veneration is seen as demanding. Prawn seed collecting is used by the Sundarbans women who practice it to provoke subtle reversals of village hierarchies — both of gender and of economy — and to engage in an alternative perception of modernity based on their terms. They reject the middle-class ideals of femininity and participate as active agents in a global trade where, with Kali the strong and violent patron goddess on their side, they see themselves as having better chances to fit in with contemporary times. By offering a contrary discourse to that of the forest workers and landowners, the prawn-seed-collecting women have carved out for themselves a space in which they bow neither to the traditional nor to the urban ideals of femininity. This uneasy space highlights a contrast between the 'imagined global' and the very dangerous materiality of working in the rivers of the Sundarbans.

Notes

1. Bengali form of 'Kaliyuga' — the last of the cosmic periods. This seems to be a well-known adage in the Sundarbans. In Bengali: *Hindu Musalman ek jati loye (niye), ghochaibe kolir dukho abtar hoye.*
2. 'Matobbor' meaning headman or a man of position, is used derogatorily in the Sundarbans. I have refrained from using the term 'village elders' and used 'village political leaders' instead, because matobbors, being between the age of twenty-five and forty-five, were far from being old. Also, I have used the word in the plural because representatives of different political groups

were always present at these meetings even though they were not always their leaders.

3. Khoti is a little shack built along an adjoining fishery by a prawn fishery owner. These serve to watch over the fishery at night and are used as a prawn seed transaction area during the day. They also become temporary living spaces for prawn dealers during the busy months.

4. Narayan is another name for the god Vishnu, *sinni* is a dish prepared for festive occasions; this worship is usually performed as an expiatory ritual. It is ironic that it should be this very worship which should be undertaken for the expiation of a Hindu–Muslim marriage because this very popular worship performed throughout Bengal is a narrative of how the worship should be celebrated by all, i.e., Hindus with folded hands calling Satya-Narayan, and Muslims with open hands calling Satya-Pir.

   For the five parts of Garjontola refer to Map 3.

5. It was public knowledge that Badal (who had never married) had famous long-standing affairs with two of his neighbours. He was far from being the only one and it was not such an issue as long as things remained discreet but, as because of this, one of the women had been killed by her husband and Badal had nearly killed himself due to the sorrow her death had caused him, this affair had become public and sometimes indirectly referred to when one wanted to discredit him.

6. By 'urban' I mean not only those living in towns and cities but more broadly, following Gombrich and Obeyesekere (1988: 4), middle- and working-class people who even though living in villages are, through their aspiration and lifestyle, clearly differentiated from peasants, fishers or forest workers.

7. Ramprasad Sen (1720–81), poet and famous composer of songs dedicated to Kali as 'Mother of the universe', couched in the words of a wayward but repentant child. The sentiments evoked by the songs are a combination of affectionate and erotic devotion in which the singer, as a naughty child, lovingly chides the fierce Mother for neglecting him and calling her, in rural slang, *magi*, i.e., slut and threatening to eat her, making tasty dishes out of her body parts. If these intensely emotive songs, called *shyama sangeet*, were and remain highly popular in the urban sphere, they are not very popular in the Sundarbans context where mainland Hinduism is making an entry, especially through the adoption of day- and night-long devotional songs (*kirtan*) sung to Radha-Krishna and the yearly celebration of Ras by the landed and gentrified elite.

   Ramakrishna (1836–86) was a priest at the Kali temple of Dakhineshwar. He had little formal training, but his saintliness and wisdom attracted a large following. Ramkrishna's message of universal religion was spread to the West by his most famous disciple Vivekananda.

8. Even though Kali's indigenous Tantric background and Sakta origin place her outside the Vedic Hindu pantheon, these aspects are increasingly being downplayed in favour of a Vaishnavic identity (see Gupta's [2003: 60–79] and Menon and Shweder's account [2003: 80–99] of her 'domestication' — in the ritual and the social realm respectively.

9. Farmed shrimp production has truly skyrocketed, rising from just 26,000 metric tons of production in the 1970s to over 700,000 metric tons in 1995 (Rosenberry 1995: 34–35).

10. Reports published by the organisation Environmental Justice Foundation (EJF) such as 'Smash and Grab: Conflict, Corruption and Human Rights Abuses in the Shrimp Farming Industry'. The study includes an extensive bibliography and concludes that the growing demand for shrimp promotes human rights abuses such as land seizure, sexual abuse, forced labour, and murder in the global south. Similar studies include: 'From Wetlands to Wastelands: Impacts of Shrimp Farming'; 'Squandering the Seas: How Shrimp Trawling is Threatening Ecological Integrity and Food Security around the World'; 'Risky Business: Vietnamese Shrimp Aquaculture — Impacts and Improvements', 'Farming the Sea, Costing the Earth: Why We Must Green the Blue Revolution', etc.

11. 'Zamindar' refers to 'landlord', especially those that emerged with the introduction of the British Permanent Settlement (Landlease) Act of 1793. Many were former revenue collectors of the Mughal period.

12. Pokrant et al. (2001: 101), quoting from chief secretary, Bengal to Govt. of India [GOI], 8/9/1888, para 3.

13. This was very much a possibility as the peak of the prawn-collecting season was the monsoon time.

14. Prawn seed collection along the rivers of both Bangladesh and West Bengal was officially banned in 2006. This study was written in 2004 from data collected between 1999 and 2003.

15. '*Ma Ganga, tumi amay bhoy dekhale? Ami tomay lobh dekhalam.*'

VI

Sharing History with Tigers

Tigers, say many islanders, have changed from meek to ferocious animals. This transformation has occurred not only because of the harsh environment but also because of the history they have undergone. Feeling that their existence was threatened in Java and Bali, tigers, the islanders conjectured, had emigrated from there. In their search for a suitable place, they passed through many different regions but were chased away from everywhere. Finally they reached the Sundarbans and stayed on as they did not feel threatened any longer.

This narrative about the tigers' history articulates much about the islanders' own histories of migration and feeling of rejection. 'Accounts of loss and recovery may,' explains Arun Agrawal in *Greener Pastures*, 'be connected less to grand allegorical images than to specific processes of change and transformation' and 'what would constitute a "real" loss would be allegorical readings of texts that ignore the specificity and historicity of the experiences that the subjects of these texts undergo' (1998: 33). This is why understanding this story of tigers, both of their supposed migration and the contemporary transformation of their character, is so important. For the islands, it underscores the background to the tensions that revolve around the two types of relatedness to tigers: one based on peace and equality and the principles of the forest left by Bonbibi, and the other on violence based on an assumed transformation of tigers after the state's brutal treatment of its underclass citizens.

What has special significance in this context is also the actual historiography of the region. In light of tiger-charmers' spells against tigers, one should be aware of the history of the connection of this profession to Sufi saints, especially in relation to land reclamation and control of tigers. Eaton argues that, at its inception in Bengal, Islam was seen more as a technique which could work magic, enabling Sufi leaders to control tigers and evil spirits (1993: 209). Present-day tiger-charmers' use of Arabic formulae to control tigers and evil spirits might be a reflection of the relationship which once existed between the 'wild' and the Sufi holy men who introduced wet rice cultivation to the Bengal delta.

A Parallel History of Fleeing

Soon after my arrival, in the course of a conversation on how the formerly inoffensive tigers had turned aggressive, the islanders mentioned that tigers were prone to attacking humans also 'because of their difficult past'.

> Tigers had travelled from Bali and Java because they were being killed for their bones. Fearing for their lives they had passed through
>
> Sumatra, Singapore, Thailand, Hong Kong, China, North Bengal before finally feeling safe in the precincts of the Sundarbans. This long exodus, during which they had met with so many rebuffs, coupled with the salty air and water of the Sundarbans to which they subsequently had had to adapt, had affected their nerves and left them bitter.
>
> They now also felt threatened by the incursions of humans into the forest as they saw these as further challenges to their new-found territory.

This strange story about the migration of tigers to the Sundarbans, which seemed to me to be a local reinterpretation of ecologists' narratives about the extinction of the Java and Bali species of tigers, intrigued me. Though rumours have it that the Bali tiger was around until the late 1970s and sightings of the Javan tiger were made in the 1990s, it is generally believed that the first species was extinct by the first half of the twentieth century and the second by the 1970s (Boomgaard 2001: 13). Most of the islanders have not studied beyond primary school and the great majority of them are not able to place Java or Bali on a map. Yet they are conversant with urban popular eco-friendly literature such as how some species of tigers have faced extinction due to the reclamation of forests for agriculture and rampant poaching for tiger bone. But this story is important not so much because it incorporates a highly sophisticated version of the Sundarbans tigers' origins but because it is, as I eventually came to understand, a narrative which permits the islanders to voice their own sense of displacement, their conceptualisation of the Sundarbans as a refuge for migrants, and their feeling of being 'second-class citizens' especially in light of the city-dwellers' view that the Sundarbans is primarily the abode of tigers.

Even though the history of the different peoples who have settled in the Sundarbans is far from homogeneous, older islanders draw parallels between histories of flight. Yet the younger islanders hardly refer to their history of migration, except at times in relation to the fact that, when their parents or grandparents first arrived on the islands, they had to 'fight off tigers and snakes, and live in huts built on raised platforms 5m above the ground and reclaim the island from the saline tidal rivers and the vagaries of violent storms by building a bund all around'. As mentioned earlier, large numbers had come to evade moneylenders and exploitative zamindars, while many others, such as freedom fighters, had initially come to avoid the reprisals of British law. Those amongst them who had arrived more recently from Bangladesh had done so in search of a better life. As with tigers, explained the Garjontola islanders, they saw their past as one where they had had to find a suitable place, fight for it, and 'make it home'.

'Tigers', they explain,

> like all Sundarbans inhabitants, are bitter beings but having gone through the same history of rejection and living in the same insalubrious conditions as the islanders, they have also been invested with the human quality of compassion.

To substantiate this point they underscored how, if tigers had so willed, they could have chased away the human migrants who had encroached on their forest, but they had not. This point draws attention to the fact that the islanders also see themselves as compassionate. To quote Prodip, 'We also could have chased tigers away, but how could we when tigers gave us a portion of their adopted homeland?' If tigers' and humans' common harsh experience has rendered them even more violent and at times blood-thirsty, it had also made them develop 'feelings' for each other. Such sentiments, coupled with the 'agreement' that Bonbibi had left for them, made it imperative that they should 'share' with each other, he explained. One important argument the islanders highlight when narrating this story is that their presence in the Sundarbans depends on honouring this tacit agreement they have with tigers, just as the tigers' presence is conditional on them respecting their end of the agreement. As long as each group respects the other's need for a piece of territory and a portion of the products of the forest they can cohabit in relative peace.

Charm-Slinging Competitions with Tigers

In contrast to the peaceful approach to the forest, many islanders believe that tigers have to be dealt with in a strong way. They point out that Dokkhin Rai, the 'king' of all the non-humans of the forest, is primarily a ruthless and greedy Brahmin and landowner and that he and his retinue of tigers, being embodiments of 'arrogance' and 'greed', have to be 'stood up to'. They say that Dokkhin Rai resents humans because he sees their charms as undermining his power and sees humans' extraction of forest products as a depletion of *his personal* wealth. Thus, he challenges those humans he considers threats. These are mainly those who know magical formulae that can outwit his own charms as well as those who pose a threat to his favourite possessions — the most important of which is wood. Arrogant as he is, the forest fishers explain, he loves taking on important adversaries in a battle of wits and his greed is so great that anyone taking anything from him, especially wood, is terrorised with the threat of death reprisal. The task of tiger-charmers or of the intrepid wood and honey workers, the islanders explain, is therefore far from enviable as it challenges Dokkhin Rai's arrogance and greed.

This point is well-illustrated through the following apocryphal story: Binod, a veteran tiger-charmer, had been hired, along with a few others from the village, to collect some huge logs which had been washed up along the sea shore, 20 km south of Garjontola. With seven other men, he sailed off in two boats with enough water and food to last ten days. By dusk they reached Kedokhali, the biggest island furthest south. Recognised as Dokkhin Rai's abode, it is also feared for its large number of tigers. Once they arrived, they decided to settle for the night in one of the canals that criss-cross the island, away from the powerful sea waves and strong winds and well-hidden from any forest boat on patrol. This was deep in the core area of the forest where humans are barred entry — had they been found, they would have been heavily fined. On their way there they were lucky and collected some logs.[1] Then, as night fell, one of the men chopped off a piece of the wood and lit it. All of a sudden they heard 'auuuu, ouuu, I'm burning, I'm burning!!' coming from the jungle. Binod ordered the man who had lit the log to extinguish the piece of wood. Then they heard a threatening voice floating down to them demanding, 'Hand me that man, he burned me.' Surprised, they turned towards the voice and saw in the distance, sitting along the river bank, what looked like a human figure, beckoning with his long arms, and calling for the man in the boat who had lit the piece of wood.

Binod had often had experiences with the nastier non-humans of the forest and was never one to be easily intimidated, so he replied, 'Come and fetch him yourself if you have the guts; it's impossible for me to deliver him to you because, having brought him to the jungle, I have the responsibility of taking him back home.' But the figure refused to leave them. So, after some time, Binod took a clay pot and a thin towel (*gamcha*) and recited some magical formulae. The figure stopped threatening them and disappeared. The recitation of his charms completed, Binod found, as he had expected, a pebble inside the pot. He plucked it out and tied it to the bow of the boat — it was Dokkhin Rai, who had been converted into a pebble. He then told his men not to worry, ordered that food be served and that they go to sleep, as the next day would be a long one.

The next morning, the occupants of both the boats woke up not in the canal where they had moored the previous night but in the middle of the sea, their anchor having mysteriously been loosened. They were totally lost, surrounded by a thick fog which clouded all sense of direction. To make matters worse, they were hit by a storm and one of the two boats capsized with most of their water and food. Directionless, cold and hungry they started wondering whether they would ever reach home again. A couple of nights after this strange happening, they heard the same voice say, 'let me go' (*amake chere de*). Every time, Binod replied, 'Take us to safety first, after that I will let you go.' Finally, after about two weeks, they reached a coast. The voice said, 'This time I could not stop you, but I'll get even later.' As they arrived, Binod kept his promise, untied the pebble and threw it into the sea. Then they felt shivers down their spine as the voice parted with a menacing, 'I am Dokkhin Rai, nobody tampers with my powers.'

They had arrived at a little fishing village in Orissa and the inhabitants, not being able to understand their language, called the police and they were sent back to WB. After a few days' rest, Binod returned to the forest as he needed some golpata leaves to rebuild the roof of his house.[2] He and the men who had accompanied him heard that voice again. It kept saying, 'Bring me that man and I will leave you alone, otherwise I will not let you cut any of my golpata.'

Binod said, 'I've had enough of you and I will cut golpata whether you like it or not.' With the powerful charms he knew, Binod managed for a second time to imprison Dokkhin Rai in his earthen pot, which he then covered with his thin towel to prevent the miniature Dokkhin Rai pebble from escaping and causing any more mischief. Dokkhin Rai pleaded to be released, but Binod replied that he would not do so until he had completed building his roof.

With Dokkhin Rai still tied, Binod came back home later that day with enough golpata leaves for his roof. On the way back, Dokkhin Rai's pleas became more insistent, 'Please, let me go, you know that I am not allowed to see women's faces, I am a bachelor, please deliver me.' Binod replied, 'After all the mischief you have done to me, how can I now be sure that you will not create more trouble? No, it's safer to release you once I have reached home.' 'Please,' pleaded Dokkhin Rai, 'I am not allowed to enter inhabited places, deliver me.' Binod turned a deaf ear to his entreaties, returned home with Dokkhin Rai in his pot, removed all the golpata from his boat and arranged them in the middle of his courtyard in preparation for his roof-building. Once he had finished, he decided Dokkhin Rai's ordeal had lasted long enough and untied the towel but, as he lifted the towel, a huge wind blew all his golpata over the river back into the forest. This was Dokkhin Rai's doing. From the pebble-like form he had been first transformed into and then released from, he had used his magic to take the form of a storm and blow the leaves back into the forest.

Thus, the manifestations of Dokkhin Rai in his 'arrogance', the islanders believe, do not restrict themselves to taking the form of spirits or of tigers. Also, Dokkhin Rai is not just 'arrogant' but also 'greedy' and 'thieving'. Indeed, if these titanic beings are seen as being able to match the powerful charms and fearlessness of certain humans, they are also believed to be 'thieves' (*chor*). This is because they attack from behind and lay claim over wood or forest products but also because they are considered to be insidious beings who disguise themselves to plant the seed of fear in humans' hearts to make them weak and cause them to die. The islanders narrate that arrogant non-humans target tiger-charmers because they know of their opponents' powers and feel threatened or challenged by them. Once one of them is killed, they know the other team members are filled with fear and will become easy prey as they will have 'caught the fear'. Most islanders recover from such fears by having it exorcised but some of them never pull through and months later die from this fear which has been eating into them.

'Why do you refer to these beings as "arrogance"?' I asked, perplexed. 'But this is what they all are. Whether it is Dokkhin Rai, tigers, monsters, or spirits, they all have a firm conviction of their self-importance, are very possessive about their wood, are vengeful and are the very embodiment of arrogance,' they replied. One person added how some friends of his had challenged a group of spirits to a charm-slinging contest. When, after an entire night's fierce competition, they fell short of charms, one of them had the sense to say, 'Please forgive us, master, we know no more.' Hearing this, the satisfied spirits left them. 'They love to feel superior to us and once we recognise that, they leave us humans alone.'

Of Fakirs, Tigers and Tiger-Charmers

Many islanders maintain that, to be in accordance with the 'ways of the forest', one has to respect certain basic 'Islamic' rules because the forest is ultimately the realm of Islam. The forest is a domain of Islam because Bonbibi reclaimed it from the Hindu Brahmin and zamindar Dokkhin Rai and restored the original understanding that had existed between humans and tigers. Tracing the present-day myths of the Sundarbans to the history of the dissemination of Islam in Bengal is practically impossible; nor would it help much in this context as it was not a history the islanders engaged with. Nonetheless, in light of the recorded history of Lower Bengal, and because the islanders kept underlining the forest as a shared territory to which both the people and tigers of the Sundarbans could legally lay claim, this history needs to be addressed.

Briefly, Eaton argues that, from 1200, Sufi holy men and their converts cleared the forests of the northern parts of the Sundarbans. Agriculture came to be intimately linked to the spread of Islam in Bengal (1993: 310). Eaton demonstrates this by arguing how, for several centuries after the beginning of the thirteenth century, the Bengal delta saw two frontiers, both of them moving. The first was a cultural frontier dividing Turk and Bengali, the second was an agrarian frontier dividing forest and field. The cultural frontier was not a clean or stable line since the advance of Indo-Turkish garrisons was itself uneven. Operating at the same time, the second frontier, he argues, was a quieter one, slowly advancing into Bengal's eastern and southern districts with wet-rice cultivating communities moving into previously forested areas. Many of these new agrarian communities started professing an Islamic identity, for it was Muslim holy men or, perhaps more accurately, men popularly endowed with charismatic authority and a Sufi identity, who played a pivotal role in this process. Indeed, in the subcontinent generally, Bengal is perhaps the only region in which the extension of agriculture is associated in popular memory with the lives of Sufi saints (Eaton 1987: 6).

This parallel conversion of forest into agricultural land and of people into Muslims continued until the eighteenth century in much of South and East Bengal (ibid.: 6). The consequent symbolic tie-up between agriculture and Islam in Bengal has been well-documented (Eaton 1993; Greenough 1982; Nicholas 1963). What has remained unexplored, however, is the persisting relationship in Bengal between Islam and the forest. There is historical evidence of a 'symbiotic relationship' between tigers and Sufi holy men (as noted by gazetteer writers Marshall, O'Malley, Wise, in Eaton 1993: 208–9; Mitra 1903, 1918). Eaton argues that, with the forest being cleared, Islam gradually shifted its link from the forest to agriculture. What has to be underscored is how this historical link between Islam and the forest was never entirely broken.

What appears to be the most common aspect shared by these holy men is their propensity to work miracles and make 'a multitude of converts by whom the wastes were gradually reclaimed'.[3] There are numerous local stories of how Islamic holy men, known as pirs,[4] received popular canonisation as patron saints of villages after coming to the aid of local rajas against the Mughals. Let me take an example. Mobrah Gazi (also known by the name of Mubarrah), a legendary pir who reclaimed jungle tracts, is believed to have come to the succour of the local king, Sadanand Chaudhri, to help him repay his debts to the Mughal emperor.[5] It is believed that he did this by appearing in a dream with his posse of tigers, scaring the Mughal emperor. He also paid up the revenue owed by the raja to the emperor from his treasure buried in the forest. After that, he returned to the forest.

The return to the forest is another recurring feature of these pirs. The stories about them tell how, even after receiving large tracts of cultivable land or initially lording over them, they always redistributed them and went back to live in the forest as recluses. Khan Jahan, for example, after obtaining from the king of Gaur a *jagir* (revenue assignment) of the lands he had cleared, eventually withdrew himself from worldly affairs and lived as a fakir. In fact, even though most pirs end up becoming the patron saints of villages, the main attachment of these holy men is said to be to the forest, an association characterised by a peculiar intimacy. This is manifested not only in their urge to return to the forest once their earthly duties are performed, but also in their control of tigers.

The earliest reference to the connection between Muslim holy men, or their tombs, and the delta's tigers dates to the seventeenth century. The Englishman John Marshall, travelling from Orissa to Hooghly, recorded on 14 February 1670:

'Tis reported That every Thursday at night a Tyger comes out and salams to a Fuckeers [faqirs] Tomb there [in Ramchandpur, near Balasore], and when I was there on Thursday at night, it was both heard and seene' (Khan 1927: 62).[6]

Hunter refers to Mobrah Gazi as a 'fakir' who had taken up residence in a part of the jungle and 'overawed the wild beasts to such an extent, that he always rode about the jungle on a tiger' (Hunter 1875: 119). Wise writes towards the end of the nineteenth century that 'no one will enter the forest, and no crew will sail through the district' without first of all making offerings to one of the shrines of the pirs.

This relation between Sufi saints and tigers was not restricted to the Sundarbans but seems to have been common all over Bengal. Francis Buchanan, a British officer, noted in 1833 that in the Dinajpur district pirs and tigers usually inhabited the same tract of woods. He says,

as these animals seldom attack man in this district, the Pir is generally allowed by persons of both religions to have restrained the natural ferocity of the beast, or, as it is more usually said, has given the tiger no order to kill man. The tiger and Faquirs are therefore on a very good footing, and the latter . . . assures the people that he [the tiger] is perfectly harmless toward all such as respect the saint, and make him offerings. (Buchanan 1833: 93)

Based on traditions collected in 1857, Wise writes how Zindah Gazi — a legendary protector of woodcutters and boatmen all over the eastern delta — was 'believed to reside deep in the jungle, to ride about on tigers, and to keep them so subservient to his will that they dare not touch a human being without his express commands' (Wise 1894: 40).

In fact, while these holy men did not take possession of land reclaimed and cultivated through their leadership, administrative records inform us that in the popular imagination they were seen as retaining control over the forest because, as pointed out by Wise, they were often the ones to decide the exact limits within which the forest was to be cut (1894: 40). However, this control was not perceived as total. As noted by Buchanan a century before Wise,

> [a] particular class of men make a profession of collecting this oil, honey, and wax. They are Mohammedans and pay a duty to the Zemeendars for liberty to follow their profession. The woods, however, are not considered as property; for every ryot [Indian peasant or cultivating tenant] may go into them and cut whatever timber he wants.[7]

What emerges is that these Sufi holy men are mentioned in two different contexts. The first sphere portrays them as 'pirs' or the patron saints of Bengali villages where their memory is sung and respectfully marked by graves and shrines. The second context depicts them as 'fakirs' controlling the forest and the living patron saints of woodcutters.

Even as late as the first two decades of the twentieth century we have evidence of an 'intimate relation' between Sufi fakirs and the forest. The first is in 1908 by O'Malley, the compiler of the gazette for the Khulna district, who reports that parts of the Sundarbans forest were associated with the charismatic authority of Muslim holy men who were visited by the 'professional woodcutters' of the Sundarbans. He reports how together they proceeded in boats to certain localities in the forests, and how each locality was presided over by a fakir 'who is supposed to possess the occult power of charming away tigers and who has undoubtedly some knowledge of woodcraft' (1908: 193–94). He describes how these 'professional woodcutters' of the Sundarbans worked six days a week, as one day was set apart for 'the worship of the sylvan deity presiding over that particular forest' (ibid.).

By the turn of the century, 'fakir' and 'bauley' denoted people doing the same kind of work — that is, leading woodcutters to the forest and possessing the ability to control tigers.[8] Gradually, the meaning shifted and today, in official discourses, 'bauley' exclusively means woodcutter, thus stripping this occupation of its association with magic and tiger-charming. For the islanders, however, 'bauley' refers specifically to those who can control tigers.

Tiger-charmers often acknowledge Islam's sovereignty over the forest and at times claim descent, usually spiritual, from the Gazi and the 'five pirs'. Islam and the ethos of the forest are conflated for the jungle workers and this link offers a greater insight into the ideology of 'egalitarianism' which they believe they have to uphold. I talk of 'Islamic egalitarianism' because 'Islam with its more democratic appeal in the social plane and a simpler code of tenets, . . . opened up an inviting vista, . . . proved to be a haven from religious and social persecution by the upper classes' (Ray 1945: 49). Because the forest is the realm of Islam, those who work there, especially those who entrust themselves to Bonbibi's care, believe they have the prerogative of adhering to what they see as Islamic rules.

The growing popularity of pirs and the pir cult in Bengal was and is, as argued by Roy (1983), both a challenge as well as an opportunity for the Brahminical priestly class. The Brahmin answer was to create Satya-Narayan as an extension of Satya-Pir so as to establish continuity between old and new beliefs with a view towards a total absorption of Islamic practices into Hinduism. Conversely, perhaps in conflating Islam and the forest, the pirs of old were doing the opposite. Somewhere along the line, the tiger became a Hindu symbol — or was it because it was already a Hindu symbol that gave weight to all these narratives about pirs controlling tigers?

In an article of the beginning of the century, 'On some Curious Cults of Southern and Western Bengal', Mitra reports a song sung by fakirs where Dokkhin Rai is considered to be the son of Bonbibi (1918: 440). The song goes like this:

The birds are calling in bush and brake. The tides are running high in the creeks.
O sons of female slaves! come, come to cut the reeds and bulrushes.
Remembering the name of our mother-goddess, we go in front.
O! come ye all with axes and hatchets and bekis [unknown word] in your hands.
The son of 'The Dame of the Forest' (Ban-bibi) is sitting alone in the forest.
O shaven-pated Mahomedan clodhoppers! Come into the midst of the mangrove.

According to Mitra, this is sung by the 'baoyalis' (alternate spelling of 'bauley'), whom he calls 'the Sundarban traders in fuel', in their worship of the forest goddess Ban-bibi (alternate spelling of Bonbibi). He says she is the 'dame of the forest' 'believed to preside over the gloomy and impenetrable jungle of the Sundarbans and to protect the baoyalis'. He then, to my mind erroneously, explains that

> (T)his goddess must be an incarnation of the terrible goddess Kali, for it is said that, over the mangrove (*bada*) or, at least, over that portion of the Sundarbans which has been reclaimed and is now tenanted by Pods, Chandals and Musalmans, many deities are believed to preside, among which may be mentioned Kali. (1918: 441)

I believe this interpretation is wrong not only because the forest fishers themselves never associated Bonbibi with Kali, but also because fringe religious practices have the unfortunate fate of being interpreted from a Hindu bhadralok's idea of Hinduism and rarely on their own terms or from a rural Bengali Muslim's point of view.

Bonbibi and the State

Islanders often told me that those who 'do the jungle' are 'insane daredevils'. Also, even if forest fishers do occasionally collect honey and wood they do not refer to these forays as '*doing* the jungle'. This is because they want to mark the fact that they are not 'professionals'; that is, they do not practise honey or wood collection in the intensive way the honey and wood collectors do. Those who 'do the jungle' on a regular basis are seen as taking enormous risks both because they actually *walk* on the forest ground (thus exposing themselves to tigers and crocodiles) and because, as seen by the forest fishers, their occupation is *threatening* to tigers. They are also called 'arrogant' and I explained earlier how this is seen by the forest fishers as the main reason why the forest is getting 'polluted' and wild animals are increasingly killing people.

I was keen to meet these people who regularly work as honey and wood collectors and learn from them how they situate themselves vis-à-vis the criticisms levelled both by the islanders and by the representatives of the state. So, one mid-April morning, I dropped by the Sajnekhali Wildlife Sanctuary to meet the honey collectors who had come to apply for permits. Once their passes are obtained, they set off for a couple of weeks in groups of about seven to work deep inside the forest. I stopped by two men who were sharing a smoke in the verandas of one of the typical little wooden bungalows built on stilts which dot the sanctuary. One, in khaki shorts, was evidently a minor forest official, the other looked as if he could have been a honey collector. The forest official went in to get me some water while the other struck up a conversation. Soon I came to learn that he worked in the forest and that he had come to collect his permit for honey collecting. When the forest official returned and learnt the purpose of my visit, he sarcastically pointed his chin towards his companion and said:

> It is only greed which makes them take up such a job, they seem to leave their senses behind and, led by guys like him who call themselves tiger-charmers, they enter in a trance.

He then mockingly explained how the gramer lok had no knowledge of the importance of the forest and its prime position in the list of World Heritage Sites. Stung, the other man retorted that there was a difference between, 'greed and need, between being in a trance and being terrified. Give up your place and we'll happily stay put in your well-fenced world heritage forest and well-paid jobs.'

This altercation is highly representative of the way forest officials often speak of islanders in general, and of forest workers in particular, in order to impress upon visitors that they are aware of the rapid depletion of the Sundarbans forest and that they are not to be blamed for it, for they are the upright guardians of the forest. However, even though the two groups argue fiercely with each other, they are often on collusive terms. It is a known fact that honey and wood collectors also work as poachers and that they would not be able to undertake poaching without the help of the forest officials. The honey collector, whose name is Shankar and who is also a tiger-charmer, explained that he was not 'greedy' but, having come from Bangladesh in the 1970s, he did not own land and there was not much else he could do. Like most jungle workers, he enumerated the different occupations he engaged in during the different seasons and stressed that he mainly worked as a crab and fish collector.

Shankar explained how the risks in honey and wood collection were so great that they were not very tempting lines of work for most people. Neither were the economic returns very lucrative. In fact, they had even dwindled over the past few years. For example, for honey collecting, in 1999 there had been forty-five groups entering the forest, but in 2000 the numbers had increased to sixty-two. This had forced the government to further reduce the amount of honey each person could collect for the entire trip and from the previous year's maximum of 50 kg the amount had been reduced to 40 kg. He also pointed out that, though tigers were taking more victims, there were greater numbers of people trying their hand at this occupation. 'Wasn't this simply an indicator of a growing desperation and not of greed?' he ruefully asked his companion, the forest guard, and me.

Poachers in general were hesitant about worshipping Bonbibi and thought she was ineffective (because, as discussed in the previous chapter, of the violence of their profession). One day, the father of my host's eldest son's friend, Atish, came to his place to thank Hori and Maloti for having let their eldest son stay over at their place for about four months and look after the house while he and his wife were trying to get their own son treated in different nursing homes and hospitals in Kolkata. The man was comfortably off, owned quite a bit of land, and had spent around Rs 50,000 trying to cure his son, Hori had briefed me. I also came to know that he was a poacher. Interested in what he might tell me about the forest I broached the subject by embarking on Bonbibi. Atish looked straight at me and said in a wry mocking tone, '*You* believe all this? Please tell me, which government gave *her* the deed of lease (*patta*) of the forest?' The man went on to explain that he 'believed in firearms' and that this was the reason why he thought that worshipping Kali was more appropriate in his line of work.

Atish sells deer meat and gave me the price list of different sizes of tiger skins. Hori then asked him: 'You are well off, you have come face to face with the terrifying image of tigers many times, you have even had close shaves and yet you persist in working in the jungle, why?' Atish's answer was straightforward,

> For me, it's not work, it's an addiction (*eta amar pesha noy, nesha*). Ignoring the pleas of my wife and children, I rush there twice a month. You ask why, I can't really answer, what I know is that you put an ill person in the jungle and he will get better, you put an insomniac in and he will find sleep — the jungle has properties you will find nowhere else, it is a sacred place.

For Atish, even if the jungle was still a 'sacred place', the animals in there were no longer sacred. Atish, like others who went poaching, believed that his job was violent and that therefore Bonbibi's blessings could not be solicited for his occupation. But people are sometimes very ambiguous about the way they divide their allegiances to gods. Subol, who is also poacher, said,

> Whether you are a doctor, a poacher or a policeman, you have to worship Kali. But, even if you worship Kali, Bonbibi is the deity of the jungle, and you have to call on Bonbibi as you enter the forest because you have to [bring yourself to] fear the tiger [*bagher bhoyta kintu kortei hobe*]. But even though I keep Bonbibi in my heart, I actually worship Kali; and that's because I need to use firearms.

Some people mentioned having become poachers after the Morichjhanpi massacre in 1979 when hundreds of migrants died, many of them shot at by the government (more on this episode later in the chapter). Then, in the 1980s, the same time as the introduction of prawn seed collection, it actually became dangerous to be killed by a tiger because the family of the dead trespasser was made to pay a hefty fine. The victim's body had to be abandoned in the forest for fear that the forest officials would get to know about it. The new widow and the victim's children were forbidden to cry and taught to say that their father had died of diarrhoea because if exposed, the family members were exhorted to pay up for the dead, and were, in effect, treated like criminals. Many islanders also argued that, if the tiger could swim over to their village (which happened very often in those days) and make off with their cattle and sometimes even human beings, they did not see why they were not allowed to be able to enter the jungle and do the same. 'The state officials think we are thieves and poachers anyway,' said a young man, 'then why not live up to their expectations?' he rhetoricised sarcastically.

The difference between forest fishers and wood and honey collectors is not simply a distinction of occupation: these activities are also typically undertaken by groups of different ages and living in different places. The crab collectors and forest fishers are principally older men who often work with their wives and live in the 'down' islands, whereas the occupational honey and wood collectors are young all-male groups from 'up' places. Although some of the honey collectors come from 'down' places such as Jamespur, Satjelia (in the Satjelia island), Pakhiralay (in the Gosaba island), Jharkhali (Basanti island), most of them come from places such as Deulbari, Kumirmari, Rampurhat, and Mollakhali, and even as far away as Katakhali, Barunhat, Hasnabad, or Hingalganj. Because these places, though part of the Sundarbans region, are relatively better-off and far removed from the forest, they are seen as offering greater opportunities for making money. The islanders of Garjontola argue that these people come because they can make relatively good money within a week.

Now, to get an idea, let us take a group of seven people each collecting the maximum amount of honey (i.e., 40 kg) allowed per person by the government during their trip. This amounts to a total of 280 kg of honey and 45 kg of wax; this gives us a total of 325 kg. (For every quintal [100 kg] of honey there is about 15 kg of wax.) The government buys the 280 kg of honey at Rs 34 per kg. This gives the team Rs 9,520 for honey. After adding 45 kg of wax at Rs 36 a kg they get a further Rs 1,620. They now have to deduct the sales tax from this. Honey and wax have the same sales tax of Rs 3.

Rs 3 multiplied by 325 kg is Rs 975 on honey and the wax deducted as sales tax. Now 12 per cent of that amount is equal to Rs 111. This amount is levied by the government as income tax. Another 15 per cent of additional sales tax on the wax has to be added (15 per cent of 135) which means Rs 20. So a total of (Rs 975 + Rs 111 + Rs 20 = Rs 1,106 has to go as tax to the government. So from the total of Rs 11,140 they make by selling their honey and wax, they have to deduct Rs 1,106 as tax. At the end of the trip they get the net amount of Rs 10,034. As they are seven, this means that they each receive Rs 1,433. Once costs like food and boat permits are deducted they are assured of taking back home between Rs 1,000 and Rs 1,200 — an important sum to make within a week and which sometimes even exceeds by double the sum the crab collectors or forest fishers make in a month.

To get good honeycombs the honey collectors have to venture deep inside the forest. Some of the prime honey areas, such as Golbhaksha, Jhille and Chamta, are avoided for the large numbers of tigers they host (presumably because of the many fresh water ponds dug there).[9] It is because the honey collectors are seen as not being afraid for their lives that they are considered to be 'arrogant daredevils'. Of all the occupations linked to the forest, the honey collectors face the greatest risk of being killed by tigers. One in every twenty-four was killed in 1999. The *Anandabazar Patrika* newspaper of 2 May 2000 reported that there were a total of seven honey collectors killed that season. This gives us a figure of 2 per cent victims for honey collectors. Unofficially though, tiger and crocodile casualties during the honey collecting season are at least double this figure, raising the death toll to a minimum of 4 per cent over a fortnight.[10]

It is a very dangerous job and if honey collectors can make a relatively good sum of money they can also lose their lives. On the other hand, the islanders explain how the honey collectors, like the wood collectors, have to invest much more than do crab collectors and forest fishers, for example, by having bigger boats. So it is economically more risky as well. Practically speaking, it is not easy to enter the smaller canals with such boats. The honey collectors can navigate their boat through the smaller canals only during high tide. Once they locate four or five honeycombs (they stick a bamboo pole on the nearest bank to where they think there is one), they dismount from their boat and set off into the forest.[11] They have to do this before the tide recedes.[12] To get to the honeycombs they have to wade in waist-deep water, holding flaming torches above their heads, walking abreast as if combing the forest at an interval of 30 m and calling out to each other to make sure they are still all advancing in the same direction. When they come across a honeycomb, they yell out to the others and start the process of chasing away the bees with smoke.[13] What makes this occupation so dangerous is that if people do not get along with each other they put at risk the whole team. Usually the cook stays in the boat and rows it back to a bigger canal before the tide recedes; otherwise the boat risks getting stranded. If this happens, not only does he put his own life at risk but also that of his colleagues as he cannot pick them up for the next ten hours. They are then completely defenceless, with no protection against tigers or crocodiles.

'To engage in violence is to die in violence' is a phrase the islanders often use when talking of honey collectors and woodcutters. Violence is seen as an inherent prerequisite as well as a consequence of being a honey collector; they have to use powerful charms which threaten non-humans. As the islanders see it, standing up violently to tigers and spirits risks arousing their deadly anger. The honey and wood collectors are, as the forest fishers explain, 'insane daredevils' because 'to do the jungle is to tempt the tiger' (*mohal kora mane bagh chesta kora*). 'Tempting the tiger' and the use of the word *cheshta* (literally 'trying') is translated as 'deliberately searching for' or 'looking for' the tiger. To 'do the jungle' means to enter the jungle in order to collect honey (or wood) with the intention of making money and in full knowledge of the danger one is incurring. This arrogance makes a mockery of the tiger and this is what the tiger resents, as tigers, too, are 'arrogant'.

There is another reason for this perception: the honey collecting teams are seen as always ending up fighting with each other. Whenever I was told stories of honey collectors having died in the forest, it was said that this was because the group had fought, as happens with such necessarily 'arrogant' people. Both the arrogance and the fighting are seen as due not only to the risks they took but also the way tasks are distributed. Each honey collecting team has a tiger-charmer, a leader (usually the person who owns the boats and holds the purse), a third person charged with the important task of holding the container below the comb, a fourth's duty is to cut the comb, a fifth — the cook — has the vital responsibility of rowing the boat when the others are out in the forest and of cooking for them. If there are other team members, usually new recruits, they are helpers. The one who cuts the comb and the cook are the two most significant people.[14] However, the three others also hold central positions. These five roles of honey collectors are seen by the islanders as being so important that those who undertake them are liable to becoming conceited and clash, thus rendering themselves vulnerable to tiger attacks.

The other reason why regular honey collectors and woodcutters are given such bad press by the islanders in general is because they are seen as being the allies of the state. The state tightly regulates these two occupations both because they are risky for those who undertake them and because they bring in a lot of revenue. During the two-week honey collection period, the forest is closed to all other occupations. Crab, fish and prawn seed collectors as well as woodcutters are not allowed to enter during that time. Besides, the state controls the entire process. The forest officials divide the jungle into plots and decide where each group goes; on certain days 'flying launches' come to collect honey and provide water to the different teams and monitor their locations and movements. The amount of honey or wood to be collected and the price at which these items are to be sold are all set by the government.[15] For the forest fishers, such protection compromises the whole ethos of the forest. They see their own collection of honey or wood as something they do 'on the side' and they neither register their boats for this nor obtain permits. Why the state has such a negative reputation in this region is partly explained in the next section, which will discuss the implications of the partition of Bengal and the perceived involvement of the state in the killing of an estimated two hundred refugees on the island of Morichjhanpi in the late 1970s.

The Brutal Evacuation of East Bengali Migrants from Morichjhanpi

As the political mobilisation for the partition of Bengal gathered momentum in the late 1930s and early 1940s, the larger Bengali cultural and linguistic identity increasingly came to be fractured along sectarian and religious lines. As a result, when partition occurred in 1947, most people increasingly looked upon themselves as Hindus or Muslims first and Bengalis afterwards (Chatterji 1994). If the richer East Bengali Hindus had started migrating towards WB in the 1930s and 1940s, in the 1950s, 1960s and 1970s it was the poorer Hindus who made the journey westwards from what had become East Pakistan and subsequently, after 1971, Bangladesh. They were usually sent to various inhospitable areas outside West Bengal, with the assurance that they would eventually be relocated in West Bengal. When talking about being the 'second-class' citizens of the state, the islanders would often give me the example of Morichjhanpi and highlight the events that occurred there in the late 1970s. What had happened there was, for many islanders, a betrayal — as much by the state, the forest officials and city dwellers, as by tigers.

As explored by Ross Mallick, the reasons leading to the Morichjhanpi massacre have to be understood in relation to the long history which led to the partition of Bengal and the intricacies of caste, class and communal differences (1999: 105). Briefly, in the colonial period, the East Bengal Namasudra movement had been one of the most powerful and politically mobilised Dalit movements in India.[16] In alliance with the Muslims, they had kept the Bengal Congress Party in opposition from the 1920s. By the late 1920s the bhadralok press started to view them with hostility and suspicion and were worried that the low-caste leaders might follow the separatist politics pursued by Muslim leaders. Gradually, when the Hindu elite saw that they were becoming a minority, they pressed for the partition of Bengal at independence so that at least the western half would return to their control.[17] Partition, however, meant that Dalits lost their bargaining power when divided along religious lines of Hindus and Muslims and became politically marginalised minorities in both countries.[18]

The upper-caste landed elite had started migrating from East Bengal before partition (already in the 1951 Census of India it was recorded that 27 per cent of Kolkata's population was composed of East Bengali refugees) into West Bengal; subsequent migrants (mainly rural middle-class cultivators and artisans, and later the landless) came after partition. Some found a niche amongst relatives and friends in Kolkata while the poorest squatted on public and private land and tried to resist eviction. Migration continued right up to the liberation of Bangladesh in 1971; it increased during periods of particular communal unrest such as the 1964 riots and the 1965 India–Pakistan War, when it is believed that 600,000 refugees left East Pakistan for India. Estimates of the total number of refugees up to 1970 are over 50 lakh (mostly to West Bengal). Another 20 lakh of the 100 lakh refugees who had entered India during the early months of the Bangladesh War of Independence (1971) stayed back after Bangladesh became independent.

Unlike their richer counterparts, who were backed by family and caste connections, many of these poorer fishing and cultivating migrants did not find shelter or ways of making a living in Kolkata. They were sent to various camps in inhospitable and infertile areas — the most famous being those of Umerkote, Malkangiri, Paralkote, and Kondagoan in the Koraput and Kalahandi districts of Orissa and Bastar district of Madhya Pradesh. Termed the Dandakaranya Project, these camps for East Bengali refugees were situated in the semi-arid and rocky place between Orissa and Chhattisgarh and were entirely removed, both culturally and physically, from the refugees' known world.

The CPIM, which was then the main opposition party, promised that when they came to power, the refugees would be settled in WB and that it would most probably be in the Sundarbans.[19] In 1977, when the Left Front came to power, they found their refugee supporters had taken them at their word and sold their belongings and land in Dandakaranya and elsewhere to return to WB; in all, 1,50,000 refugees descended upon WB (Visharat et al. 1979 [1993]: 100 in Mallick 1993: 8).[20] Fearing that an influx of refugees might jeopardise the prospects of the state's economic recovery, the government started to forcibly deport them back. Many of them, however, managed to escape to various places inside WB, one of these being the Sundarbans where they had family and where they would be able to survive by working as fishers in the forest. From the month of May 1978 onwards, about 30,000 refugees, most of them SC, sailed to Morichjhanpi and set up a settlement there (Sikdar 1982: 21 in Mallick 1993: 100).

Many migrants, especially those from Khulna, had preferred settling in the inhabited islands of the Sundarbans — where they had erstwhile neighbours and relatives who had come from Khulna to clear the forests in the West Bengal part of the Sundarbans during the 1930s and 1940s — rather than go to the totally alien area of Dandakaranya. In 1975, many of those who had been sent to these camps started to move to a sand band called Morich chak which was part of Morichjhanpi island in the Gosaba police station. It was thought to be possible to settle 16,000 families there, another 30,000 refugees in nearby Dattapasur, and in other Sundarbans places that had 'cultivable waste land' (Maudood 1981: 224).[21]

The migrants from Dandakaranya were joined by people from the villages of the adjoining Sundarbans islands of Satjelia, Kumirmari, Puinjali, and Jharkhali. A lot of them also shared close blood ties with the migrants, ties which were reignited through visits and gifts of paddy and vegetables. Young landless couples were urged to settle with the Morichjhanpi dwellers; their intimate knowledge of that part of the forest and generous lending of boats and dinghies recompensed by the migrants' eagerness that they too settle on Morichjhanpi to strengthen their case. The settlers initially built some makeshift huts along the cultivated area of the island, beneath the government's coconut and tamarisk trees. Most survived by working as crab and fish collectors in the forest, and with the help of the islanders, by selling their products in the nearby villages. In contrast to the ruling elite of their villages, composed essentially of large landowners who aspired to migrate towards Kolkata, the islanders saw the East Bengali leaders as wanting to settle there and, therefore, more apt to represent them. They explained that this was because they were poor, rural and low caste and hence not afraid to take up manual work, such as fishing, and knew, through the twists of fate what it was like to fight for their rights and have the moral courage to face the Kolkata ruling class with their rural concerns. The islanders expressed awe at the way the East Bengali refugees rapidly established Morichjhanpi as one of the best-developed islands of the Sundarbans — within a few months tube-wells had been dug, a viable fishing industry, saltpans, dispensaries and schools established, and this contrasted lamentably with the islands they came from, where many of these facilities were, and are, still lacking.[22]

Stories abound about the spirit of bonhomie and solidarity between migrants and islanders whose similar experiences of marginalisation brought them together to bond over a common cause which was fighting for a niche which became a metaphor for the reclamation of voice in the new Left Front WB. The islanders explained the migrants' eagerness to stay on in Morichjhanpi as a dignified attempt to forge a respectable identity for themselves as well as an attempt to reclaim a portion of the West Bengali political rostrum by the poorest and most marginalised. They had also hoped that this would be taken up by the government as an opportunity to absolve itself of the wrong it had done to the poorer refugees by sending them away from West Bengal. When narrating their memories, if some of the islanders evoked their dismay at finding their ponds emptied of water overnight due to the migrants' initial dependence on the adjoining islands' pond water for their survival, most islanders drew on memories of fraternal bonding.

Unrepentant, and despite this display of self-help and cooperative spirit, the government persisted in its effort to clear Morichjhanpi of the settlers. This was even though Morichjhanpi island had been cleared in 1975 of its mangroves and replaced by a governmental pro-gramme of coconut and tamarisk plantation to increase state revenue. But even though this was not an island covered in mangrove forest, the state government was in no mood to tolerate such a settlement. It stated that the refugees were 'in unauthorised occupation of Marichjhapi which is a part of the Sundarbans government Reserve Forest violating thereby the Forest Acts' and that refugees had come 'with the intention of settling there permanently thereby disturbing the existing and potential forest wealth and also creating ecological imbalance'.[23]

On 31 January the police opened fire killing thirty-six persons. The media started to highlight the plight of the refugees of Morichjhanpi and wrote in positive terms about the progress they were making in their rehabilitation efforts. Photographs were published in the *Amrita Bazar Patrika* of 8 February 1979 and the opposition members in the State Assembly staged a walkout in protest of the way the gov-ernment was treating them. Fearing more backlash, and seeing the public growing warm towards the refugees' cause, the chief minister declared Morichjhanpi out of bounds for journalists and condemned their reports saying that these contributed to the refugees' militancy and self-importance and suggested that the press should support their eviction on the grounds of national interest.

After the failure of the economic blockade (announced on 26 January — in an ironical twist on Republic Day!), in May of the same year the government started forcible evacuation. Thirty police launches encircled the island thereby depriving the settlers of food and water; they were then tear-gassed, their huts razed, their boats sunk, their fisheries and tube-wells destroyed, and those who tried to cross the river were shot at. To fetch water, the settlers had now to venture after dark and deep into the forested portion of the island and were forced to eat wild grass. Several hundred men, women and children were believed to have died during that time and their bodies thrown in the river (Mallick 1993: 101). The Kolkata High Court ordered a two-week lifting of the ban but this was not properly implemented. 'At last, the Left Front Government was able to claim that it had succeeded in "freeing" Marichjhanpi from the illegal encroachment of "deserters" from Dandakaranya' (Kudaisya 1996: 36).

Based on Sikdar and Biswas's pieces, Ross Mallick estimates that in all, 4,128 families who had come from Dandakaranya to find a place in West Bengal perished of cholera, starvation, disease, exhaustion, in transit while being sent back to their camps, by drowning when their boats were scuttled by the police or having been shot to death in Kashipur, Kumirmari and Morichjhanpi by police firings (Sikdar 1982: 22 and Biswas 1982: 19 in Mallick 1993: 100–101).[24] How many of these deaths actually occurred in Morichjhanpi we shall never know. However, what we do know is that no criminal charges were laid against any of the officials or politicians involved. Even Prime Minister Morarji Desai, wishing to maintain the support of the communists for his government, decided not to pursue the matter. Many refugees and islanders had voted for the government coalition based on their stated commitment to resettling the refugees in West Bengal. The argument that this might be a precedent for an unmanageable refugee influx from Bangladesh was also heatedly argued as baseless. Ross Mallick argues that by then the last wave of East Bengali refugees had been forcefully driven out of the state and those who would have settled in Morichjhanpi would not have been a financial liability for the state government (1993: 100–101).

The refugees saw the brutality of the government as one that had been possible because it was backed by the bhadralok who perceived them and the Sundarbans islanders as lesser beings who came behind tigers in their classificatory scheme of importance. With the betrayal of Morichjhanpi, the islanders voiced how they felt that the distinction between the urban as central and the rural as peripheral was reinforced.

Morichjhanpi: A Double Betrayal

In the islanders' memories, these events were recounted as a 'war' between two groups of people, one backed by state power and modern paraphernalia, the other dispossessed and with only their hands and spirit of companionship. Jayanta, an islander who had gone there as a young man with his wife and baby child, gave a poignant narrative of the course of events at Morichjhanpi. He remembered how when the refugees saw their children dying of cholera and starvation they tried to break the cordon formed by the police and the military launches. They sent arrows made with wood, aimed pieces of brick and dried mud from their slings and verbally abused the government officials. The officials urged the police to retaliate by throwing tear-gas bombs and using firearms. A 'war' was on, one group fighting with wooden arrows and stones, the other with tear-gas, guns and loud-speakers. For greater protection, the thirty launches were covered with wire netting and police camps were established in the surrounding villages. As one islander put it, the launches looked like 'stinging swarms of floating bee-hives'.

The ease and brutality with which the government wiped out all signs of the bustling life of the past eighteen months were proof for the islanders that they were considered completely irrelevant to the more influential urban Bengali community, especially when weighed against tigers. In two weeks' time all the plots had been destroyed and the refugees 'packed' off. 'Were we vermin that our shacks had to be burned down?' rhetorically asked one of the islanders. The migrants were then forcefully put in launches and sent to Hasnabad where lorries carried them back to central India or to the Andamans. Many of the islanders who had been rounded up along with the refugees, now fled, often with some of their new-found migrant companions from the lorries taking them back to Dandakaranya. They came back to their former islands and settled along the embankments. Others built shacks along railway lines or in places like Barasat, Gobordanga or Bongaon — in West Bengal.

To understand the identification of the islanders with the refugees, the social context of the differences between Kolkata and life on these islands has to be underlined. The Sundarbans region is also referred to as 'Kolkata's servant' (*Kolkatar jhi*), due to the large number of its inhabitants working as servants in the houses of Kolkata's affluent. As mentioned earlier, before the introduction of prawn seed collection in the 1980s, the islanders had barely enough to eat. For many islanders, especially those who owned no land, working in the forest was the only way of making a living. Jayanta, reflecting on the hope the arrival of the settlers had brought them, had longed to start a new life in Morichjhanpi where for once, the aspirations and rights of the lowest would be established. But he and his family had barely been there five months when their shack was burned down by the police. He wondered why the government was bent on reclaiming Morichjhanpi for tigers when it wasn't even part of the tiger reserve. The other sore point was that the refugees had been promised land in the Sundarbans. He saw the 'treachery' by the government as proof that for the Kolkata bhadralok they were just 'tiger food' — disposable people who could be shot and killed because they wanted the home-stead they had been promised.

Within the CPIM there were divisions over the way the party leadership had handled the matter. The CPIM cadres felt that the management had washed themselves off the responsibility of the poorer migrants in a 'bureaucratic way' when it could have used the issue to develop a mass movement against central government discrimination and neglect towards Bengali refugees vis-à-vis the Punjabi ones. However, the CPIM State Committee *Political-Organisational Report* was keen to close the matter and issued a statement saying that there was now 'no possibility of giving shelter to these large number of refugees under any circumstances in the state'.[25] Accusations were made, including the Land Revenue Minister Benoy Chowdhury's unsubstantiated allegation that 'foreign agencies' were behind Morichjhanpi; the CPIM also blamed vested interests, reactionary forces, Congress (I) and P. C. Sen for using the issue for political gain and claimed that it had met the challenge and had ultimately achieved success with the return of the refugees to Dandakaranya in May 1979.[26]

The islanders had bonded with the migrants not only because they shared with them a common place of origin which was eastern Bengal but also because they could identify with the terrible hardship they had gone through. Stressing his affinity with them, Jayanta, an inhabitant of Garjontola, recounted how during the time they had settled in Morichjhanpi they had 'all become one big family' as they had 'the same hopes, went through the same ordeal, fought on the same side. That was until the moment 'Kolkata let us down'.

After that, he said, 'we each went back to the islands or camps we had come from with broken hearts and bloody hands; a broken, disunited and utterly weakened group.' The chapter was quickly closed. A few journalists questioned the capacity of the upper-class people, whether they called themselves communists or something else, to represent the poorest strata of Bengali society. As noted by a journalist in the Bengali paper *Jugantar*:

> The refugees of Dandakaranya are men of the lowest stratum of society. . . . They are mainly cultivators, fishermen, day-labourers, artisans, the exploited mass of the society. . . . So long as the state machinery will remain in the hands of the upper class elite, the poor, the helpless, the beggar, the refugees will continue to be victimised.[27]

'Why have our dead remained unaccounted for and un-mourned by the babus of Kolkata, forced to hover as spirits in the forest, while a tiger who enters our village and then gets killed puts us all behind bars?' asked Jayanta voicing a general bitterness.[28]

The New Repository of *Bhadralok* Violence: The National Royal Bengal Tigers

Now half-broken embankments and the few fruit trees planted by the settlers during their stay remain as the only vestiges of past human habitation on Morichjhanpi, the rest having been reclaimed by the forest. We shall never know exactly how many people lost their lives. According to many of the islanders only 25 per cent of those who had come to Morichjhanpi left the island alive. This figure is important more because it reflects what the islanders feel rather than for its factual veracity. The main thrust of the argument about the bloody events of Morichjhanpi was that the people of the Sundarbans felt that they had been betrayed by the government and the Kolkata urbanites. The islanders explained that tigers, annoyed at the disturbances caused by the violence unleashed in the forest had started attacking people and that this was how they ended up getting a taste for human flesh. Others argued that it was the corpses of killed refugees that had floated through the forest that had given them the taste. 'After Morichjhanpi, tigers had become "arrogant",' I was often told. As an old woman explained, 'tigers initially were fine animals that were afraid of people. They were compassionate and were agreeable to the fact that the products of the forest and rivers were to be shared with people. But now,' she lamented,

> due to the legitimising of killings in their name, they had turned egotistical and did not hesitate to attack people. Now tigers were no longer the neighbours with whom the forest had to be shared but 'state-property', and backed by the ruling elite they had begun to treat the islanders as 'tiger food'.

For the islanders, some of the measures taken by the government, such as building fresh water ponds and the introduction of 'hybrid' tigers, which, it was widely believed, came straight from city laboratories, had endowed *their tigers* with the arrogance of knowing that their species was superior. Tigers, they said, now felt they were invincible as they had state protection. Besides, they were the national animal both of Bangladesh and India as well as the current popular trademark for global conservation. These imaginary tigers were called 'hybrid' because they were considered to be a cross between a kind of jackal and a dangerously ferocious species of tigers. The islanders explained to me how these tigers had a long snout not unlike that of a mole and that their bodies were so long that they 'looked like trains'. The islanders further elaborated that because of tigers' access to the fresh water ponds built by the government and because of their 'hybridity' they had grown impervious to charms and reproduced faster.

This narrative reminds one of the story reported by the former park director to the author Amita Baviskar on the 'absurd fears that villagers entertained'. The Director reported that the villagers (pastoralists) had told him that 'under the eco-development programme, a special kind of leopard had been released in their forests'; this leopard was believed to have been imported from America, fed chiefly on sheep and goat and even sported an identification tag in its ear which read 'Made in America' (2003: 285). Both this story as well as the one on 'hybrid' tigers are 'real' at some level because, and I shall use Baviskar's words, these are 'telling metaphors' which try to make sense of the imported concept of conservation which seems to be 'consuming and alienating local resources' (ibid.).

Here, through the rejection of the tiger as an animal one needs to be proud of (due to its 'national animal' stature in both Bangladesh and India) as well as its renown in conservation circles, the islanders' narratives of tigers highlighted their perceptions of a harsh history and an unjust contemporary society (especially in relation to both their own beliefs in a forest-based equality as well as Hamilton's ideals of a co-operative society). What is important is how the Sundarbans islanders internalised the injustice they felt had been levelled at the poorer migrants' claims for settlement in West Bengal and why they thought their request had been trivialised.

Just as in a final show of desperate anger, the migrants had cut down the government plantation of coconut and tamarisk before being forced to leave the island of Morichjhanpi, now, every time the islanders are angry with the representatives of the state they destroy public property — cut down trees, break solar lights, loot from the various government schemes. 'As we are treated as lesser beings, we act as is expected of us,' said one of the islanders. Another reason why Jayanta had said that they now had 'bloody hands' and 'broken hearts' was because 'after this massacre, I couldn't continue working with peace in my heart and I started to work as poacher'.

The decline of the Namasudra movement, which started with the bhadralok's call for the partition of Bengal, and which led to the death of thousands of refugees, not only marked a growing unequal access to West Bengal in general, and Kolkata in particular, and the associated disparate resource distribution, but also revealed a dilemma of a greater order — that of being a Bengali, yet not a bhadralok. The proof of this lies in the fact that those killed in the Morichjhanpi massacre are yet to find justice, and their stories are yet to appear in histories.

Notes

1. The collection of timber from wrecked vessels is another trade in the Sundarbans: 'Such flotsam and jetsam were collected in secret until some few years ago, when a case occurred in which the authorities refused to interfere. Since then the trade is openly carried on' (as noted by Westland 1871, in Hunter 1875: 314–15).
2. A bush with a kind of broad palm-like leaves. The leaves are used to thatch roofs by those who do not have enough land, therefore not enough straw (from paddy), for a roof.
3. The statement on making converts is said to be that of Pir Umar Shah, who is said to have come to the jungles of Noakhali from Iran in the 1700s and lived in a boat (Webster 1911: 100–101).
4. I shall indiscriminately use 'fakir', 'pir' and 'Sufi saints' to mean Muslim holy men and to distinguish them from their Hindu counterparts, the 'sadhus'.

5. Mobrah Gazi's territory included Basra which is in the Maidanmal Fiscal Division, Baruipur Subdivision, situated on the Bidyadhari river.
6. Khan also mentions how this tomb at Ramchandrapur is that of Muhammad Khan Shahid, one of Kala Pahar's commanders. He believes that Marshall may have heard some local legend regarding this tomb and confused it with that of a fakir (1927: 84).
7. 'An Account of a Journey Undertaken by Order of the Bd. of Trade through the Provinces of Chittagong and Tipperah in Order to Look Out for the Places Most Proper for the Cultivation of Spices' (March–May 1798) in Eaton (1987: 1).
8. Mitra reports how 'bauley' was a word used both for 'woodcutter' as well as for 'fakir' and how no work was begun in the forest until 'the fakir' had gone through his charms and incantations (1918: 440).
9. Refer to Map 1.
10. Even though the family of a tiger victim is compensated with Rs 55,000 (Rs 10,000 from the Block Development Office, Rs 25,000 from the Janata Life Insurance Policy, and Rs 20,000 from the Tiger Project), they unfortunately lose at least half of this sum in the process of claiming it at the hands of unscrupulous middle-men and politicians.
11. In learning how to 'read the jungle', they learn that, when the flight of bees is light and swift, they are in search of flowers, whereas when their flight is heavy and drowsy, nearer the ground, it means that they are laden with their booty.
12. After taking into account the force and direction of the wind, the flux of the tides and currents along with whether they are in a small or a big canal, as the flow and the level of water is different depending on whether a canal joins a river or a creek.
13. Each comb has a minimum of 10 kg of honey and a maximum of 25 kg, and usually they manage four or five combs per day.
14. The cook is the one least at risk as he is not supposed to alight; he has to have sharp ears and be physically the strongest as he has to be able to row the boat single-handedly as quickly as possible to the bank where his friends call him to collect them. For all practical reasons, the cook, explained the honey collectors, took on the role of the 'mother' and had to give them moral support and tend to their ills by applying medicine to their bruises (as they often get cut and scratched), encourage and console them, and generally keep up their spirit of companionship.
15. In addition to the taxes, when teams overstay the two-week period, they have to pay fines of Rs 3 per day per person.
16. Mallick (1999) uses the term 'Untouchable'. As this group excludes the non-Untouchable Scheduled Castes, the Scheduled Tribes and Other Backward Castes, I prefer using the more widely used term Dalit — which means 'oppressed' and is widely recognised both by Dalits and non-Dalits in the political sphere — even though it is a term not commonly used in WB.

17 Mallick (1999). This is in line with the arguments made by Bandyopadhyay (1997) and Chatterji that the demand by the bhadralok for the partition of Bengal became more vocal after the Poona Pact of 1932 where it was decided that seats would be reserved for the 'Depressed Classes' out of general electorate seats in the provincial legislatures and that in the 18 per cent of the seats in the central legislature would be reserved for them (1994: 15, 33).

18. See Mallick (1999).

19. See Flibbertigibbet (1967: 633).

During the B.C. Roy government in the 1950s and early 1960s, Jyoti Basu, then the leader of the opposition, had presented their case in the Legislative Assembly. As late as 1974 he had demanded in a public meeting that the Dandakaranya refugees be allowed to settle in the Sundarbans. In 1974–75 leading members of the subsequent Left Front government, including Ram Chatterjee, the minister of the State Home (Civil Defence) Department, had assured the refugees that, if the Left Front came to power, they would arrange their resettlement in WB. At a meeting of the Eight Left Front Parties in 1975 it was resolved that the refugees would be settled in the Sundarbans.

20. As noted: 'now that the Congress is out of power, would the refugees be far wrong in expecting the CPI(M) to practise what they preached?' (Chaudhuri 1978: 1098–99, in Mallick 1993: 100).

21. *Ananda Bazar Pátrika*, 23 June 1975.

22. This concords with the information provided by Mallick (1993: 100).

23. Letter from the deputy secretary, Refugee Relief and Rehabilitation Department, Government of WB addressed to the zonal director, Ministry of Home Affairs, Office of the Zonal Director, Backward Classes and ex-officio deputy commissioner for Scheduled Caste and Scheduled Tribes, eastern zone, Subject — 'Problems of Refugees from Dandakaranya to West Bengal', no. 3223-Rehab/DNK-6/79, in Mallick (1993: 100).

24. Sikdar, (1982: 22); Biswas (1982: 19) in Mallick (1993: 101).

25. Communist Party of India (Marxist), West Bengal State Conference, Rajnaitik-Sangathanik Report ('Political-Organisational Report') adopted 14th Plenary Session 27 December 1981–1 January 1982 (Calcutta: West Bengal State Committee, Communist Party of India–Marxist, 1982), p. 14.

26. *The Statesman*, 19 February 1979.

27. Sikdar (1982: 23), quoting *Jugantar*, 29 May 1979, in Mallick (1993).

28. For more on the way government policies have caused resentment amongst Sundarbans islanders, read 'The Sundarbans: Whose World Heritage Site?' (Jalais 2007).

VII

Unmasking the Cosmopolitan Tiger

One afternoon, after trouble had broken out earlier in the day between the forest guards and the prawn seed collectors of the villages adjoining the forest, a meeting was hurriedly summoned. That morning, around 200 fishing boats had laid out their nets for prawn fishing when suddenly forest guards had swooped down upon them, blaring from their microphones that they wanted everybody out. In one of the boats two men started arguing with each other and were slower than the others in dismantling their nets. The forest guards, losing patience, abused them in foul language and beat them up. The incident sparked widespread anger amongst the islanders of the area. The president of the Prawn Collective Union, Bhuban, called a meeting and persuaded the prawn seed collectors and the local forest state dignitaries to attend. There is a long history of radical politics in the Sundarbans. In contrast to other parts of rural Bengal, where such language and beatings might be tolerated by those considered the 'depressed classes', here it was seen as a grave offence, serious enough to call for the presence of the range officer himself. He came with two policemen, his subordinates.

The meeting opened with the president of the Prawn Collective Union calling on everyone's cooperation so that the meeting would not break out into violence; the aim was 'to come to a greater understanding between two groups — forest officials and prawn seed collectors'. He started by saying that, when the range officer had arrived for the meeting, his first words on stepping out of his launch had been to ask about the condition of the two men who had been beaten. Bhuban said that this had touched him and from there he tried to set the tone of the meeting by invoking the metaphor of kinship, a theme which then ran through all the speeches of the meeting. He said:

> We live next to each other as neighbours — meaning forest officials and prawn seed collectors — and are therefore like brothers. Yet two of us have been beaten up mercilessly. The pain is not so much physical as emotional, hurting not only two of us but all of us here.

He ended the speech emotionally by saying how his heart went out to the families of the three prawn seed collectors from nearby villages who had been killed the previous week by tigers.

The young RSP leader, Ratan, was the next person to deliver his speech. After saying how they were honoured to have the range officer amongst them, he thanked him for having come in person. He then said that they knew that this was a National Park, and that entering it was illegal but that, by the sudden closing of the forest, the prawn seed collectors had been prevented from making a living. He then used kinship, not to mark a bond like the range officer and the Prawn Collective Union's president, but to highlight the differences between the two groups. He asked with hardly veiled hostility,

> Which mother's children are these guards who beat up and abuse our brothers? We are neither poachers nor illegal woodcutters, why treat us in this insulting way? Those who have got jobs at the forest department are an example we tell our children to emulate. Why do they turn against us? Is it because they have put on a uniform that they have changed their blood?

Then, on a more threatening note he added, 'Remember that you cannot save the forest or tigers without us.' After that Kalidas Mondol, the village ex-headman, who was famous for his fiery speeches, got up. He had the public waiting breathlessly for him. He started,

> I have come here to do the work of street dogs; I have come to bark. Let me start with Sukanto's idiom — 'land unfortunately belongs to those who never walk on it' — and place this in the context of the Sundarbans [forest].[1] Who are the ones getting jobs at the forest department to save the Sundarbans? Not us. Why? Tell us, how many policemen and guards will you keep sending here to save yourselves, in the name of saving the forest? How many of us will you go on beating and killing? Remember the ex-range officer Rathin Banerjee and the pot of prawn he kicked with his foot? Remember how he was taken into the middle of the Dutta river and he had to send desperate messages for one of you range officers to come and save him? You have the power to sever the head of any poacher but you prefer using your power to break open the head of a poor prawn catcher. Now let me give you a piece of judicial information. You are allowed to arrest and seize but you have no right to beat any of us. This is a crime, a violation of human rights. And anyway, are you not ashamed

of having broken open a head? The point is, we have no other options. The Prawn Collective Union does not consist of people organised along factional or political lines but is the party of the hungry, with the same spirit of cooperation and hope infused amongst us all.

He continued,

Hungry people are even fiercer than tigers. Those who go without food do not know any party except the party of the hungry. We have nothing to lose and are therefore ready for anything. You Kolkata people have no blood relation with us here. You have good jobs with fine salaries, how will you feel our pain, how will you feel the fire that burns our stomach? Is that why you grab even the morsels of food which we lift to our mouths? We do not do politics on a pedestal: our politics is to bark at you like roadside dogs. Yet, let looks not deceive you, though you see us as dogs, *we* are the real tigers of the Sundarbans.

The islanders clapped and cheered but the speech had deeply moved one of the two policemen who accompanied the range officer. He asked Bhuban if he could be permitted to speak. In his short speech he was keen to re-establish the ties of kinship between Kumirmari (where he came from) — considered an 'up' island even though not very far from Satjelia and a relatively wealthy island because land there is of better quality — and Satjelia, a 'down' island where most of the inhabitants live as forest workers and prawn seed collectors.

We are not foreigners. If you search a little, you will see that we are cousins, we have uncles and aunts in villages around here. I am from Kumirmari, from this very region. It is only the tediousness of the job which makes us behave like this. Do you know that we are the ones who get into trouble when you enter the forest? On behalf of the [forest] staff at Sajnekhali, let me tell you that I am really ashamed of what happened today.

Once he was done with this speech the range officer finally got up to speak.

We are not from outside. True, I am from Kolkata but that is not so very far, you know. I am sorry for what happened. Thank you for having kept such exemplary law and order in this organisation, and please do not mention bloodshed. You all know that if there were no law or control from the state then the jungle would go and with it your livelihood, so we are forced to set limits. You prawn, fish and crab catchers are our friends and we count on you to let us know about poachers. But recently some of you have used the cover of prawn seed collection to poach and this will not be tolerated. Two of our boats were sunk three days ago and our officials have to face a lot of insults from you.

Here Kalidas cut him off and said,

This is all very well but tell us concretely, what are you going to do for these men. We want them taken to Kolkata and treated in a private nursing home and not in the crowded cowsheds that are the government hospitals, plus we want compensation for the number of days they will not be able to work — what will their wives and kids eat while they recover from your beatings?

The range officer replied: 'The government will undertake the medical cost of these two victims but it will not be possible to provide three days' salary to them apart from giving it from my own pocket.'

Kalidas retorted: 'Tiger victims are compensated, and these men are the victims of your tigers so . . .' Everybody laughed. It had surprised me to see so many prawn seed collectors assembled — and evidently across the range of political groups. Even though it had only about 500 registered members, who each paid Rs 2 per year, the group was generally believed to have political potential as Bhuban, its leader, was often seen hobnobbing with the range officer and other forest personnel. Now, Bhuban was clearly glad that the range officer had come all the way from Garjontola to attend the meeting — it proved that his association had been given legitimacy and that his authority had been respected.

When Ratan, the RSP leader, spoke of the 'sudden closing of the forest' he was referring to the new rule that the islanders were legally allowed entry but only up to 2 km inside the jungle for the collection of prawn seed. The islanders had pressurised the forest officials to allow them further on condition that they would restrict their hours from dawn to dusk and never enter during the night. It was under cover of darkness that poachers caught deer and tigers, collected wood, etc. The islanders had been given the permission to enter only 2 km into the forest on the understanding that they would not carry out nor condone poaching.

At the end of the meeting Bhuban issued a leaflet titled 'An important announcement'. In it, those present were reminded that wildlife had to be protected. The announcement also laid out the tariffs that would be incurred by anyone breaking rules. Not only would poachers be instantly apprehended but could also get seven years' imprisonment. The notice now stipulated that the fine for entering the forest rivers illegally was Rs 1,000 (in fact, members of the Prawn Collective Union were normally released after they had paid just Rs 200). The notice also stated that those buying illegal deer, tortoise or wild pig meat (these were greatly sought after by the landed elite and the school teachers who had the means) were also offenders and would have to pay a fine if caught. Anybody reporting an offence would be rewarded, the reward being at least Rs 10,000 for information about a tiger skin.

The Prawn Collective Union had another meeting at the end of May, where they said that the range officer was not prepared to grant this favour of letting the prawn seed collectors enter 2 km into the forest any longer and that henceforth the fines would be what the government had stipulated. Some of the islanders said that they were happy that fines would be increased as that would lead to fewer people practising the occupation and therefore bring some stability to the highly fluctuating prawn seed prices. Others said that they had had enough of bearing the brunt of the officials as, of all the occupations linked to the forest, prawn seed collectors were always the ones blamed for poaching or at least of helping poachers. A prawn seed collector can make up to Rs 30,000–35,000 per year, a very reasonable sum which allows a few of the islanders to buy rifles and cartridges and thus become poachers either during the lean months or after their daily stint as prawn seed collectors. Of course, this is only for those brave enough to face the tigers as well as the dacoits, who are notorious for their brutality.

Reflecting on these events, what I would like to stress is the way that kinship ties are invoked both by the islanders and the representatives of the state. Where the government officials and the head of the Prawn Collective Union use kinship terms to emphasise that they share a relatedness of 'brotherhood' with prawn seed collectors, the prawn seed collectors deliberately refused this metaphor of relatedness to state officials and stress their relatedness to each other and, in effect said that tigers too are their kin and that they are the ones who can protect tigers best. The village representatives highlighted the ruthlessness of the guards, and how they had 'changed their blood' because they were now 'service holders'. The idiom of kinship was used throughout to subtly threaten the range officer and his subordinates with the islanders' unity and force — as seen by the fact that they spoke in one voice and threatened to rise as one body — the meeting itself being a good example. The two policemen had obvious Brahmin names and the trappings of bhadralok comfortable urbanity unavailable to the prawn seed collectors. As explained earlier, for the islanders, the 'Babus' were of a different 'kind' altogether and were often derogatorily referred to as 'poultry' — fair-skinned and feeble, prone to heart attacks at the slightest scare or mishap. In contrast, the prawn seed collectors — especially because they saw themselves as having to flout both the traditional rules as well as the state laws about the forest — saw themselves as hardy and as violent as tigers. This is exemplified in the following anecdote: One evening, while on my way to watch a play with a group of young men, I was asked what my study consisted of. I replied that it was the study of their, that is, Sundarbans islanders' history and culture. To which one young man replied, 'But why would anyone want to study our history and culture? Don't you people consider us from the Sundarbans just tiger food?'

The representation of the Sundarbans as a 'down' place and a veritable moger muluk pirates' den corresponds in the mind of many islanders to the idea that, for the rest of the world, they are just 'tiger food' — dispensable citizens — and starkly contrasts with the other image of the Sundarbans: that of the glamorous World Heritage Site with beautiful flora and fauna that belongs to the elite, whether they are the Kolkata bhadralok or international tourists. And the Sundarbans possesses the elite of fauna — the Royal Bengal tiger.

State-Making in the Sundarbans

'Within the next fifty years the Sundarbans will disappear.' This was how the islanders sometimes chose to introduce me to their region when I first arrived. I was struck by the conviction with which they held this view. Why did they hold such a view?

In the colonial period, the Sundarbans was designated a virtually unpopulated 'wasteland'. In the twentieth century this 'wasteland' is now a World Heritage Site and as such has attracted considerable global funding over the last couple of decades. Yet this seeming transformation in which 'wasteland' has become the 'preserve of wildlife' has continued to reinforce the idea that humans do not belong. The origins of this representation lie in the negative colonial perceptions of the Sundarbans (Greenough 1998).

How does this compare with the islanders' own relation to their histories and the history of the region? In one sense there is some similarity — the emphasis on the physical milieu. Even though they originally come from a number of different regions in WB, or India more widely, or Bangladesh, and although they belong to different jatis and religions, the islanders believed that it was their environment in the Sundarbans that has bound them together in its physicality: its harshness, its brackish saline waters, its unpredictability. The other important factor about their environment is the special status of the forest, which is seen, especially by the Sundarbans living bhadralok, as the receptacle of civilisation. What is particularly striking is that, although the islanders do speak of their identity as migrants, they have no interest in engaging with the history of the places their forefathers came from. Seeing themselves as migrants *to* the Sundarbans rather than migrants *from* somewhere else, they can *all* lay equal claim to the Sundarbans. Seeing their past in the past of their environment, the Sundarbans — a past similar to that of tigers — legitimises their claim to the forest. People in the Sundarbans do not see themselves as 'insular', nor do they dwell on their status of migrants even though they see it as being one of the reasons of their bond with tigers. Rather than celebrate their ancestral places of origin, the wish is to exhibit the forest as a sort of museum of past civilisations (by the Sundarbans bhadralok) as well as an area offering common ground for food sharing between the islanders and tigers (by the forest workers). These are ways of reclaiming the forest by and for themselves. In part, their urge to have me, seen as a bhadralok, albeit a strange one, visit the forest when they understood that I had come to write about life in the Sundarbans was to do with the fact that they wanted me to know that they lived in a place just as impregnated with 'culture' as the 'up' places.

One interesting historical feature of the forest is the presence of certain large tanks, masonry structures and high embankments. Their significance is disputed. In some accounts they are seen as evidence that the region in earlier times enjoyed a degree of prosperity and was formerly a widespread civilisation which was ultimately destroyed by pirates (as mentioned in Chapter I). In other accounts they are relics of the Portuguese and Mag pirates who 'displaced' the 'original' population of the Sundarbans and lived off salt-making and piracy, preying on the numerous merchant ships which passed through the region (Campos 1919: 105; De 1990: 12–13; and the earlier accounts of Bernier and Rennell, who travelled though the region during the 1600s and 1700s). *The Calcutta Review*, July 1889, was happy to report the second explanation of the potentially prestigious ruins: 'these two facts [piracy and salt making] go some way to explain the existence of many masonry remains without resorting to the theory of a former widespread civilisation' (De 1990: 51).

The history of the Sundarbans under the British was briefly recounted in Chapter One: as soon as the East India Company had acquired the *diwani* (civil administration) of Bengal in 1765, it set out to reclaim the Sundarbans, waging a campaign against the pirates, especially the Portuguese. Portugal had been the pioneer of European commerce in this part of the world, and so powerful that their position in Bengal at the beginning of the seventeenth century was comparable to what that of the British would become by the middle of the eighteenth century.[2] Various schemes were drawn up for the best use of the so-called 'wastelands' and in 1770 the first land reclamation efforts by the British were undertaken.

From the start, the power of the East India Company in the Sundarbans was challenged by landowners, who advanced claims on the basis of their 'ancient rights' against the government's claim of 'inherent title' on the grounds that, prior to their arrival these tracts were 'wastelands'. (The international law doctrine of *terra nullius*, that land could be legitimately acquired if it was found to be 'the land of no one', may have been a factor in this designation.) Regulation XXIII of 1817 sought to put a stop to this litigation. Maintaining the government's 'inherent title' to a share of the produce of all lands cultivated in the Sundarbans, it re-classified these lands as 'encroached' upon by the zamindar landowners. Despite this, many landholders persisted in advancing claims. Regulation III of 1828 then declared that these tracts of land had always been government, not private property (notably under the Mughals) and that therefore they should remain so (Pargiter 1934: 22). The Sundarbans were proclaimed the property of the state — and as having in no way been alienated from landholders, as the area had lain 'waste' at the time of the Permanent Settlement of 1793, and therefore not included in its provisions for zamindar landownership (ibid.: 12). Finally, in 1830, the boundary of the Sundarbans was determined. Called the Dampier-Hodges line,

it still partly stands as the line demarcating the Sundarbans region
from the rest of WB.

Meanwhile, keen that the lands be reclaimed, and revenue ex-
tracted from them, the government granted leases from early on in its
administration. However, due to the hostility of zamindars, periodic
cyclones and tidal bores, many grantees, being speculators, simply
made a quick profit from the wood on their land and sold off their
property as soon as they found a purchaser. The grantees also found
it difficult to collect the labourers they needed to settle on the lands
permanently. To recruit labourers, the maximum rent was fixed at
the low sum of Rs 1.50 per acre. The government also encouraged
peasants to take up leases, thus creating a body of peasant proprietors
holding land directly from the government. By 1810, the areas down
to Sagar island in the west and the south-east and the eastern part
of the Sundarbans (now in Bangladesh) were cleared. In the centre
of the Sundarbans, land started being cleared under Tilman Hunkell
(giving his name to Hingalganj), magistrate of Jessore.

To foil lease-holders' attempts to exploit the wood and leave
the land un-reclaimed, rules were stipulated in 1853 by which the
grantee was required to reclaim one-eighth of his land in five years,
one-fourth in ten, one-half in twenty, and the whole in thirty years.
Also, to make the deal more attractive, land tax was reduced to a
fourth of what it was previously and grants were leased for ninety-
nine years to the highest bidder. In 1863, the 'Waste Land Rules'
further provided for exemption from tax in cases of outright sale.
However, even in this case, and even though they were allowed to
pay by instalments, many would-be purchasers were unable to pay
the purchase money (De 1990: 17).

Various schemes were drawn up for the location of a port, and
several surveys of rivers and the suitability of areas in the Sundarbans
were undertaken. The area had become highly attractive since the
creation of a vast network of railway lines across India from 1853
onwards required unprecedented amounts of timber. In 1858 Port
Canning was set up along the river Matla and a municipality was
established there with a big scheme to develop a township. A railway
connecting Port Canning to Kolkata was constructed in 1862. Soon,
however, the British had to abandon their plans. The once-thriving
Diamond Harbour port lost four-fifths of its population in 1864 and
in 1867 the Canning port and town was reduced to nothing when
a huge tidal wave and storm destroyed the whole place. Also, the
Matla river started rapidly silting up and the few farmers and grant

holders who had taken up residence there left the place and stopped investing in the Sundarbans.

In the face of these events, the British soon became dissatisfied with their ventures in the Sundarbans. An appropriate revenue system had not been found and levying revenue on the cultivable lands soon became too cumbersome. On the whole, cultivation in the Sundarbans yielded such mixed results that the British administration abandoned the idea of reclaiming the south-west portions of the Sundarbans for agricultural purposes and concentrated instead on tapping it for timber for railroads and fuel resources. In 1862, Brandis, conservator of forests in Burma, urged the government to conserve the forests of Bengal and from 1871, the Bengal Forest Rules came into force. Even so, parts of the forest continued to be leased out for cultivation. The geographical differences between east and west Bengal were, in turn, deepened by the separate political measures concerning these two regions. In Khulna (east), the forest was 'Restricted' and thus protected. In the 24 Parganas (west), the forest was merely 'Protected' and left open either for leasing and thus clearing, or for timber production. It was in the west that the rivers, much used by trading ships, began to silt up and become brackish, whereas the eastern soil and rivers proved to be very fertile: nearly 90 per cent of the land was reclaimed from forests in the district of Bakarganj — the eastern-most district of the Sundarbans.

During all this time, the only local people we hear about are the litigious zamindars, who in fact rarely lived in the locale. The contrast between the history narrated by the islanders and the history buried in colonial records is remarkable. The islanders, even though migrants, see themselves as being part of the history of the Sundarbans, while the colonial records maintain an eerie silence about them. As noted in Chapter One, when people were finally written about, in 1875, by the gazetteer writer W. W. Hunter, they were catalogued directly after similar — but longer — lists of snakes, birds and fish.

Here we learn nothing about the occupational groups common at this time, such as deer hunters, lime-preparers and ship scavengers. Greenough believes that this rhetoric of portraying the Sundarbans as a sodden largely uninhabited wasteland was in fact geared to-wards the utilitarian needs — especially for wood — of British rule in India (1998: 240). Why else, Greenough wonders, did Hunter take the trouble to write at such length about a region apparently so dismal? It is Greenough's contention that the widespread depiction of the Sundarbans, both historical and contemporary, as a risky and repulsive place is to be traced to this single Victorian essay written by Hunter. Four decades later O'Malley describes the Sundarbans in a similar vein, as a region of total desolation where rivers are dying, industries languishing, villages left with no vitality, and courts deserted. In this place where 'there is nothing to induce an influx of immigrants', 'even the fecundity of the inhabitants seems to be sapped by endemic fevers and epidemic diseases' (O'Malley 1914: 26).

The British government had chased off the Mag and Portuguese pirates and dispossessed the landowners who laid claims to the forested areas of the Sundarbans (and presumably the woodcutters and forest fishers, though there is no mention of them). Those who could have eventually claimed rights over the territory and who actually worked as forest fishers or woodcutters in the area were given the equivalent of Gästarbeiter status by the gazetteer writer Hunter (Greenough 1998: 253).

> The southern portion of the Sunderbans, which comprises the jungle tract along the seashore, is entirely uninhabited, with the exception of a few wandering gangs of woodcutters and fishermen (Hunter 1875: 317).

It is important to realise that the practicalities of 'state-making', as discussed by Sivaramakrishnan (1999), went hand-in-hand with the conceptualisation of the region as a wasteland, though rich in fascinating flora and fauna. In such a representation, there was and is no place for humans, especially when these are poor and marginalised and seen as threats to the resources of state-owned forests.

The islanders have their own view of the multiple thwarting of the colonial state's grand designs for the Sundarbans: it is the expression of an environment which refuses to be controlled, a subtly different version of the dominant account. For the islanders, the periodic destruction of the region is a core feature of the Sundarbans; they cite the near annihilation of Diamond Harbour and Canning port in the 1860s to make their point. By the 1870s these two places had been completely abandoned. Hence, for them the Sundarbans represent an area where struggles have been played out and where those who 'had nothing to lose' were ultimately the only ones to stay on. The image of the Sundarbans as a locale not fit for humans has thus had important repercussions in the way the contemporary islanders of the Sundarbans feel that, both for the state and for those who live outside the Sundarbans, they are at best 'illegitimate' inhabitants of the area, or at worst mere 'tiger food', invisible in official colonial records, listed in a secondary position after the (literally) 'natural' inhabitants of the area — the local flora and fauna — and the unimportant remnants of a forgotten lot for successive leaders of bhadralok politics.

The contemporary wildlife 'heritage' status of the Sundarbans also perpetuates the colonial heritage. What today adds to the feeling of being 'illegitimate' inhabitants of the area are the various public speeches made by the very highly regarded and popular environmentalist NGO activist, Tushar Kanjilal, in which he invariably mentions scientists' predictions that in the next fifty years the Sundarbans will disappear. In his book *Who Killed the Sundarbans?* published in 2000, he blames prawn seed collection. Of course, prawn seed collection and the disappearance of the Sundarbans have often been correlated (Sarkar and Bhattacharya 2003; Vidal 2003) but it is Kanjilal who has popularised the issue in the public domain. But what alternatives have been offered — especially for women? Prawn seed collection may be 'big business' on the global front but it is also a desperate necessity for people living in the region.

Since the first settlements in the Sundarbans in 1770, the population of the West Bengal Sundarbans has risen by 200 per cent to its present population of around 50 lakh. The sea level in the Sundarbans has increased by an average rate of 3.14 cm a year over the past two decades, while the global average has increased by only about 2 mm a year. Indeed, it has been foreseen that, if the sea level rises by just one metre, 1,000 sq. km of the Sundarbans will be inundated (Bhaumik 2003: 1).

The Importance of Taking Part in 'Party Politics'

Taking part in 'party politics' is seen as a prerequisite to keeping checks and balances on different groups of people. This was what was at stake in the other issue discussed at the meeting mentioned at the start of this chapter: the prawn seed collectors' demand that they be allowed in the forest for longer hours. Behind the scenes, however, the Prawn Collective Union's president Bhuban and the RSP leader, young Ratan, had struck a deal with the range officer. The range officer had offered Ratan and Bhuban the contract to build a fine meshed fence along the forest islands adjoining the villages if they succeeded in stopping people from their village collecting prawn seed in the forest. A public secret, this had evidently annoyed a section of the prawn seed collectors and was another reason why Badal had thought he could be the alternative political party representative and had joined the BJP.

A few days after these events, the Gram Sansad meeting was held.[3] This meeting is supposed to provide a forum for village-level political leaders and the general public to meet and discuss.[4] I was asked by different people which path I would take to arrive at the little club-hut (which had been built by an NGO and was therefore 'neutral' ground) chosen for the meeting. Puzzled by these questions, I asked why people were asking me about this, but soon realised that the RSP, the TMC and the BJP supporters took different routes and shouted different slogans while on their way there. Upon arrival, they even sat on opposing sides. The whole village, especially married men and women between the ages of twenty-five and forty-five, was attending and I decided to follow Maloti's path and sit in her group, amidst loud cheers from that group and some heckling from the others. (It goes without saying that, when I returned to my house-to-house surveys in the days following, I was given a lot of unsolicited advice on whether I had made the right choice.) The Gram Sansad meeting, after starting off well, was ended when a scuffle broke out, with the RSP and the BJP coming to blows. The meeting had to be called off. But the islanders were actually proud that, in their village, they had debated for two hours before breaking into a row and that the meeting had not been called off even before they had sat together as in many of the other villages. In the other villages the various parties had marched up and down the village with their 'weapons', ensuring the boycott of the meeting.

Participation in politics took up a substantial amount of people's time and energy. Even the innocuous issue of the school vote to elect parent representatives to its governing body became the occasion for all the leaders and active supporters of the four main parties to congregate around the school. They sat in little groups along the four paths leading to the school and exhorted the islanders to vote along party lines. All the parents had come to vote — the fields lay empty and the fishing temporarily given a respite. There were long queues outside the school and the whole day was marked by febrile excitement over which party would dominate. At the end of the day, once the votes had been counted, the TMC and RSP members, following their usual habit, took different paths, the TMC breaking the still night air with shouts of '*Bande Mataram*' (Hail to the Mother[-land]) and the RSP with '*Inquilab Zindabad*' (Long Live the Revolution).

Politics is an important part of life in the Sundarbans because, as the islanders saw it, they had to 'bite and bark' or their voice would never reach the government officials in Kolkata. A large number of people mentioned how ridiculous it was that when one of their politicians, a landowner, was offering a plan to reduce the number of crocodile victims amongst the prawn seed collectors, he had suggested they be given rubber boots. They also talked about how the WB Irrigation Department was more concerned about the erosion of the Ganga–Padma delta in Malda and Murshidabad than with repairing the breaches of the embankments of the Sundarbans. *The Statesman*, a Kolkata-based newspaper, in its edition dated 17 June 1995, published a report of how a Dutch-based organisation's offer to co-operate with Tushar Kanjilal's NGO (the TSRD) had ended in a fiasco. The Dutch along with the TSRD were offering to provide technical and financial assistance to the government but this met such hostility from the engineers and contractors of the WB government's Irrigation Department that finally the scheme had to be abandoned. The article concluded with Tushar Kanjilal delivering his standard message (see previous section) that, if there was no concerted effort from the government to ally itself with en-vironmental NGOs to solve the bund and embankment problem, the region would be wiped off WB's map within fifty years.

Sizing up the Colonial Tiger

In 1758 Linnaeus classified the tiger as *Felis tigris*. After that, different categories of tigers were given various generic names by naturalists. About a hundred years later, the Indian subspecies (and particularly the one from Bengal), by virtue of being the largest, was given the name *Tigris regalis* by J. E. Gray in 1867 (Mazak 1981: 1). However, the basis of this classification was almost immediately supplemented by Fayrer, who felt that physique alone was not sufficient to warrant the term '*regalis*'. Far from challenging this appellation he offered further justification with a description of the tiger's 'habits and mode of life' to prove why this animal was indeed 'royal'. In *The Royal Tiger of Bengal: His Life and Death*, published eight years after Gray's book, Fayrer argued that, even though its physical aspects were considered superior to those of the lion, the tiger had been unfairly prevented from acceding to the 'royal' title because its 'nature' had been misunderstood: the beast had wrongly been taken to be a 'natural man-eater'. Fayrer took it upon himself to rehabilitate the tiger's image. He tried to reason that the Bengal tiger had 'fallen into evil ways', its man-eating habit was not natural but acquired; and that in any case this habit was 'not of much consequence' (Fayrer 1875: 32) being largely due to the 'superstition' of islanders.[5]

Fayer's account of what he believed to be the tiger's *true* 'psychology', so to speak, implied that for the subspecies to regain its due or 'natural' regal status, it had to forego its nasty man-eating habit. There was only one solution, according to Fayrer: to stop tigers from killing humans one had to 'stand up to them'. This explains how he attributes the tiger's man-eating habits to the 'superstition' of islanders: according to Fayer, they were too frightened to face the beast down. If their 'superstitions' prevented them from dealing with the tigers themselves, he continued, they would nevertheless be happy to be rid of this animal that caused villages to be deserted, roads to be abandoned, and humans and livestock to suffer great loss of life.[6] The fear caused by these animals amongst the local population thus functions for Fayrer only to highlight the courage of the English sportsmen who killed the Bengal tiger, at the rate of about 1,200 tigers per year. By hunting them, Fayrer implies that the British government not only rid the villagers of this scourge but also rid the tigers of their 'evil man-eating ways' (1875: 44).

The nature of the relationship that the British had with the tiger was, to say it gently, problematic. This was because they were seen both as a tremendous threat to governmental agrarian revenue ('The tiger often figured in colonial hunting narratives as an oppressive figure terrorizing the rural populace with the spectre of arbitrary violence' [Pandian 2001: 84]) and as an emblem of enemy Indian monarchs. This might explain the virulence of the description of tigers by sport hunters; they talk of it as 'a cunning, silent, savage enemy', 'a pleasure to outwit and shoot'. This dual image of a 'royal' animal (because of both its association with South Asian kings and its qualities of beauty and intelligence) and flesh-eater that dared to eat *people* (emphasis in Rangarajan 2001: 25) must have brought the British some mental satisfaction as well as justification when engaging in a sport that was causing an alarming decline in the number of these felines.

It is certainly true that the tiger stood as the symbol of Indian monarchs, and this reference is implicit in Tipu Sultan's famous carved musical instrument representing a tiger pouncing on a British soldier. In a similar, though inverted symbolism, the curbing of the revolt of 1857 is represented in a painting by Edward Armitage called *Retribution* where Britannia is depicted, not unlike the goddess Durga, slaying a tiger. That the British associated the metaphor of the tiger, a 'worthy' enemy, with the control of the Pathans has been noted by Bayly (1990). Kipling's *Jungle Book* character of Sher Khan is an animal representation of the Pathan.[7] The tiger's 'royalness' was thus a symbol the British were keen to highlight, as it gave them the pleasure of measuring themselves against an 'equal' who stood his ground by virtue of his strength; therefore, killing a tiger (or any big cat, for that matter) added extra prestige to the sport of hunting because of the tiger's potency in symbolising the power of Indian monarchs.

Protecting the National Animal

A century later, the prestige of hunting and killing tigers has been replaced by the prestige of being part of the 'save the tiger' or 'adopt a tiger' conservation project. But the discussions about tigers in WB still centre on the supposed 'naturalness' of Bengal tigers' man-eating ways. It is now required of the tiger not only to fit comfortably its old epithet of 'royal' but also to rise to its current position of national animal, as well as its new cosmopolitan trademark image for wildlife conservation. Unfortunately, the high number of people killed annually by tigers in the Sundarbans prevents this.

It is important to remember this dilemma when we underscore how, in the 1970s and 1980s, scientists performed a number of experiments investigating the inordinately aggressive character of Sundarbans tigers, seeking both explanations and potential remedies. (Between 1975 and 1982, the official number of humans killed by tigers in the Sunderbans was around fifty per year; while I was there between 1999 and 2002, the figure was about twenty-five per year officially but at least one hundred unofficially for the whole of the Sundarbans.) The Sundarbans tigers, in contrast to tigers from other regions, seemed to defy the norms of tiger behaviour as observed by tiger experts. The Sunderbans tiger displayed a positive predilection for human flesh.[8]

In 1975, after months of research in the WB Sundarbans, Hubert Hendrichs, a German scientist, concluded that the primary reason for tigers in the Sundarbans killing high numbers of people was the increased brackishness of the WB rivers. According to Hendrichs, who in fact is the only one to have studied the man-eating aspects of Sundarbans tigers, 'the man-killing by tigers is not of recent origin, nor is it caused by lack of other prey as has often been assumed' (1975: 184). Hendrichs argued that the number of casualties from tigers is not correlated with utilisation of the forest by humans nor with the density of spotted deer and wild boar, the main tiger prey. He found that it appears to be positively correlated with the salinity of water and high water level and negatively cor-related with variety of vegetation and variety of mammal fauna (1975: 194). He concluded that the high salinity of the rivers had forced Sundarbans tigers to depend on the 'sweetness' (his term) of human blood to obtain a certain dietary balance.[9] This was why, it was generally argued that, contrary to tigers elsewhere which attack humans only when they are old and impaired, young tigers of the Sundarbans were seeking out humans by swimming over to villages or lifting people off boats to satisfy their hunger.

This observation initiated a series of articles (e.g., Choudhury 1979; Diamond 1979; Chakrabarti 1986; Rishi 1988) and counter-articles in which the 'naturalness' of the Sundarbans tigers' man-eating was fiercely debated. Most scientists concurred that the cause was mainly environmental. Apart from the brackishness of the water, it was suggested that because in the Sundarbans the rivers are tidal and wash away the boundaries of any territory that a tiger usually marks with its urine, the tigers of the Sundarbans have no idea of what constitutes a specific territory — and this was why they swam into villages and attacked cattle and people. Others maintained that it might have to do with the fact that tigers have to keep swimming for hours to stay afloat during high tide. Still others said that because monkey and deer flesh in the Sundarbans was salty, their meat was not good enough and had to be supplemented with human flesh. Madhusudan and Mishra, however, argue that while the non-availability of fresh drinking water could be considered an important cause of the problem, 'his [Hendrich's] claim is largely unsubstantiated by the data he presents' (2003: 47).

The government decided to devise tricks to curtail the tiger's penchant for human flesh. Between November 1986 and October 1987, it placed four electrified dummies dressed in used clothing (to give them human smell) in strategic spots in the forest. The idea was that tigers, through aversion therapy, would stop attacking humans after they received an electric shock (a safety fuse and a low current of 20 to 25 milliamps ensured that it was not fatal to the animal).[10] The government also set up the very expensive project of digging freshwater ponds surrounded by raised mud banks in different corners of forested islands so that tigers could drink fresh water. Fresh water in Bangla is called 'sweet water', and drinking 'sweet' water as opposed to salt water is believed to have the effect of turning crabby natures into 'sweet' or amiable ones, which would both tone down their irritability and, in the process, incite them to reproduce faster. I was also told how, with a similar logic, government officials left out palm sugar for tigers' consumption in different spots in the forest.

These developments were by and large followed by the islanders, who were indirectly made to contribute toward the rehabilitation of tigers' nature by becoming the unwitting guinea pigs for these experiments. The government distributed free of charge 2,500 plastic masks to honey collectors and woodcutters permitted to work in the buffer zone of the Sundarbans reserve. It was observed that tigers generally attacked from the back. Hence, wearing a mask at the back of one's head was believed to have the effect of puzzling the tiger, who, seeing what appeared to be a pair of eyes peering back at him, would forever abandon the idea of attacking.

The WB government was very pleased with these experiments. The dummy trial was believed to have reduced the incidence of man-eating by half (Sanyal 1987), and the mask experiment was seen as a total success because no one wearing a mask was killed. Nonetheless, the official statistics showed the usual figures, with thirty people killed during the twelve-month-long experimental period. But the government highlighted that these had been people who were 'too superstitious' (Rishi 1988) to wear a mask. While the government officials believed that these measures had made tigers less aggressive, the islanders were seemingly not so convinced. Going by their own observations, the killings had actually increased. They argued that discovering whether tigers were 'natural' or 'unnatural' man-eaters was a futile endeavour.

Fayrer, in the nineteenth century, argued that tigers were man-eaters because of the superstition of villagers, too afraid to 'stand up' to the tiger. This characterisation is echoed in twentieth-century scientists' beliefs that islanders refuse to use masks because they are too superstitious. This unfortunately also finds resonance in contemporary city-talk in which the islanders are blamed for the deterioration of the flora and fauna of the Sundarbans. Nobody can dispute the fact that Sundarbans tigers, as far as records go back, have always killed people. The earliest records of travellers (who used the interlacing rivers of the Sundarbans to get to the trading centres of Bengal) mention the threat Sundarbans tigers posed to humans. Bernier describes how tigers were able to carry people off boats in the middle of the night and swim back with them to the forest (1891: 443). The causal link, whether this makes them 'natural' or 'unnatural' 'man-eaters', is a question that will probably always remain unanswered. But what remains unquestioned is the fact that neither of these representations of tigers permits an engagement with the local ways of understanding tigers. The tiger's 'nature', first understood along colonial lines of ruler and subject, was now to be understood along lines of inferior villagers and superior tigers, with a new rhetoric on conservation reformulated along the Bengali bhadralok stance towards inequality and social structure.

Sundarbans Islanders and Bengal Tigers

'Before writing about us you have to understand the *ways of the forest*,' Mihir had said when, sometime during the first week of my arrival in the Sundarbans, I was naively telling him about the nature of my research. Unlike tourists, I had told him, it was not tigers and wildlife that interested me but *people*. I wanted to record the lives of people like him and Maloti and Hori, my hosts, and all the Garjontola people. For a long time I mistook the eagerness with which he and other islanders suggested I work on the forest, thinking that they had misunderstood the reasons for my presence amongst them. The usual attraction for any visitor to these parts of the Sundarbans is the forest and its formidable wildlife. Visiting relatives are often packed into little boats and taken for short excursions through the criss-crossing rivulets into the forested archipelago. 'Wait till you have seen the forest and understood its ways.' I was repeatedly warned, 'Then you will believe our stories about tigers and this will help you write about our lives.'

It was some time until I took on the force of the islanders' remarks that, if I actually wanted to 'understand' and write about them — the people — I had to 'start with the forest or the jongol and tigers and their daily struggles'. My initial sense was that I needed to correct the dominant perception of the Sundarbans as the realm of nature — a wilderness, a preserve of wild beasts — by a simple reversal and then finally break the silence and talk about people. But the Sundarbans people I was living with were telling me that I would not be able to comprehend their lives if I looked at just one side of the river, that of the village or the abad. They wanted me to look also at the jongol and appreciate 'their' tigers precisely in order for me to value their lives and what gave them the distinct identity of being islanders of the Sundarbans. For Mihir the forest and its beings had to be *experienced* to be properly understood. As the days went by, the islanders made great efforts not only to explain verbally through narratives the risks entailed in the different occupations they practised in the forest or its rivers but also to have me actually accompany them (even though these forays were then fraught with even greater danger for them) so that I would not only *hear* stories but also *see* and *feel* the forest for myself.

Towards the end of my stay, Nonibala, a neighbour and prawn seed collector, came up to me and said, 'You've accompanied the forest working groups many times but you have never come and pulled the net for tiger prawn seeds with us. Meet us tomorrow at 4 a.m. We want you to know how difficult it is.' It had never occurred to me to try working in the river to fish tiger prawn seed because it had initially not seemed directly relevant and also because I was terrified of crocodiles. I had on a few occasions seen one basking in the sun or floating just below the surface of the river — whereas I never saw a tiger.

Pulling the net is strenuous. It takes intense effort to walk against the current in fast-flowing hip- to chest-deep water without slipping. Like going into the forest to cut wood, this experience too struck me by its sheer physicality and seemed like it was the perpetually defining moment of one's existence as a forest- or river-working individual living in the Sundarbans. It was this physical intimacy with the elements — the cyclones, the salt water one had to contend with daily, the strong winds and fiery sun — that many islanders saw as the reason why, in the Sundarbans, their tigers' behaviour was what it was; in their own words: 'irritable and prone to violent bouts of anger'. This kind of 'nature' was not limited only to tigers. They believed that they, too, because they shared the same geography with tigers, shared the same characteristics. Such occasions lead me to stress that, for the islanders, it is crucial to understand the intimate symbolic and physical connections between the abad — the inhabited world of humans — and the jongol, the sphere of the non-humans, if one is to write about the Sundarbans and its people. This is why this book has tried to give a systematic account of the processes by which these two aspects are negotiated within the daily lives of those who live there.

As mentioned earlier, the urban literature on the Sundarbans focuses principally on its physical as well as metaphorical transformation, that is, how it has metamorphosed from being a 'waste' or 'drowned' land under early colonial administrators into 'a beautiful and exotic garden' culminating in a World Heritage Site where the glamorous national animal, the Royal Bengal tiger, lives. The tiger has now become the urban middle classes' rallying point — everybody wants to save it or, at least, be seen as espousing the cause of nature and wildlife. Protecting this cosmopolitan tiger is thus a badge of one's own cosmopolitanism, a sign of moving beyond the parochialism of one's location within the confines of urbanity and one's nation-state. In this view the cosmopolitan 'save the tiger' tiger, because it is a shared symbol crossing national boundaries, should be subjected to a study reflecting on the transnational cosmopolitan issues of social justice, human rights and global politics. This is where the Sundarbans people come in and ask me to look at a more local tiger, *their* tiger.[11]

What is a Tiger?

The fact that tigers are socially constructed leads to a number of questions for anthropologists. Must we restrict ourselves to describing as best we can the specific conceptions of tigers that different cultures have produced at different times? If not, should we look for general principles of order enabling us to compare the seemingly infinite empirical diversity of human/tiger complexes? Philippe Descola, who asks these questions in relation to 'nature', says that the only alternative is to go beyond both relativism and universalism, as neither provides suitable solutions. Relativist positions presuppose the existence, in each culture, of a specific system of meanings that arbitrarily code an unproblematic natural world whose implicit measuring rod, however, remains its Western conception. Indeed, claims Descola, this leaves unchallenged Western culture's epistemological privilege of the nature–culture divide itself (1996: 84–85).

But supposing, he asks, we take the second alternative and believe that there exists some very general or universal pattern in the way in which people construct representations of their social and physical environment, where do we start looking for traces of their existence and *modus operandi*? Ethnobiological taxonomies have been elaborated to this effect, but how much do they tell us about the 'social objectivation of nature' — which is 'the process by which each culture endows with a particular salience certain features of its environment and certain forms of practical engagement with it' (1996: 85)?

Should we then, asks Descola, analyse these 'underlying patterns' through Lévi-Strauss's universalising grid and see tigers as symbolic manifestations of a classificatory mode of thought whereby people understand similarities and differences? But for Lévi-Strauss, plants and animals are useful in the constitution of humans' cognitive need for understanding only to the extent that these classifications can be *contrasted* with the cultural world of human beings (1962). For him, peoples' concrete knowledge of the world they live in is meaningless unless transposed to the abstract level, where it can be used to classify and order the social. Thus, Lévi-Strauss's schema, based on difference and analogy, proves problematic because it means that the practical experience of, or communication with, animals (or plants) is irrelevant per se. But for the islanders of the Sundarbans, if tigers were interesting, it was not only when *making sense* of their social world but because they were *part of* their social world.

The 'animal world' for any society, says Adrian Franklin (1999), is never an indivisible category but a historically constituted and morally loaded field of meanings that derives from the human habit of extending social logics, complexities and conflicts onto the natural world, and particularly onto animals. The possibilities for differentiations in meaning and practice in human–animal relations, he says, are multiplied everywhere by the social differentiations that stem from class, regional affiliations, gender, and religion. But in this case, whatever their regional affiliations, gender and religion, the urban middle classes the world over are 'united' in a particular perception of tigers and the 'protection' of wildlife.

If, following Descola and Franklin, ideas of nature are fundamentally intertwined with dominant ideas of society, we need to address what ideas of society and its ordering become reproduced, excluded or validated through images of nature, or, in this case, tigers. This is because, as they argue, not only are understandings of nature predicated by reference to the human domain but also ways of thinking about it are ultimately informed by ideas and practices concerning 'self' and 'otherness' (Descola 1992: 111; 1996: 85). This leads to two questions: What ideas of 'self' and 'otherness' are perpetuated through ideas of the cosmopolitan tiger and of nature for urban children around the world? Were the islanders trying to familiarise me with *their* tiger so that I understood what 'self' and 'otherness' — and by extension 'social life' — is all about in the Sundarbans?

The Sundarbans islanders often explained that, because the locale had become more violent for them all, it had unified humans and non-humans by investing them both with a common cantankerousness. The islanders, in turn, believed that this increased each group's aggressiveness, which again affected both the *lived* and *thought* environment of which tigers were a part. These constant threats to the other's existence were therefore in reality seen like threats to one's own existence, having adverse effects on the 'psychology' of all beings, both human and non-human, who lived in this environment. This was the reason why, argued the islanders, they shared with non-humans, especially tigers, an irritable, angry nature.

Also, just as they saw the locale as influencing them and making them more cantankerous, they believed that history, especially the violence witnessed in the politics of the Sundarbans, was increasing the harshness of their environment. In other words, the islanders explained that the growing violence of humans expressed through their polluting paraphernalia such as motorboats, prawn seed collectors' mosquito nets and poachers' rifles, and the more dangerous religious and political violence, affected the locale of the forest, which in turn affected tigers and other non-humans' need for peace and security. This made tigers even more ferocious and increased the danger of working in the Sundarbans. The two (humans and non-humans), however, are 'sealed' together by this common environment of the Sundarbans — the locale of Bengal tigers.

When I pressed the islanders to tell me more about *their* tigers, they explained that their tigers had changed, primarily because the government was replacing them with a new, more aggressive species that bred much faster. As one honey collector pointed out,

Tailormade in city labs with no prior knowledge of the difficult Sundarbans terrain, what do they know of the hardships of migration and of the harsh Sundarbans geography?

These tigers were called 'hybrid' because they were considered to be a cross between a kind of mole and a dangerously ferocious species of tigers and were believed to have been introduced by the government with the specific intent of seeing the tiger population of the Sundarbans increase.[12] I have no proof of the introduction of such a species of tiger, but according to the islanders as well as the tiger census-takes, it is agreed that there has been an increase in the tiger population since the early 1970s.

Not all the Sundarbans islanders agree on what tigers are. Some highlight how they share with tigers a history of displacement and a terribly dangerous environment, which leads them to be very protective toward 'their old tigers'. Others argue that the lines of relatedness between tigers and people have been redrawn so that now they are pitted against each other. Their grievance is that the state's investment in tourism and wildlife sanctuaries is instituting an unequal distribution of resources between humans and tigers and that this is therefore a betrayal of them, the inhabitants of the Sundarbans, by the state. Correspondingly, tigers, by becoming 'cosmopolitan', have become 'high-status' animals and have moved on to the other side of the overarching socio-economic divide. This cosmopolitan tiger has been created as an animal needing a locale bereft of people. It is *this* tiger, one that is constructed by the state, conservation NGOs and urbanites, that the islanders argued they were trying to fight against, not *their* old tigers.

Can there be a Cosmopolitan Anthropology?

The problem with the Western notion of nature, which Descola has called 'naturalism', is that it is used to justify a greater control over not only people but also, in this case, 'tigers'. If we stretch Descola's argument, could we ask if the protection of Royal Bengal tigers is silencing the Sundarbans islanders' ways of engaging with non-humans? Kuper argued, against postmodern critiques of anthropology, that we should aspire to contribute 'a comparative dimension to the enlightenment project of a science of human variation in time and space'. 'Our object,' he continues, 'must be to confront the models current in the social sciences with the experiences and models of our subjects, while insisting that this should be a two-way process' (1994: 551). But as Fardon (1990) and others have pointed out, most anthropological conversations are regional — so how do we extend them cross-regionally?

On the other hand, how do we extricate the local Sundarbans tiger from the cosmopolitan one? Appiah (2006) suggests that, rather than seeking 'agreement' with everyone, we should 'get used to one another' before possibly rising to the next level of sympathetic engagement. He argues that ideally, cosmopolitanism amounts to 'universality plus difference'. To be properly able to do this, one needs to pause and reflect on what constitutes 'universality' and 'difference'. The location of something as common as a toy or a poster of a tiger in a child's room needs to be recognised within the influence both of successive polities and of the current politics around tigers and their protection. The earlier negative connotations of 'wilderness' have today been replaced by the idea of 'wilderness' as positive — validated — both in the name of ecology and wildlife preservation as well as of tourism; and the implications of such a transformation are significant. And so, too, is the continuity of certain perceptions, such as the inference that humans do not belong in the Sundarbans.

The Sundarbans have been 'territorialised', not only in the decisions made about the use of the Sundarbans forest but also in the kind of meaning with which the place has been invested. It is therefore crucial to draw the links between how administrative classifications, law making and discourses on nature and science have 'represented' the Sundarbans, its tigers and its islanders. What is even more important is to see how the Sundarbans islanders situate themselves within this portrayal. These links need to be highlighted because it is only by spotting them that the new imperialisms propagated in the name of conservation be revealed.

'Nature is forever being made and remade in speech and text, not least when science and the state collaborate to alter the fate of highlighted species' (Greenough 2003: 201). One of the reasons for the islanders' keenness that I should 'know the forest' and 'understand tigers' might have been their urge for me to materially 'feel the fear' — as they call it — of tigers. It might also have been because they wanted to debunk my idea of tigers in connection with tourism, hunting or the raj. The transformation of the *Tigris regalis* to the status of Royal Bengal tiger and trademark for global conservation and tourism has reduced discussions about this animal to those bounded by the terms of environmental discourse. Such a discourse is often limiting, as it refuses to engage with alternative understandings of tigers. What is interesting in the different narratives of tigers of Sundarbans islanders was how some saw them as invested with the human qualities of 'understanding' and 'kindness', while others saw them as the state's killing machines. If ideas of society and of its ordering become reproduced, legitimated, excluded, validated, and so on, through appeals to nature or the natural, as Macnaghten and Urry (1998: 15) argue, the project that remains is to determine what is natural. And this, as they say, is as much a social and cultural project as it is a 'purely' scientific one. Through the islanders' rejection of the 'tourist tiger', voicing instead their own narratives, dilemmas and arguments in terms of '*their* tigers', they express their feelings of marginalisation and also belonging. Highlighting the transformations of *their* tigers is also a way for the islanders to reclaim the forgotten pages of a history that has relegated them to oblivion, an injustice they feel they have been done by the urban folks who believe tigers are more precious than them, the islanders of the Sundarbans.

Notes

1. This refers to Sukanto Bhattacharya (1926–47), young revolu-tionary poet who organised student movements for India's independence and whose poetry is famous for being dedicated to the struggle for liberation and social justice.
2. Chittagong had belonged to the king of Arakan; it had been almost entirely in the hands of the Portuguese (Campos 1919: 101). In the seventeenth century, while in the service of the king of Arakan, the Portuguese were infamous for having, along with the Mags, committed 'frightful depredations all along the banks of the rivers in the Sundarbunds carrying off Musalmans and Hindus as captives. Between 1621 and 1624, the Portuguese brought to Chittagong 42,000 slaves' (ibid.: 105).
3. The Gram Sansad meetings were launched in the late 1990s to strengthen local-level government. It meets about once a year to discuss and approve projects for the coming year.
4. It has been argued that these meetings were rarely quorate and that it was questionable whether they contributed to any meaningful participation (Hill 2003: 16; Bhattacharyya 2002). In the 'down' islands the most insignificant political meeting became the hub for secret meetings and visits both before

and after and was always heavily attended, as both groups came to each house to recruit people to come with them to make a show of *dol bhar* — the 'heaviness' or 'importance' of the group.

5. Fayrer claims that it is both because of the 'apparent indifference of villagers and cowherds with which they regard the brute' (1875: 37–38) and because 'the natives of India, especially the Hindoos, hold the tiger, as they do the cobra, in superstitious awe' (ibid.: 41–42). I will not develop here the broad generalisations that permit Fayrer to make these claims. He uses examples from Chotanagpur, concerning the Ghond and the Khurkoo, to conclude that the victims of man-eating tigers are considered social outcasts on the ground that they are 'labouring under the displeasure of the Deity' and that these tiger victims are 'prescribed sacrifices' offered by these 'wild and ignorant aborigines' who believe that the man-eating tiger is in fact the deity (ibid.: 46).

6. Fayrer accepts that the tiger population has increased since 1857, but he is sceptical of the figures concerning loss of life (even though he tells us that in Lower Bengal alone, from 1860 to 1866, tigers killed 4,218 people) and property (it amounted annually to 100 lakh pounds [1875: 47]). He invites the reader to consider this destruction as being 'not so great' when one bears in mind that 'the population of India, including the native states, is nearly 250,000,000' (ibid.: 55)! Even at the turn of the century, in 1908, the number of people killed by tigers was as high as 909 (Sukumar 1994: 306).

7. The tie-up of the symbol of the tiger to 'royalty' needs to be further explored (even if one should add that the Mughals had lions as emblems on their flags).

8. Experts have come up with many reasons as to why tigers turn into man-eaters. The famous hunter Jim Corbett suggests in one of the most notable of his books, *Man-eaters of Kumaon*, that big cats become man-eaters if unable to pursue 'normal' prey through injury or if for some reason they get the taste for human flesh by tasting human carcasses (1946).

9. 'Forced to get by with salty water, the felines undergo a chemical imbalance that can be corrected by eating humans, who constitute high-quality food' (quoted in Diamond 1979: 37).

10. The dummy and the mask experiences have been considered successful examples (Sukumar 1994: 311) of 'psychological warfare' led against animals so that they learn to fear humans.

11. At this point I must stress the fact that never once did I hear the islanders questioning the need for tigers to exist. What they do have an issue with, however, is whether it needs to be 'protected' — with all the patronising and universalising elements of 'control over nature' embodied in both this word and the project it entails — at least via the policies it is currently being protected.

12. The choice of the mole is interesting and symbolically revealing. Projecting the duplicitous and 'lowly' status onto the Royal Bengal tiger makes it lose much of it regal nobility and national standing.

VIII

Conclusion: Beneath the Tiger Mask, the Human Face of the Sundarbans

The Sundarbans islanders believe that they share with tigers a unique geography, a shared history, and a set of common laws — and, crucially, 'interactive experiences'. Tiger-charmers are those most apt to take up the responsibility of negotiating with tigers because they are understood to have similar qualities to tigers. Tigers 'understand' them best because, they argued, like them the tiger-charmers, they have very strong 'egos' and are inclined to greed and short-temperedness. Tiger-charmers, especially in the old days, were believed to be able to 'shout back at tigers' (a bit like Fayrer!) and, like them, take on magical appearances and transform themselves into animals, birds or insects. Indeed, all those working in the forest saw their 'interactive experiences' with tigers as possible not only because they felt they shared with tigers a certain fearlessness but also because they saw tigers as invested with 'human' dispositions and emotions.

How was this sharing of disposition and emotion seen as some kind of 'relatedness'? There is no one singular underlying pattern of understanding 'relatedness' in the 'down' islands of the Sundarbans when it comes to human ties. Equally, the Sundarbans islanders have different ways of positioning themselves in relation to tigers as well as their environment. It is remarkable how forest fishers believe that they share with tigers a history of displacement and a dangerous environment, which makes them very protective towards 'their old tigers'; their stories of oratorical battles of wits between tigers and famous tiger-charmers are narrated with some fondness. But, if forest fishers are able to empathise with tigers, at the other end of the spectrum the prawn seed collectors and the poachers have redrawn the lines of relatedness between tigers and people. Far from finding some sort of identity or empathy with the tiger, they see the events of Morichjhanpi and the state's investment in tourism and wildlife sanctuaries as instituting an unequal distribution of resources between humans and tigers and, therefore, a disloyalty towards the inhabitants of the Sundarbans. It is not so much that tigers and people are no longer seen as related; rather some tigers are now related to a different class of people. In the allied discourses of the state, environmental NGOs and the tourism industry, tigers now occupy the elevated status of 'bhadralok', tourist or cosmopolitan tigers.

Thus there is a clear split among the Sundarbans islanders, with contrasting kinds of interactions both with the forest and in ways of 'relating' to tigers. If the forest workers persist to this day in their belief in continuity and that the best way forward is still to pacify tigers and keep treating them as 'conniving mates', then the prawn seed collectors, on the other hand, believe that their relation with tigers, and by extension with the other non-humans of the rivers and forests (notably crocodiles), and with each other, has been irretrievably broken. They see tigers as the symbol of a state ruled by the rich and powerful bhadralok cosmopolitan, a state in which they feel that, as gramer lok, they are discriminated against. As for the bhadralok themselves, focusing as ever on land when talking of the Sundarbans, the stress is on vestiges of past civilisations. Many of them hope that they will come across old coins and statues when labourers dig up their fields; any 'find' thought to be 'ancient' is neatly arranged in glass show cases. These objects reassuring them about belonging to the greater 'imagined community' of cultured and educated Bengalis.[1]

Are Tigers Good to Think with?

The social construction of the realm of nature and the environment, the forest and its non-humans, most important of which in this context are tigers, leads us to consider the 'social objectivation of nature': 'the process by which each culture endows with a particular salience certain features of its environment and certain forms of practical engagement with it' (Descola 1996: 85). As mentioned earlier, Descola identifies a common feature in all conceptualisations of the natural world — that it is always predicated by reference to the human domain and that ways of thinking about it are ultimately informed by ideas and practices concerning 'self' and 'otherness' (1992: 111; 1996: 85). He suggests that anthropologists should analyse different patterns that societies have elaborated to represent the non-human just as they would different kinship systems. These patterns, which can neither operate nor be studied independently of cultural and historical contexts, provide a framework within which a study of the conceptualisations of the tiger in the Sundarbans can be deployed as a way of understanding social bonds in the Sundarbans.

The structure of the book implicitly draws largely on Descola because his insight offers an alternative way of approaching social relations not only in the South Asian realm, where caste and religion are important analytical grids, but also to grasp international north–south relations in the domain of wildlife conservation. An understanding through different societies' perception of animals, or the complex relationship between particular social systems and their deemed 'natural environment', lags behind in the social sciences. Similarly, instead of looking at discrete entities whose boundaries are set by administrative or social units such as the 'village' or the 'district', understanding the islanders' life worlds through the categories of 'up'/ 'down', bhadralok/gramer lok, human/non-human, etc., is necessary to reflect categories which made more sense for them. This is why tracing how the ecological/environmental dynamics of the place have been interwoven in its specific history, culture, social and political institutions, relationships with the state, remains important.

Whose World Heritage Site?

In 2002, the Supreme Court ordered the eviction of fishermen from the island of Jambudwip — an island customarily used by fishermen as their base to catch and dry fish during the fishing season. The reason for their eviction? To make way for a Rs 540 crore tourism project of the Sahara India Group. The plan was to build a 'world class city-centre spread over 250 sq km of water surface', and to include a business centre, a cinema theatre, a cultural centre, club houses, health clubs, a helipad, etc. Advertising 'virgin islands' and beaches of 'pristine glory', this 'dream' tourist destination guaranteed a service of 'global standing' on floating boat houses where one was assured of finding all at the same time a casino, scuba diving facilities, and a tiger breeding centre. In other words, it guaranteed to be, in the words of Sekhsaria, 'a modern tourism blockbuster' (2004).

The problem with this hugely ambitious Sahara venture is that it posed an important threat to this already extremely fragile ecosystem. The impunity with which the environmental and social concerns were neglected in the planning of the project could, and I quote from Sekhsaria again, 'certainly be called spectacular, if indeed they were not so serious and "deadly"' (ibid.). However, the timely efforts of a team of independent observers, the People United for Better Living In Calcutta [PUBLIC]), Kolkata; Bombay Environment Action Group [BEAG], Mumbai, and the Bangalore-based EQUATIONS that works on issues related to tourism) and of renowned novelist Amitav Ghosh (2004b) raised the alert and the Sahara project was stalled, at least for the time being.

What I would like to dwell upon, through the contrasting images of fishermen being evicted from Jambudwip on the one hand, and the Sahara India Group's advertisement of their project on 'virgin islands' on the other, are the current implications for the wider world of the far from uniquely contemporary view (continuing from the past that humans do not or should not fit in the Sundarbans. The Sahara Goup's projection of the Sundarbans is yet another representation, in a long list of such depictions in which the islanders of the Sundarbans are seen as superfluous. This will to omit people from images of the Sundarbans or see them as detrimental to the survival of the forest and tigers must be addressed. It is a prerequisite of engaging with the concerns raised by Rangarajan and Shahabuddin — the need for more knowledge-sharing between biologists and social scientists (2006: 361). Without such shared knowledge, the perception that humans are excess baggage, whether in the sphere of wildlife preservation or in current bids at rebranding the place for the purposes of global marketing, will persist, and will ultimately lead to an increased alienation between the inhabitants of the Sundarbans and its wildlife.

Environmental plans for the Sundarbans have been dominated by discourses dictated in the name of an eco-science that never took into account the islanders of the Sundarbans; but these discourses need to be addressed from the point of view of the Sundarbans inhabitants. The lesson of Descola is that we cannot properly begin to address the issue of 'nature' without first entering into a study of social re-lations as rendered through the discourse around non-humans (in this case the tiger) — both as a part of the cosmology of the forest and the embodied reality one faces. In the islanders' different images of tigers, the rhetoric of having to stand up against tourist tigers, or tigers that have 'opted out' of their historic connivance with the islanders to ally themselves instead with urbanites and state officials, needs to be understood if the region is to remain a shared space for both tigers and the inhabitants of the Sundarbans.

The history of conflict in the Sundarbans, or, rather, the battle between subaltern groups of people who live in the Sundarbans and
dominant groups (the zamindars, the British, the Left Front government), is very often referred to in islanders' discourse on their marginalisation. A rumour which circulated widely in the Sundarbans in
the late 1990s was that the WB government had 'given the tender'
of the whole Sundarbans to a powerful rich foreign multinational
called the WWF which 'has no love lost' for people but very much
wants to see tigers flourish. This is the context in which to understand
the violence that often erupts in the Sundarbans today. It is seen as a
fight against a state representing only the urban middle classes and
not the Sundarbans islanders' interests.

In the context, it is important to draw links between how administrative classifications, law making and discourses on nature and
science have 'represented' the Sundarbans and in turn have 'evolved'
a particular perception of the inhabitants of the Sundarbans. These
links need to be exposed because it is only by doing so that the new
imperialisms propagated in the name of conservation can be
denounced. Over the last two decades, 'natural' science studies in
India have accentuated the link between the process of imperialism
and techno-scientific development (Kumar 1991: 6; Worboys 1991:
13–15; Arnold and Guha 1996; Sangwan 1998). Guha has described
how, in their pursuit of a self-professed brand of forest preservation, the
British colonial administration of the forest broke with the traditional
pattern of authority which was normative and flexible (1989a). In
the Sundarbans, even though there never was a 'traditional pattern
of authority which was normative and flexible' before the British —
there were merely landlords usurping the products of the forest —
there has been, through official discourse, both colonial and national,
an imperious 'making' of a tiger, a forest, and a people.

What better way to combat this subjugating and imperious
'making' of a region and its people than allowing the inhabitants
of the region to say what they have to say about themselves and
their region? Following the growing emphasis in Subaltern Studies,[2]
especially after the publication of Ranajit Guha's *Elementary
Aspects of Peasant Insurgency in Colonial India* (1983) on rural
communities' consciousness, as shown through the study of rural
movements in colonial Bengal, I wanted to record the islanders'
voice, or voices. It is with this in mind that I tried to focus less on
caste or religious discourse as structural themes when looking at

marginalisation and resistance from the islanders' point of view. This is because, like Ruud, I believe that the tendency to consider 'the Subaltern' in light of overpowering cultural or structural domination severely reduces the scope for understanding subaltern action (1999b: 690). It is also because, more practically, this allowed me to use the islanders system of referentials. By this I mean, to use Scott's words, 'the culture that peasants fashion from their experience' — their 'offstage comments and conversations, their proverbs, folksongs, and history, legends, jokes, language, ritual and religion — it should be possible to determine to what degree, and in what ways, peasants actually accept the social order propagated by either' (Scott 1985: 41). In this case, I decided to use the organising element I found most prevalent, which was the language of 'human and non-human', and see how this system articulated and transcended, among other concerns such as social mobility, politics and the effects of globalisation, the all-consuming topics of caste and religion. Here the environment is analysed as a narrative device (for example, humans and tigers sharing a can-tankerous nature because of a harsh geography and a common history of displacement) and as a practical experience of working in the forest as collectors of crab, fish or honey, especially in contrast with landowning cultivators. As I have tried to explain, these different groups have diverse understandings of the environment, which highlight distinctions between bhadralok/gramer lok — a frame of reference that enables me to better grasp social relations in the Sundarbans.

This is not to say that understanding religious practice is of no importance; on the contrary. This is why I was keen to draw the distinctions between those worshipping Bonbibi and those who thought Bonbibi was not 'cool' or 'modern' or 'global' enough and chose to worship Kali instead. It was a way for these women to assert their identities as not just working women (which woman in rural India does not work?) but specifically as 'earning women' and therefore women with power and clout who could now start to negotiate for a share of social status. The worship of Kali offered social mobility and a better position within the sphere of Bengali respectability as it allowed them to partake of an imagined sense of 'emancipated' Bengali womandom.

Privileging religion over all else distracts attention from the equally important economic and political spheres, and from alternative, less well-known cultural spheres. If on a theoretical level, the contending elements in being both 'Bengali' (unfortunately too readily conflated with 'Hindu' in West Bengal and 'Muslim' in Bangladesh) and 'Muslim' have often been highlighted, those of being 'Bengali' and gramer lok have rarely been addressed.[3] In the case of the Sundarbans, the framing of community consciousness is undertaken not only through the valorisation of religion, caste, ethnic or communitarian identity per se but also through an overarching divide along the lines of bhadralok/gramer lok. It is through this main distinction, which is expressed through the local narratives about tigers, that the different groups of Sundarbans islanders highlight their perceptions of 'self' and 'other'.

To speak of a single 'Bengali Hindu community' is to invoke an 'imagined community' (Chatterji 1994: 43); this is why in this case it was interesting to see how narratives of the tiger and of the forest are used to subvert dominant categories of caste and class and, by extension, of an imagined community. The story of Bonbibi against the Brahmin landowning Dokkhin Rai could well have been penned in the early stages of a peasant consciousness against high-caste bhadralok domination — just as today stories of hybrid tigers made in laboratories by scientists and released by the WB government are a way for the islanders to voice their resentment against what they consider to be a highly unjust situation. Which is why it is important to note the tangible tension that exists when one is 'Bengali' but not a bhadralok to comprehend why the islanders believed that they had become 'just tiger food'.

An Answer to the Masks

While preparing for fieldwork in the Sundarbans ten years after my high-school episode with the masks, Fayrer's 1875 text on *Tigris regalis* brought back memories of the conversations my friend and I had had with the forest guards and the scientists who had been involved in the government research on stopping Sundarban tigers from eating humans. Nothing seemed to have changed. During my studies I also read the following quote from a Dutch text, which could just as easily have been said by someone British: '(I)f it is the lion who rules Africa, it is undoubtedly the tiger who is the tyrant of the Indian jungles and forests. It is a beautiful animal — black stripes against a yellow and white background — graceful in his movements, but of a mean, cruel disposition, so that one could compare him with a Nero or a Philip the Second' (Hartwig 1860: 61, in Boomgaard 2001: 1). The sport hunters who shot the tiger in huge numbers saw the animal in a largely negative light, at best a worthy antagonist.

It was 'a cunning, silent, savage enemy', 'a pleasure to outwit and shoot', to end 'the fearful ravages' it committed against people.

The transformation of the *Tigris regalis* into the contemporary status of Royal Bengal tiger and trademark for global conservation and tourism has now reduced discussions about this animal to those bounded by the terms of 'scientific' environmental discourse. Such a discourse, by refusing to engage with the social reasons which favour the existence of man-eating in the first place, is in itself an inherently repressive knowledge. The Sundarbans islanders' refusal to wear masks is, as I came to learn during fieldwork, one among many possible ways of defying, or at least complicating, the legitimisation of a state-backed 'scientific knowledge' of tigers' appetite for humans. Even though local narratives of the tiger interweave a rational observation of these animals with the social problem of man-eating, and have, one could argue, as much scientific purchase as the narratives of scientists, they have consistently been ignored.

This is not a plea for 'deep ecology'.[4] What we need to recognise is the relevance in Latour's claim that modernity did not succeed in, and indeed, cannot separate the natural from the cultural/human; there can only be hybrids and networks of humans and non-humans (1993 [1991]: 23). The implications of Latour sensitise me to look for hybrids and networks in the various understandings of Sundarbans tigers. This is so as to dismantle the assumed superiority of certain forms of knowledge — here the one highlighted by the state and which is assumed 'scientific' and above the knowledge of the 'indigenous'. Instead of focusing on the conflicting scientific debates on the 'naturalness' of Sundarbans tigers' man-eating habits, the question I would pose is why the Sundarbans islanders believe that they have now become 'tiger food'.

The narratives developed by the islanders about the history they share with tigers is another aspect they see as 'bonding' them to non-humans. Those who have to ensure that the agreement left by Bonbibi is respected are the tiger-charmers. Their history is a long one — which highlights both the Islamic heritage of the forest as well as the pirs' rather strained relationship with central powers such as the Mughal state. The tiger-charmers of today have many aspects which link them to Sufi pirs. The fact that the forest is the realm of Islam is increasingly seen as problematic for the islanders — especially the landowners. For those who work as poachers the dilemma is of a different order. When the state officials use firearms to protect themselves against tigers, the islanders do not see why they should use masks. The islanders who opt for rifles thus do not want to carry the attributes which mark them as inferior because seen as at best 'anti-modern', or at worst 'superstitious' in relation to the bhadralok. They argue that if Kali and firearms work for the forest guards, Kali and firearms will work for them too.

The key question put by the islanders which undermines nearly 200 years of 'scientific' discourse on the tiger is: Why are attacks made by tigers justified on the 'scientific' grounds that the Royal Bengal tiger of the Sundarbans forest is a *man-eater*? Scientists for the last forty years have been studying the reasons which might account for the predilection of the Sundarbans tiger for human flesh. But how 'true' are these 'scientific truths'? There are just as many arguing the opposite, that is, that these are not 'natural' man-eaters. Either of these purported 'scientific truth' discourses about the peculiar habits of Sundarbans tigers cannot be understood on their own. As Goody (1977) and Latour (1986) point out, dichotomous distinctions are convincing only as long as they are enforced by a strong asymmetrical bias that treats the two sides of the divide or border very differently. Developing this argument, Latour says that these 'great divides' do not provide any explanation, but on the contrary, are the very things to be explained (1986: 2). What needs to be addressed, therefore, is not why tigers are 'natural' man-eaters but why some scientists and the state insist that they are.

What was more important for the islanders, as we have seen, is that the old tigers, even though violent and arrogant, had been sensitive to them because they shared their harsh past and difficult surroundings. 'Their' tigers had a 'human' quality, not only because they had huge egos and were keen to establish their rights over the forest, especially over wood, but also because their migratory history and difficult geographical environment had given them some feeling of compassion and taught them to share with their fellow human neighbours. In contrast, the new tigers were seen as being violent and arrogant in a nasty way: they killed 'for fun' to prove they were the 'real' tigers the tourists expected them to be. Because they were dis-cussed by the powerful — the influential representatives of the government, the scientists and the increasingly interested foreign NGOs like the WWF — and were the national animals of both India and Bangladesh, 'these new tigers', as elucidated by the islanders, thought they were invincible even though they had become mere 'tourist tigers' or 'killing machines'. If, for the old tigers, the islanders were 'equals', these new tigers were treating them as 'tiger food'.

Notes

1. The 'imagined community' as famously developed by Anderson in his book on the origin and spread of nationalism (1983).
2. See studies by Sarkar (1985; 1987); Dasgupta (1985); Cooper (1988); Bose (1993); Bhadra and Chatterjee (1997).
3. Being both Bengali and Muslim is discussed by Chatterji (1996), Ahmed (1981), Islam (1973), Roy (1970).
4. Briefly, Guha describes 'deep ecology' as 'conservation imperialism'. Deep ecology's central tenets, as criticised by Guha, are: 'the distinction between anthropocentrism and biocentrism, the focus on wilderness preservation, the invocation of Eastern traditions, and the belief that it represents the most radical trend within environmentalism'. Guha criticises these four points on the grounds that the distinction between anthropocentrism and biocentrism is of little use in understanding the dynamics of environmental degradation; the implementation of the wilderness agenda is causing serious deprivation in the Third World; the interpretation of Eastern traditions is highly selective; and in different cultural contexts (e.g., West Germany and India) radical environmentalism manifests itself quite differently (1989b: 71).

Afterword

Sixty two years after Independence, even though the Sundarbans region lies a mere three hours away from Kolkata, it is a spectacular administration of 'lackings'. The cultivated prawns are sold and an untold amount of foreign exchange is entering the country. The prawn fisheries owners seem to fatten and burst at the seams. But the collectors, they live like animals in hovels, they don't even have brick roads to walk on, no midday meals are distributed to their children, they won't get job cards, and even if they get them, they won't be able to work for more than 100 days. They will not have ration cards, and even if they do manage one they will not get the basic necessities, and if one amongst them manages by mistake to enter a college, he will not get the scholarships announced by the government. Even if the place has been called 'under-developed' the poor will get no peace, they will have no opportunities. (Ghosh 2008: 8 [translated from Bengali by the author])

Since leaving the Sundarbans in 2001, I've returned on visits about once every year. The last time I was there was January 2009. This time I also travelled to other islands to get a sense of what changes might have taken place over the last ten years. What surprised me was to see how little had altered. This was despite three new additions. A bridge now exists between Shonakhali and the island of Basanti. With the Parliamentary elections round the corner (April and May 2009) work had also started on two other bridges at major intersections of the tidal rivers: one across the Matla in Canning and the other across the Ichamati in Hingalganj. The second big change was the mushrooming of the unlicensed local tourist industry, with tourist launches making greater incursions into the forest areas. The third, and perhaps the most important transformation for the islanders, was the presence of phone towers on some of the inhabited islands of the Sundarbans. Communication was not always possible but still, if one walked long enough, for a couple of rupees one could enter into direct communication with the connected world.

However, most places in the Sundarbans still don't have electricity, a dispensary or even a brick road. Politics has remained incendiary (often literally) and the murder of political activists is just as rampant as before. I decided to travel to Kumirmari, the village just north of the island of Morichjhanpi, to meet the headman and enquire if they were going to mark the thirty years since the Morichjhanpi massacre. The headman was not at home; in fact he had absconded after allegations that he had taken part in a murder. So I met with the ex-headman, who said that he would strongly recommend people do not organise a memorial ceremony for the victims of Morichjhanpi as it would likely be hijacked by the TMC and violently opposed by the CPIM. 'It is best that old bones, even if they had never been laid to rest, remain forgotten rather than spilling new blood over them,' he said in an ominous whisper.

All through the months of November and December 2008, I kept seeing pieces about the Sundarbans in the Kolkata newspapers: tigers were swimming into villages and attacking people or people had been killed by tigers while working in the forest. These attacks and deaths were so frequent that the current chief minister of West Bengal, Mr Buddhadeb Bhattacharya, asked the Sundarbans Biosphere Reserve to conduct a survey to find out whether tigers 'straying into human settlements [were] leaving their habitats because of lack of food or due to any change *in their nature*' (*The Statesman* 30 December 2008; italics added). How strange it was to see that the old question about the man-eating 'nature' of the Sundarbans tiger was still being asked. While nowadays people generally get to know about tiger attacks and deaths more often and more quickly through mobile telecommunication and the internet, the old anxieties keep resurfacing. Had the number of these attacks increased or were they just better reported by the mainstream media?

The threat of wild animals to life and livelihood — especially to the disadvantaged, whose way of life necessarily exposes them to constant danger — is not limited to the Sundarbans. What makes it poignant in the case of the Sundarbans is that here, like many parts of the global south, resources are so unjustly distributed. What has changed, however, in the South Asian context, is the emergence of a new rural activism 'à la Chipko movement', as Rangarajan dubs it. More politically conscious, they do not hesitate to 'take up mobilisation against dominant groups' (Rangarajan 2003: 218). But what happens in places such as the Sundarbans where people have not really organised themselves into eco-conscious pressure groups to demand more from their government?

Madhusudan and Mishra have described how, every year, despite all their efforts to save their crops, South Asian villagers living in the elephant roaming zones lose nearly 15 per cent of their paddy to raiding elephants; marauding leopards and tigers also devour some 12 per cent of their livestock. Occasionally, even villagers themselves are killed by elephants and tigers. The result 'is a deep gnawing resentment among villagers about large and dangerous animals that come into direct conflict with them, inflicting losses to life and property. Often, this resentment spawns angry reprisal: large carnivores are poisoned at kills, elephants are shot in crop fields, forests are set on fire' (Madhusudan and Mishra 2003: 31). Large herbivores in the Sariska Tiger Reserve in Rajasthan destroy up to 18 per cent of the annual production of certain crops (Sekhar 1998), while in the Bhadra Tiger Reserve in Karnataka, elephants inflict crop losses averaging about 15 per cent (Madhusudan and Mishra 2003: 40). It is estimated that livestock constitutes 26 per cent of the diet of the Asiatic lion of the Gir National Park in Gujarat (Chellam 1993; Khan et al. 1996 in Madhusudan and Mishra 2003: 42).

This scenario repeats itself all over the global south. Like most Indians, the majority of Africans do not visit the wildlife parks of their countries nor do they receive much tangible benefits from them. Yet they, especially those who live in close proximity to these parks and forests, are the ones paying the greatest price: the cost of their life, the loss of their livelihood. Here in the Sundarbans, for example, through the latest ban on prawn seed fishing or woodcutting or hunting, the indirect economic costs are borne by the poorest: because government revenues are siphoned off to pay for parks instead of schools or hospitals. Fifteen years ago Sukumar argued that 'to mitigate the impact of wildlife on people, a variety of social security schemes should be made a part of conservation plans. Project Tiger did take this into account by providing compensation for livestock killed by tigers or leopards near reserves. Many schemes are in operation now but in practice some of these are not adequate' (Sukumar 1994: 314).

Such schemes are still not adequate today. Justice Potti, from the Bombay-based Indian People's Tribunal for Human Rights, suggested that, in trying to find alternatives that might defuse the situation, compensation for victims of animal attacks should equal what is paid to the families of airline crash victims (Rangarajan 2003: 219). The analogy is an important one. Fifteen years ago, Sukumar was talking of how local people see sanctuaries or national parks 'as simply the pleasure resorts of the affluent' (Sukumar 1994: 315). Things have not changed, and today it is still, as it was, 'a certain section of society, the marginal farmers and tribals', who 'bear the entire cost of depredatory animals' (ibid.: 303–04).

For Sivaramakrishnan, 'General reflections on the state of democracy and society in India are a necessary point of departure for the study of environmental politics in the subcontinent' (2003: 384), as he says in the chapter aptly named 'Conservation Crossroads: Indian Wildlife at the Intersection of Global Imperatives, Nationalist Anxieties, and Local Assertions'. As with Chipko protests, rural activists have started to call the shots over the last two-and-a-half decades and, consequently, 'urban intellectuals have gone from studying alternative systems to favouring a radical shift in the power structure to meet the dual demands of conservation and human livelihoods' (Rangarajan 2003: 217). Their stance tends to be that this step towards disadvantaged groups getting empowered in relation to their rights vis-à-vis nature is in the right direction so long as it is not anti-conservation. Even though those Rangarajan calls the 'urban intelligentsia' are trying, in their bid to preserve nature, to find more locally rooted systems and depend less on governmental regulations, I believe it should be more of an exchange between the two. Locally rooted systems are not static reservoirs of tradition. They change over time as people make adjustments to their changed environments. Equally, without the concerted efforts of nation-states (both individually and together) in regulating human use of the natural world there is very little of the natural world that is going to remain.

However, a more mutually positive exchange can occur between the Sundarbans islanders and the guardians of the state (and in the islanders' case more specifically, the officials who are supposed to be guarding the wildlife of the region) only if people feel that those in power are listening. As argued by Rangarajan and Saberwal, a failure to provide people with a stake in conservation will simply result in alienating these communities, an alienation that has, in the past, resulted in active undermining of state-initiated conservation policies (2003: 2). 'Listening' can occur only when more attention is paid to the way that local people conceptualise eco-systems and try to deal with their changing world. This will allow a 'cultural ecology' concerned not only with 'ecologically caused aspects of culture' but also and especially, in Viveiros de Castro's words, with 'culturally created aspects of ecology' (1996: 184).

The two really go together. In the case of the Sundarbans, for example, if the human element is brought back in by documenting and highlighting existent local knowledge and practices, then such studies would be potentially in a position to redress the conflicts between the different warring factions we have looked at in this book. Anthropology as a discipline can play a key role. By ethnographically documenting local perspectives on wildlife, the Sundarbans could find what Breitenmoser calls a 'cultural contextualization of wildlife that could help achieve a more locally sensitive wildlife management policy' (1998: 288).

The forests, pastures and hillsides of South Asia have been privileged sites of attention for social scientists over the last quarter century (at least in the domain of ecological history): see, for example, the seminal books edited by Arnold and Guha (1995; 1996), Sivaramakrishnan (1999, 2003), Saberwal and Rangarajan (2003), Rangarajan and Shahabuddin (2006; 2007). Yet there is practically no work on the Sundarbans, the only exceptions being Anuradha Banerjee's *Environment, Population and Human Settlements of Sundarban Delta* (1998), Amites Mukhopadhyay's yet unpublished thesis 'Doing Development: Voluntary Agencies in the Sundarbans of West Bengal' (2003), and an assemblage of papers by various writers in Bengali in 'Shundorbon Bishesh Shonkha: Shamokala Jiyonkathi' (2007), edited by Nazibul Islam Mondol. Even the work on the agrarian landscape of Bengal has mostly neglected the deltaic region. What clearly lags behind are ethnographies of human/non-human co-existences and conflicts. Actually, ethnologies about people–wildlife have generally been few and far between the world over and have attracted little analytical attention even though, for the continued existence of wildlife, I really believe that understanding and studying the human content is a necessary part.

One of my return visits to the delta over these ten years included travelling to the Bangladesh Sundarbans. There, I met the couple, Elisabeth and Rubaiyat Fahrni Mansur, who have been behind wildlife initiatives in Bangladesh and who have conducted long-term investigations on dolphins in the Sundarbans. Their book *Sundarban: A Basic Field Guide* (2006), raising awareness about the flora and the fauna of the Sundarbans, and their work on dolphins, are welcome initiatives. I also had the privilege of meeting Dr Gertrud Denzau who, with her husband, has spent many years working on the ecology of the Bangladesh Sundarbans, and Adam Barlow who was then conducting fieldwork for a Ph.D. on Sundarbans tigers. Given the previous dearth of sustained biological work on the Sundarbans, it was reassuring to find scientific work being undertaken on the current state of the Sundarbans' fauna. I was also fortunate to engage in discussions on the Sundarbans with wildlife photographer Sirajul Hossain. In West Bengal, at a conference organised in December 2008 in the Sundarbans I had the occasion of meeting Anamitra Anurag Danda who has conducted doctoral research in the Sundarbans and has written *Surviving in the Sundarbans: Threats and Responses. An Analytical Description of Life in an Indian Riparian Commons* (2007).

In both WB and Bangladesh, one of the reasons why anthropological research on the Sundarban islands has been lacking is not just the harshness of the terrain but, also, the difficulty of obtaining permits and visas to conduct such a study. Barlow's investigation, as part of his doctoral research 'The Sundarbans Tiger: Adaptation, Population Status and Conflict Management' (2009) highlights the scarcity of knowledge on Sundarbans tigers:

> Very little is known about the ecology of tigers in the Sundarbans or what measures need to be taken to ensure their continued survival . . . [there is] no monitoring programme in place to track changes in the tiger population over time, and therefore no way of measuring the response of the population to conservation activities or threats (ibid. 16).

The positive result of this study is that the information gathered by Barlow and his team has helped formulate the draft Tiger Action Plan involving the Bangladeshi Forest Department for Bangladesh for the years 2009–17.

All this research and publishing activity, it goes without saying, is very welcome in creating an awareness about the Sundarbans. But very little in these books deals with the way people make sense of their day-to-day lives in such close proximity with tigers, crocodiles, sharks, and snakes. An expansion into this area of study is now imperative. I want to end this Afterword with the following anecdote. Early one morning, I was visited by Murari Mondol, a rising political leader of Annpur. He had come, he announced, to take me to his village so that I would write 'about the plight of being attacked by tigers and crocodiles'. I replied wearily that it was enough for my thesis to concentrate on Toofankhali, that I wasn't a journalist and that I didn't believe much would come of my note-taking anyway as this was 'just' an ethnographic study. He refused to be dissuaded and insisted he take me back to his place. I summarise and quote from memory the long conversation we had on our way there: 'How can you get an idea if you don't ask us? You might not be able to do much today, but I want what we, from Annpur, will say, to haunt you until you do. Your job is to write. Besides, they're not only *our* tigers, they're *yours* too! Come, listen and write about how we have to live with them.'

I have lived uneasily with these words for many years; and hope that by recording them here, I have begun to fulfil some of Murari's expectations. 'Write', he had ordered, 'write, so that along with tigers, we islanders too may survive'.

Glossary of Selected Terms and Acronyms

abad Refers specifically to those Sundarbans islands which were reclaimed and cultivated.

Adivasi Literally means 'original inhabitant'; it usually refers to people who belong to a Schedule Tribe group.

babu Middle- or upper-class male. It is seen as a badge of *bhadralok* status, and is a frequently used term of respect all over West Bengal when addressing a social superior.

bagda Refers to what is commonly known as the 'tiger prawn'. The tiger prawn is considered to be one of the most delicate in taste. It is the largest Indian marine paneid prawn to be farmed. Its scientific name is *Penaeus monodon*. The bagda hatchlings are usually at the post-larval stage PL 20, 9–14 mm and are commonly known as 'prawn seed', though the literature also refers to them as 'post-larvae'/'juveniles'/'seedlings'.

bauley Tiger-charmer. Term previously used for woodcutters.

bhadralok i.e., 'gentle-folk'; from *bhadra* which is translatable as 'civility' with resonances of middle-class sensitivity to culture and refinement, and *lok* which is 'group' or 'people'. The word carries connotations not only of landed wealth, but also of being master (as opposed to servant), and frequently of upper-caste exclusiveness and of possessing education, culture and Anglicisation. This word has its origin in the rentier class, called *zamindar*, who enjoyed tenurial rights to rents from land appropriated by the Permanent Settlement introduced by the British in 1793. The Permanent Settlement set up a system of parasitic landlordism that led to the subinfeudation of the peasantry. Shunning manual labour, the

	bhadralok have always been very careful to keep social distance between themselves and their social inferiors (Chatterji 1994: 5).
bhotbhoti	Local name for mechanised boats.
bhite	Homestead. It is the consecrated piece of land where one's house is built and includes the courtyard and the adjoining non-cultivated land surrounding the house.
bhog	Ritual offering made at a feast.
bidi	A thin and cheap Indian cigarette made of tobacco wrapped in a tendu leaf.
bigha	Unit of land measurement roughly equal to one-third of an acre.
Bonbibi	Name of the deity of the forest, from *bon* which means forest and *bibi*, woman.
BJP	Bharatiya Janata Party.
bund	Raised mud quays called *bādh* in Bengali which protect islands from the saline tidal rivers by holding back their twice daily high tides.
bunding	The process of enclosing an island with a bund. There are 3,500 km of bund around most of the southern inhabited islands of the Sundarbans.
chor	Sandbars created from newly deposited silt.
CPIM/CPM	Communist Party of India-Marxist. Largest party constituting the WB Left Front government; often simply referred to as 'party'.
cycle-van	Three-wheeled cycles with raised platforms which carry goods and people.
dacoit	Anglicised version of the Bengali word *dakat*. Dacoits are infamous as armed robbers or pirates who not only plunder and loot but also perpetrate atrocious cruelty, defy local authorities, rob entire villages, and sometimes even murder their victims. They are legendary in rural Bengal.
Dalit	Means 'oppressed' and widely recognised by Dalits and non-Dalits in both social and political spheres.
dargah	Literally, 'court'; the seat of spiritual authority represented by the shrines and tombs of pirs or saiyeds.

dokkhin	South.
gram sansad	Village council.
jaghir	Revenue assignment.
jati	The Bengali *jati* is especially used, like 'caste', to mean 'genus', 'kind' or 'ethnic groups'. It also provides room for other collective identities such as those established along the lines of religion, regional affiliation and gender.
jongol	Commonly used for 'forest' with the word '*bon*' but specifically meaning 'wilderness' and in the Sundarbans specifically the sphere of non-humans. I have kept the word as it differs in its meaning from the English word 'jungle' and the idea of an impenetrable thicket of tropical vegetation.
khoti	Are little shacks built along an adjoining fishery by a prawn fishery owner. These serve to watch over the fishery at night and are used as a prawn seed transaction area during the day. They also become temporary living spaces for prawn dealers and their helpers during the busy months.
mal	Traditionally it meant land held on which revenue was required to be paid. In the Sundarbans context referred specifically to the piece of earth on the forest ground which was 'checked' when tiger-charmers said their charms on alighting from boats.
matir manush	Literally, 'people of the earth' or 'earthen people'; refers more specifically to a gentle, amiable person.
maun	Unit for measuring wood. It represents about 40 kg.
modhuwala	Bee-keeper.
mohal or *mahal*	Administrative unit; roughly equivalent to 'country' or 'sub-district'. It is a term which gained currency during the Permanent Settlement and means 'one's own place'. It comes from the word *mohalla* which means 'neighbourhood'; in the Sundarbans context it strangely denotes

both a loose group of families all related by blood and also a geographical part, like a 'village mohalla' or a 'forest mohal'. By extension, the islanders often refer to the forest with this term.

mouley Honey collector.

nishana Pole erected in the forest where a person has been killed. Usually a thinly spun towel called *gamchha* or a garment of the dead person is attached to its top. It is interesting to note that it also refers to the flag and pole erected in the compound of a *dargah*.

OBC Other backward castes.

panchayat Elected self-governing body at village cluster, development block and district levels.

parganas Unit of revenue administration equivalent to subdistrict or county/basic territorial unit of administration of the Mughals. The South 24 Parganas and the North 24 Parganas are today's administrative names for two districts in southern WB.

patta Certificate of landholding.

pir 'Saint'; respectful name given to Saiyeds alive or dead; Saiyed lineage name; 'teacher'.

puja Hindu worship.

rai or *ray* King or lord. It was a title many zamindars took up and it subsequently became a surname.

RSP Revolutionary Socialist Party. The most prevalent political party in the Sundarbans and part of the Left Front Government of West Bengal.

SC People belonging to a schedule (list) of castes or parts of groups within castes that are economically and socially disadvantaged and are therefore entitled to protection and specified benefits under Article 341 of the Indian constitution in order for such groups to be eligible for positive affirmative action. The bulk of Scheduled Castes were former 'Untouchables' — called 'Harijans' by Gandhi — who prefer the term 'Dalit' (meaning 'oppressed' or 'broken') in self-recognition of their historical oppression. The 1991 census tabulated 13.8 crore SC members throughout India, representing about 16 per cent of the total Indian population. The schedule in the constitution does not list the SCs by name.

ST   Schedule (list) of tribes or tribal communities that are economically and socially disadvantaged and are entitled to specified benefits guaranteed by Article 342 of the Indian constitution. The tribes are listed in the Fifth Schedule. The 1991 census tabulated 6.78 crore members of Scheduled Tribes throughout India, representing about 8 per cent of the total population.

TMC   Trinamool Congress. Party headed by Mamata Bannerjee who allied with the NDA to fight against the Left Front government. Mamata was briefly minister of transport in the NDA government.

Tiger prawn   (see *bagda*).

TSRD   Tagore Society for Rural Development. NGO headed by Tushar Kanjilal. Projects carried out by this NGO have worked specifically in Orissa, Jhargram, Bihar, and West Bengal.

WB   West Bengal.

zamindar   'Landlord', especially those that emerged with the introduction of the British Permanent Settlement (Landlease) Act of 1793. Many were former revenue collectors of the Mughal period (1526–1858); (see *bhadralok* for more details).

Bibliography

Acharya, Poromesh, 1985. 'Education: Politics and Social Structure'. *Economic and Political Weekly*, 20 (42): 1785–789.

Agarwal, Bina, 2000. 'The Family in Public Policy: Fallacious Assumptions and Gender Implications'. NCAER Golden Jubilee Seminar Series Ninth Lecture. New Delhi: National Council of Applied Economic Research.

Agrawal, Arun, 1995. 'Dismantling the Divide between Indigenous and Scientific Knowledge'. *Development and Change*, 26: 413–39.

———, 1998. *Greener Pastures: Politics, Markets and Community among a Migrant Pastoral People*. Durham: Duke University Press.

Ahmed, Rafiuddin, 1981. *The Bengal Muslims 1871–1906: A Quest for Identity*. New Delhi: Oxford University Press.

Anderson, Benedict, 1983. *Imagined Communities: Reflections on the Origin and Spread of Nationalism*. London: Verso.

Anon, 1989. 'Maneaters and Masks', Newsletter of the IUCN SSC Cat Specialist Group, in *CatNews*, 11: 12.

Anon, 1993. 'Shrimp Farms Ravage the Environment and People in Bangladesh', *World Shrimp Farming*, 18 (5): 8–9.

Appadurai, Arjun, 1996. *Modernity at Large: Cultural Dimensions of Globalization*. Minneapolis, London: University of Minnesota Press.

———, 2001. Grassroots Globalization and the Research Imagination. *Public Culture* 12 (1): 1–19. Durham: Duke University Press.

Appiah, Kwame Anthony. 2006. 'A Thinker Builds on a World Where "Everybody Matters"'. *Philadelphia Inquirer*, http://www.mywire.com/pubs/PhiladelphiaInquirer/2006/01/26/1170719?extID=10037&oliID=229, accessed on 30 April 2007.

Arnold, David and Ramachandra Guha (eds), 1995. *Nature, Culture, Imperialism: Essays on Environmental History of South Asia*. New Delhi: Oxford University Press.

Arora, Dolly, 1999. 'Structural Adjustment Programs and Gender Concerns in India'. *Journal of Contemporary Asia*, 29 (1): 328–61.

Ascoli, F. D., 1910. 'The Rivers of the Delta'. *Journal and Proceedings of the Asiatic Society of Bengal*, 6 (10): 543–56.

Assayag, Jackie and Gilles Tarabout (eds), 1997. *Altérité et Identité: Islam et Christianisme en Inde*. Collection Purusartha 19. Paris: École des Hautes Études en Sciences Sociales.

Athreya, Vidya, 2006. 'Is Relocation a Viable Management Option for Unwanted Animals? The Case of the Leopard in India'. *Conservation and Society*, 4 (3), September: 419–23.

Bandopadhyaya, Manik, 1973. *Padma River Boatman*, Barbara Painter and Yann Lovelock (trans.). St. Lucia, Queensland: University of Queensland Press. Original *Padma Nadir Majhi*, 1934. Calcutta: Granthalaya.

Bandyopadhyay, Alapan and Anup Matilal (eds), 2003. *The Philosopher's Stone: Speeches and Writings of Sir Daniel Hamilton*. Gosaba, Kolkata: Sir Daniel Hamilton Estate Trust.

Bandyopadhyay, Sekhar, 1981. Caste, Class, and Census: Aspects of Social Mobility in Bengal Under the Raj, 1872–1931. *Calcutta Historical Journal*, 5 (2): 93–128.

—— 1997. *Caste, Protest and Identity in Colonial India: The Namasudras of Bengal 1872–1947*. Richmond, Surrey: Curzon Press.

—— (ed.), 2001. *Bengal: Rethinking History*. New Delhi: Manohar, International Centre for Bengal Studies (ICBS).

Banerjee Anuradha, 1998. *Environment, Population and Human Settlements of Sundarban Delta*. New Delhi: Concept Publishing.

Barlow, Adam C. D., 2009. 'The Sundarbans Tiger: Adaptation, Population Status and Conflict Management'. Unpublished PhD dissertation, University of Minnesota.

Barraclough, Solon and Andrea Finger-Stich, 1995. 'Some Ecological and Social Implications of Commercial Shrimp Farming in Asia' in Alfredo Quarto, Kate Cissna and Joanna Taylor (eds), 'Choosing The Road To Sustainability: The Impacts of Shrimp Aquaculture and the Models for Change', Submitted for the International Live Aquatics 1996 Conference, Seattle, Washington, 13–15 October 1996. http://www.earthisland.org/map/rdstb.htm, accessed on 15 January 2004.

Basu, Amrita, 1992. *Two Faces of Protests: Contrasting Modes of Women's Activism in India*. Berkeley CA: University of California Press.

Basu, Dipankar, 2001. 'Political Economy of 'Middleness' Behind Violence in Rural West Bengal'. *Economic and Political Weekly*, 36 (16), April 21: 1333–344.

Basu, Srimati, 2001. The Blunt Cutting Edge: The Construction of Sexuality in the Bengali 'Feminist' Magazine 'Sananda'. *Feminist Media Studies* 1 (2): 179–96.

Baviskar, Amita, 2003. 'State, Communities and Conservation: The Practice of Ecodevelopment in the Great Himalayan Park', in Vasant Saberwal and Mahesh Rangarajan (eds), *Battles Over Nature: Science and the Politics of Conservation*, pp. 267–99. New Delhi: Permanent Black.

Bayly, Christopher Alan, 1990. *The Raj: India and the British 1600–1947*. London: National Portrait Gallery.

Bernier, Francois, 1891 (originally 1670–72). *Travels in the Moghul Empire, 1656–1668*, trans. and ed. London: A. Constable.

Bertocci, Peter, 1987. 'Notes Towards an Ethnosociology of the Bengal Sundarbans'. Paper presented at workshop on 'The Commons in South Asia: Societal Pressures and Environmental Integrity in the Sundarbans', Smithsonian Institution, Washington, DC, 20–21 November. Also published in John Seidensticker, Richard Kurin and Amy K. Townsend (eds), *The Commons in South Asia: Societal Pressures and Environmental Integrity in the Sundarbans*. Washington, DC: The International Center, Smithsonian Institution, 1991.

Béteille, André, 1986. 'Individualism and Equality'. *Current Anthropology*, 27 (2): 121–34.

Bhadra, Gautam and Partha Chatterjee (eds), 1997. *Nimnabarger Itihas (The History of the Subaltern Classes)*. Calcutta: Ananda Publishers.

Bhattacharyya, Asutosh, 1947. 'The Tiger-cult and its Literature in Lower Bengal'. *Man in India*, 27 (1): 49–50.

Bhattacharyya, Dwaipayan, 1999. 'Politics of Middleness: The Changing Character of the Communist Party of India (Marxist) in Rural West Bengal (1977–90)'. In B. Rogaly, B. Harriss–White and S. Bose (eds), *Sonar Bangla? Agricultural Growth and Agrarian Change in West Bengal and Bangladesh*, pp. 279–300. New Delhi: Sage Publications.

Bhattacharyya, Harihar, 2002. *Making Local Democracy Work in India: Social Capital, Politics and Governance in West Bengal*. New Delhi: Vedam.

Bhaumik, Sankar Kumar, 1993. *Tenancy Relations and Agrarian Development: A study of West Bengal*. New Delhi, London: Sage Publications.

Bhaumik, Subir, 2003. 'Fears Rise for Sinking Sundarbans', BBC World News, UK edition, 15/9, pp. 1–4.

Bhowmick, P. K., 1976. *Socio-cultural Profile of Frontier Bengal*. Calcutta: Punthi Pustak.

Bird-David, Nurit, 1992a. 'Beyond "The Original Affluent Society": A Culturalist Reformulation'. *Current Anthropology*, 33: 25–47.

———, 1992b. 'Beyond "The Hunting and Gathering Mode of Subsistence": Observations on Nayaka and Other Modern Hunter-gatherers'. *Man*, 27: 19–44.

———, 1999, '"Animism" Revisited: Personhood, Environment, and Relational Epistemology'. *Current Anthropology*, 40 (Supplement): S67–S91.

Biswas, Atharobaki, 1982. 'Why Dandakaranya a Failure, Why Mass Exodus, Where Solution?' *The Oppressed Indian*, July.

Blower, J. H., 1985. 'Sundarbans Forest Inventory Project, Bangladesh. Wildlife conservation in the Sundarbans'. Project Report 151. Surbiton, UK: ODA Land Resources Development Centre.

Blurton, T. Richard, 2006. *Bengali Myths*. London: The British Museum Press.

Bonner, Raymond, 1993. *At the Hand of Man: Peril and Hope for Africa's Wildlife*. New York: Alfred A. Knopf.

Boomgaard, Peter, 2001. *Frontiers of Fear: Tigers and People in the Malay World, 1600–1950*. New Haven, London: Yale University Press.

Bose, Pradip, 1993. *Peasant Labour and Colonial Capital: Rural Bengal Since 1770*. Cambridge, New York: Cambridge University Press.

——— (ed.), 2000. *Refugees in West Bengal: Institutional Practices and Contested Identities*. Calcutta: Calcutta Research Group.

Bose, Sugata, 1986. *Agrarian Bengal: Economy, Social Structure and Politics, 1919–1947*. Cambridge: Cambridge University Press.

Bouez, Serge, 1992. *La déesse apaisée: norme et transgression dans l'hindouisme au Bengale*. Paris: Éditions de l'École des Hautes Études en Sciences Sociales.

Breitenmoser, Urs, 1998. 'Large Predators in the Alps: The Fall and Rise of Man's Competitors'. *Biological Conservation*, 83: 279–89.

Buchanan, Francis, 1833. *A Geographical, Statistical, and Historical Description of the Districts, or Zila, of Dinajpur*. Calcutta: Baptist Mission Press.

Campos, J. J. A., 1919. *History of the Portuguese in Bengal*. Calcutta, London: Butterworth & Co.

Carsten, Janet (ed.), 2000. *Cultures of Relatedness: New Approaches to the Study of Kinship*. Cambridge: Cambridge University Press.

Centre for Women's Development Studies (CWDS), 2000. *Shifting Sands: Women's Lives and Globalisation*. Calcutta: Stree.

Chakrabarti, Kalyan, 1986. 'Tiger (*Panthera tigris tigris*) in the Mangrove Forests of Sundarbans—An Ecological Study'. *Tigerpaper*, 13 (2): 8–11.

Chakrabarti, Ranjan, 2001. 'Tiger and the Raj: Ordering the Maneater of the Sundarbans 1880–1947'. In Ranjan Chakrabarti (ed.), *Space and Power in History: Images, Ideologies, Myths and Moralities*. Kolkata: Penman.

———, 2007. 'Introduction'. In Ranjan Chakrabarti (ed.), *Situating Environmental History*. New Delhi: Manohar.

Chakrabarty, Dipesh, 1989. *Rethinking Working-class History: Bengal 1890–1940*. Princeton, NJ: Princeton University Press.

———, 1996. 'Remembered Villages: Representation of Hindu Bengali Memories in the Aftermath of the Partition'. *Economic and Political Weekly*, 31 (32), August: 2143–151.

Chatterjee, Nilanjana, 1992. 'Midnight's Unwanted Children: East Bengali Refugees and the Politics of Rehabilitation'. Unpublished PhD thesis, Brown University, Providence.

Chatterjee, Partha, 1982. 'Agrarian Relations and Communalism in Bengal, 1926–1935'. In R. Guha (ed.), *Subaltern Studies I: Writings on South Asian History and Society*, pp. 9–38. New Delhi: Oxford University Press.

———, 1984. *Bengal 1920–1947: The Land Question*. Calcutta: K. P. Bagchi.

———, 1986. 'The Colonial State and Peasant Resistance in Bengal 1920–1947'. *Past and Present*, 110: 169–204.

———, 1988. 'For an Indian History of Peasant Struggles'. *Social Scientist*, 16 (11): 3–17.

———, 1993. *The Nation and its Fragments: Colonial and Postcolonial Histories*. Princeton, NJ: Princeton University Press.

———, 1997. *The Present History of West Bengal: Essays in Political Criticism*. New Delhi: Oxford University Press.

——— 1998. 'Community in the East'. *Economic and Political Weekly*. 33 (6), February: 277–82.

Chatterjee, Partha and Anjan Ghosh (eds), 2002. *History and the Present*. New Delhi: Permanent Black.

Chatterjee, Piya, 2001. *A Time for Tea: Women, Labor, and Postcolonial Politics on an India Plantation*. Durham, London: Duke University Press.

Chatterji, Joya, 1994. *Bengal Divided: Hindu Communalism and Partition 1932–1947*. Cambridge: Cambridge University Press.

———, 1996. 'The Bengali Muslim: A Contradiction in Terms? An Overview of the Debate on Bengali Muslim Identity'. *Comparative Studies of South Asia, Africa, and the Middle East*, 16 (2): 16–24.

Chattopadhyay, Tushar, 1961. 'Dakhin Ray: A Popular Folk God of 24-Parganas'. In *Census 1961: West Bengal, District Census Handbook, 24-*

Parganas, vol. II, Appendix III, pp. 25–26. Calcutta: Deputy Superintendent of Census Operations, Government of West Bengal.

Chattopadhyaya, Haraprasad, 1987. *Internal Migration in India: A Case Study of Bengal*. Calcutta: K. P. Bagchi.

———, 1999. *The Mystery of the Sundarbans*. Calcutta: Rajeev Neogi.

Chaudhury, A. B. and A. Choudhury, 1994. *Mangroves of the Sundarbans— India*, Vol. I, Geneva: IUCN.

Choudhury, S. R. 1979. 'Predatory Aberration in Tiger'. *International Symposium on Tiger. pp.* 79–90. New Delhi: Project Tiger, Department of Environment, Govt. of India.

Chowdhury, M. K. and Pranabes Sanyal, 1985a. 'Use of Electroconvulsive shocks to control tiger predation on human beings in Sundarbans Tiger Reserve'. *Tiger Paper*, 12 (2): 1–5. http://www.wcmc.org.uk/igcmc/s_sheets/worldh/ sundarba.html, accessed on 30 May 2003.

———, 1985b. 'Some Observations on Man-eating Behaviour of Tigers of Sundarbans. *Cheetal*, 26 (3/4): 32–40. http://www.tigers.ca/Tigerworld/ tigersearch.cgi?as=0&searchterm=Maneaters, accessed on 30 May 2003.

Clifford, James and George E. Marcus (eds), 1986. *Writing Culture: The Poetics and Politics of Ethnography*. Berkeley, CA: University of California Press.

Cooper, Adrienne, 1988. *Sharecropping and Sharecroppers' Struggles in Bengal 1930–1950*. Calcutta: K. P. Bagchi.

Corbett, Jim, 1946. *Man–eaters of Kumaon*. London, New York: Oxford University Press.

Dalal, Meenakshi N., 1995. 'Rural Women of India and the Global Economy'. *Development* 3 (September): 40–42.

Danda, Anamitra Anurag, 2007. *Surviving in the Sundarbans: Threats and Responses; An Analytical Description of Life in an Indian Riparian Commons*. Published PhD dissertation, University of Twente.

Das, Amal Kumar, 1968. *Trends of Occupation Pattern Through Generations in Rural Areas of West Bengal*. Special Series No. 10. Calcutta: Scheduled Castes and Tribes Welfare Department, Govt. of West Bengal.

Das, Amal Kumar, Sankarananda Mukherji and Manas Kamal Chowdhuri (eds), 1981. *A Focus on Sundarban*. Calcutta: Editions Indian.

Das, Sharmila, 1991. 'Development of Fisheries in South 24-Parganas District: Problems and Prospects'. *Geographical Review of India*, 53 (2): 69–79.

Das, Veena, 1976. 'The Uses of Liminality: Society and Cosmos in Hinduism'. *Contributions to Indian Sociology* (n.s.), 10 (2): 245–63.

Das Gupta, Sanjukta, 2001. 'Peasant and Tribal Movements in Colonial Bengal: A Historiographic Overview'. In S. Bandyopadhyay (ed.), *Bengal: Rethinking History*, pp. 65–92. New Delhi: Manohar, International Centre for Bengal Studies.

Dasgupta, Swapan, 1985. 'Adivasi Politics in Midnapur, c. 1760–1924'. In R. Guha (ed.), *Subaltern Studies IV: Writings in South Asian History and Society*. New Delhi: Oxford University Press.

Davies, Marvin. 1983. *Rank and Rivalry: The Politics of Inequality in West Bengal*. Cambridge: Cambridge University Press.

De, Amalendu, 1974. *Roots of Separatism in Nineteenth-century Bengal*. Calcutta: Ratna Prakash.

De, Rathindranath, 1990. *The Sundarbans*. Calcutta: Oxford University Press.

De, S. K., 1962, *Bengali Literature in the XIXth Century*. Calcutta: Firma.

Descola, Philippe, 1992. 'Societies of Nature and the Nature of Society. In A. Kuper (ed.), *Conceptualizing Society*, pp. 107–26. London, New York: Routledge.

———, 1996. 'Constructing Natures: Symbolic Ecology and Social Practice'. In Phillipe Descola and Gíslí Pálsson (eds), *Nature and Society: Anthropological Perspectives*, pp. 82–102. London, New York: Routledge.

Devalle, Susana B. C., 1992. *Discourses of Ethnicity: Culture and Protest in Jharkhand*. New Delhi; Newbury Park, California: Sage Publications.

Dewan, Ritu. 1999. 'Gender Implications of the "New" Economic Policy: A Conceptual Overview'. *Women's Studies International Forum*, 22 (4): 425–29.

Diamond, Stuart, 1979. 'Thirsty Tigers'. *Omni*, 1 (11): 37.

Dimock, Edward C., Jr, 1969. 'Muslim Vaisnava Poets of Bengal'. In D. Kopf (ed.), *Bengal: Regional Identity*, pp. 23–32. East Lansing: Michigan State University Asian Studies Centre Occasional Papers.

Drayton, Richard H., 2000. *Nature's Government: Science, Imperialism and the 'Improvement of the World'*. New Haven, CT: Yale University Press.

Eaton, Richard Maxwell, 1987. 'Human Settlement and Colonization in the Sundarbans, 1200–1750'. Paper presented at workshop program 'The Commons in South Asia: Societal Pressures and Environmental Integrity in the Sundarbans', Smithsonian Institution, Washington, DC, 20–21 November 1987.

———, 1993. *The Rise of Islam and the Bengal Frontier 1204–1760*. Berkeley, CA: University of California Press.

Edney, Matthew H., 1997. *Mapping an Empire: The Geographical Construction of India, 1765–1843*. Chicago, IL: University of Chicago Press.

EJF (Environmental Justice Foundation), 2003a. 'From Wetlands to Wastelands: Impacts of Shrimp Farming', *Society of Wetland Scientists Bulletin*, Vol. 20, No. 1, March. Report researched, written and produced by Coralie Thornton, Mike Sanahan and Juliette Williams. London: EJF.

———, 2003b. 'Risky Business: Vietnamese Shrimp Aquaculture—Impacts and Improvements'. Report researched, written and produced by Dr Mike Sanahan, Coralie Thornton, Steve Trent and Juliette Williams. London: EJF.

———, 2003c. 'Smash and Grab: Conflict, Corruption and Human Rights Abuses in the Shrimp Farming Industry'. Report researched, written and produced by Dr Mike Sanahan, Coralie Thornton, Steve Trent and Juliette Williams. London: EJF.

———, 2003d. 'Squandering the Seas: How Shrimp Trawling is Threatening Ecological Integrity and Food Security Around the World'. Report researched, written and produced by Annabelle Aish, Steve Trent and Juliette Williams. London: EJF.

EJF (Environmental Justice Foundation), 2004. 'Farming the Sea, Costing the Earth: Why We Must Green the Blue Revolution', report researched, written and produced by Steve Trent, Coralie Thornton, Mike Sanahan and Juliette Williams. London: EJF.

Fahrni Mansur, Elizabeth and Rubaiyat, 2006. *Sundarban: A Basic Field Guide*. Dhaka: Mowgliz Production.

Fardon, Richard, 1990. *Localising Strategies: Regional Traditions of Ethnographic Writing*. Edinburgh: Scottish Academic Press.

Fayrer, Joseph Sir, 1875. *The Royal Tiger of Bengal: His Life and Death*. London: J & A Churchill.

Flibbertigibbet, 1967. 'A Calcutta Diary: "'Laying on a Conspiracy of a Lay-off'"'. *Economic and Political Weekly*, April 1: 633–34.

Foucault, Michel, 1980. *Power/Knowledge: Selected Interviews and Other Writings, 1972–1977*. Brighton: Harvester University Press.

Franklin, Adrian, 1999. *Animals and Modern Culture: A Sociology of Human–animal Relations in Modernity*. London: Sage Publications.

———, 2002. *Nature and Social Theory*. London: Sage Publications.

Fruzzetti, Lina M., 1982. *The Gift of a Virgin: Women, Marriage, and Ritual in a Bengali Society*. New Brunswick, NJ: Rutgers University Press.

Fuller, Chris, 1992. *The Camphor Flame: Popular Hinduism and Society in India*. Princeton, NJ: Princeton University Press.

Gadgil, M. and R. Guha, 1992. *This Fissured Land: An Ecological History of India*. New Delhi: Oxford University Press.

———, 1994. *Ecology and Equity: The Use and Abuse of Nature in Contemporary India*. London, New York: Routledge.

Ganguly-Scrase, Ruchira, 2003. 'Paradoxes of Globalization, Liberalization, and Gender Equality: The Worldviews of the Lower Middle Class in West Bengal, India'. *Gender & Society*, 17 (4), August: 544–66.

Gardner, Katy, 1991. *Songs at the River's Edge: Stories from a Bangladeshi Village*. London: Virago.

Gee, E. P., 2000 (1964). *The Wildlife of India*. New Delhi: Harper Collins.

Ghosh, Amitav, 2004a. *The Hungry Tide*. London: Harper Collins.

———, 2004b. 'Folly in the Sundarbans: A Crocodile in the Swamplands'. *Outlook India*, 18 October.

Ghosh, Kaushik, 1999. A Market for Aboriginality: Primitivism and Race Classification in the Indentured Labour Market of Colonial India. In G. Bhadra, G. Prakash, and S. Tharu (eds), *Subaltern Studies X*, pp. 8–48. Also available at http://www.lib.virginia.edu/area-studies/subaltern/ss09.htm and http://www.lib.virginia.edu/area-studies/subaltern/ss11.htm

Ghosh, Sanjoy, 2008. '*Aporishim bonchona o birup prokriti, ei niyei shundorboner adibashira benche achen*'. In *Sangbad Manthan*, South 24 Parganas.

Giddens, Anthony, 1992. *The Transformation of Intimacy: Sexuality, Love and Eroticism in Modern Societies*. Cambridge: Polity Press.

Gold, Ann Grodzins with Bhoju Ram Gujar, 1997. 'Wild Pigs and Kings: Remembered Landscapes in Rajasthan'. *American Anthropologist*, 99 (1): 70–84.

Gombrich, Richard and Gananath Obeyesekere, 1988. *Buddhism Transformed: Religious Change in Sri Lanka*. Princeton, NJ: Princeton University Press.

Goody, Jack, 1977. *The Domestication of the Savage Mind*. Cambridge: Cambridge University Press.

Greenough, Paul, R. 1982. *Prosperity and Misery in Modern Bengal: The Famine of 1943–1944*. New York: Oxford University Press.

———, 1998. 'Hunter's Drowned Land: An Environmental Fantasy of the Victorian Sundarbans'. In R. H. Grove, V. Damodaran and S. Sangwan (eds), *Nature and the Orient: The Environmental History of South and Southeast Asia*, pp. 237–72. New Delhi: Oxford University Press.

———, 2003. 'Pathogens, Pugmarks, and Political "Emergency": The 1970s South Asian Debate on Nature'. in Paul Greenough and Anna Lowenhaupt Tsing (eds), *Nature in the Global South*, pp. 201–30. Durham, NC: Duke University Press.

Guha, Ramachandra, 1989a. *The Unquiet Woods: Ecological Change and Peasant Resistance in the Himalayas*. New Delhi: Oxford University Press.

———, 1989b. 'Radical American Environmentalism and Wilderness Preservation: A Third World Critique'. *Environmental Ethics*, 11 (1): 71–83.

———, 2003. 'The Authoritarian Biologist and the Arrogance of Anti-Humanism: Wildlife Conservation in the Third World', in Vasant Saberwal and Mahesh Rangarajan (eds), *Battles Over Nature: Science and the Politics of Conservation*. New Delhi: Permanent Black.

Guha, Ranajit, 1983. *Elementary Aspects of Peasant Insurgency in Colonial India*. New Delhi: Oxford University Press.

Gupta Akhil, 1995. 'Blurred Boundaries'. *American Ethnologist*, 22 (2): 375–402.

———, 1996. 'The Implications of Global Environmentalism for Peoples and States'. Paper presented at Anthropology Dept., University of Massachusetts.

Gupta, Akhil and James Fergusson, 1992. 'Beyond "Culture": Space, Identity, and the Politics of Difference'. *Cultural Anthropology*, 7(1): 6–23.

———, 1997a. *Anthropological Locations: Boundaries and Grounds of a Field Science*. Berkeley, CA: University of California Press.

———, 1997b. *Culture, Power, Place: Explorations in Critical Anthro-pology*. Durham, NC: Duke University Press.

Gupta, Dipankar, 1993. 'Hierarchy and Difference: An Introduction'. In D. Gupta (ed.), *Social Stratification*. New Delhi: Oxford University Press.

Gupta, R. D., 1987. 'Save the Sundarbans'. *Sunday, Calcutta*. 27 September– 3 October 1987: 40.

Gupta, Sanjukta, 2003. 'The Domestication of a Goddess: Carana-tirtha Kalighat, the Mahapitha of Kali, In R. McDermott, and J. K. Jeffrey (eds), *Encountering Kali: In the Margins, at the Centre, in the West*, pp. 60–79. Berkeley, CA: University of California Press.

Hamilton, Sir Daniel, 1910. *India: The Finances of the Government and of the People*. London: Waterloo and Sons Limited.

———, 1930. *New India and How to Get There*. London: British Museum Press.

Hardin, Garrett, 1968. 'The Tragedy of the Commons'. *Science*, 162: 1243–248.

Harriss, John, 1993. 'What is Happening in Rural West Bengal? Agrarian Reform, Growth and Distribution'. *Economic and Political Weekly*, 28 (24), 12 June: 1237–247.

———, 2003. 'How Much Difference Does Politics Make? Regime Types and Rural Poverty Reduction Across Indian States'. In P. Houtzager and Mick Moore (eds), *Changing Paths: The New Politics of Inclusion*. Ann Arbor: University of Michigan Press.

Hendrichs, Hubert, 1972a. 'Man-eating Tiger Problem'. *Oryx*, 11 (4): 231.

———, 1972b. 'Project 669 Tiger: Study of Man-eating Problems in the Sundarbans'. *WWF Yearbook, 1971–72*, pp. 109–15.

———, 1975. 'The Status of the Tiger Panthera Tigris (Linne 1758) in the Sundarbans Mangrove Forest (Bay of Bengal)'. *Saugetierkunaliche Mittelungen*, 23: 161–99.

Herring, Ronald, 1987. 'The Commons and its "Tragedy" as Analytical Framework: Understanding Environmental Degradation in South Asia'. Paper presented at workshop program 'The Commons in South Asia: Societal pressures and Environmental Integrity in the Sundarbans'. Smithsonian Institution, Washington, DC, 20–21 November 1987.

———, 1990. 'Rethinking the Commons'. *Agriculture and Human Values*, 7 (2): 88–104.

Hill, Douglas, 2003. 'Policy, Poverty and Chronic Poverty: The Experience of Bankura District, West Bengal'. Paper presented at the International Conference on '*Staying Poor: Chronic Poverty and Development Policy*', pp. 1–26. IDPM, University of Manchester, 9–7 April 2003, http://idpm.man.ac.uk/cprc/Conference/conferencepapers/hillDouglas2%2018.03.pdf accessed on 30 December 2003.

Hunter, W. W., 1875. *A Statistical Account of Bengal. Vol.1. Districts of the 24–Parganas and Sundarbans*. London: Trubner & Co.

Inden, Ronald and Ralph Nicholas, 1977. *Kinship in Bengali Culture*. Chicago, IL: Chicago University Press.

Indira, 1992. 'Conservation at Human Cost: Case of Rajaji National Park'. *Economic and Political Weekly*, 27 August: 1647–650.

Ingold, Tim, 1988. *What is an Animal?* London: Unwin Hyman Ltd.

———, 1990. 'An Anthropologist Looks at Biology'. *Man* (n.s.), 25: 208–29.

———, 1993. 'The Temporality of the Landscape'. *World Archaeology*, 25 (2): 152–74.

Islam, Mustafa Nurul, 1973. *Bengali Muslim Public Opinion as Reflected in the Bengali Press 1901–1930* (Original: *Samayik Patre Jiban o Janamat 1901–1930*/Or, *Life and Public Opinion in the Periodical Literature*). Dhaka: Dhaka University Press.

Jalais, Annu, 2005. 'Dwelling on Morichjhanpi: When Tigers Became "Citizens", Refugees "Tiger-Food"'. *Economic and Political Weekly*, 40 (17), 23 April: 1757–762.

———, 2007. 'The Sundarbans: Whose World Heritage Site?' *Conservation and Society*, 5 (3): 1–8.

———, 2008. 'Unmasking the Cosmopolitan Tiger'. *Nature and Culture*, 3 (1): 25–40.

Kanjilal, Tushar, 2000. *Who Killed the Sundarbans?* Calcutta: Tagore Society for Rural Development.

Khan, Shafaat Ahmad (ed.), 1927. *John Marshall in India: Notes and Observations in Bengal, 1668–1672*. London: Oxford University Press.

Kudaisya, Gyanesh, 1996. 'Divided Landscapes, Fragmented Identities: East Bengal Refugees and their Rehabilitation in India, 1947–79'. *Singapore Journal of Tropical Geography*, 17 (1): 24–39.

Kumar, Deepak, 1991. 'Colonial Science: A Look at the Indian Experience'. In D. Kumar (ed.), *Science and Empire: Essays in the Indian Context (1700–1947)*, pp. 6–12. Delhi: National Institute of Science, Technology and Development Studies

Kuper, Adam. 1994. 'Culture, Identity and the Project of a Cosmopolitan Anthropology'. *Man* (n.s.), 29 (3): 537–54.

Lahiri, R. K., 1973. *Management Plan of Tiger Reserve in Sundarbans, West Bengal, India*. Calcutta: Department of Forests, Govt. of West Bengal.

Lambert, Helene, 2000. 'Sentiment and Substance in North Indian Forms of Relatedness'. In J. Carsten (ed.), *Cultures of Relatedness: New Approaches to the Study of Kinship*, pp. 73–89. Cambridge: Cambridge University Press.

Latour, Bruno, 1986. 'Visualization and Cognition: Thinking with Eyes and Hands'. *Knowledge and Society*, 6: 1–40.

———, 1993 (1991). *We Have Never Been Modern*. Harvard, MA: Harvester Wheatsheaf.

Lawrence, Patricia, 2003. 'Kali in a Context of Terror: The Tasks of a Goddess in Sri Lanka's Civil War'. In R. McDermott, and J. K. Jeffrey (eds), *Encountering Kali: In the Margins, at the Centre, in the West*, pp. 100–123. Berkeley, CA: University of California Press.

Lévi-Strauss, Claude, 1962. *Totemism*. London: Merlin Press.

Lynch, Owen M., 1969. *The Politics of Untouchability: Social Mobility and Social Change in a City of India*. New York, London: Columbia University Press.

Macnaghten, Phil and John Urry, 1998. *Contested Natures*. London: Sage/TCS.

Madhusudan, M. D. and Charudutt Mishra, 2003. 'Why Big, Fierce Animals are Threatened: Conserving Large Mammals in Densely Populated Landscapes', in Vasant Saberwal and Mahesh Rangarajan (eds), *Battles Over Nature: Science and the Politics of Conservation*. New Delhi: Permanent Black.

Mallabarman, Adwaita, 1992. *A River Called Titash*. (Originally written in 1956) trans. Kalpana Bardhan. New Delhi: Penguin.

Mallick, Ross, 1993. *Development Policy of a Communist Government: West Bengal Since 1977*. Cambridge: Cambridge University Press.

———, 1999. 'Refugee Settlement in Forest Reserves: West Bengal Policy Reversal and the Marichjhapi Massacre'. *The Journal of Asian Studies*, 58 (1): 104–25.

Marcus, George E., 1995. *Technoscientific Imaginaries: Conversations, Profiles, and Memoirs*. Chicago, IL: University of Chicago Press.

Mathur, K. S., 1972. 'Tribe in India: A Problem of Identification and Integration'. In K. S. Singh (ed.), *Tribal Situation in India*. Simla: Indian Institute of Advanced Studies.

Maudood, Elahi K., 1981. 'Refugees in Dandakaranya', *Refugees Today*, International Migration Review (spring–summer), 15 (1/2): 219–25.

Mazak, Vratislav, 1981. 'Panthera tigris'. *Mammalian Species*, 152: 1–8.

Menon, Usha and Richard A. Shweder, 2003. 'Dominating Kali: Hindu Family Values and Tantric Power'. In R. McDermott and J. K. Jeffrey (eds), *Encountering Kali: In the Margins, at the Centre, in the West*, pp. 80–99. Berkeley, CA: University of California Press.

Mitra, Sarat Chandra, 1903. 'Exorcism of Wild Animals in the Sundarbans'. *Journal of the Asiatic Society of Bengal*, LXXII (Part III): 45–52.

———, 1917. 'The Worship of the Sylvan Goddess'. *The Hindustan Review*, March 1917: 185–86.

———, 1918. 'On Some Curious Cults of Southern and Western Bengal'. *The Journal of the Anthropological Society of Bombay*, XI, as read on 29 August, Bombay: British India Press.

Mitra, Satish Chandra, 1963. *Jasohar-Khulnar Itihas, Vol. I*. Calcutta: Dasgupta and Co.

Mondol, Nazibul Islam (ed.), 2007. *Shundorbon Bishesh Shonkha: Shamokaler Jiyonkathi*. Kolkata, Joynagar: Jibon Mondal Hat.

Montgomery, Sy, 1995. *Spell of the Tiger*. Boston, New York: Houghton Mifflin Co.

Moore, Henrietta L., 1988. *Feminism and Anthropology*. London: Polity Press.

Moore, Henrietta L. and Megan Vaughan, 1994. *Cutting Down Trees: Gender, Nutrition and Agricultural Change in the Northern Province of Zambia, 1890–1990*. London: James Currey.

Mosse, David, 1994. 'Idioms of Subordination and Styles of Protest Among Christian and Hindu Harijan Castes in Tamil Nadu'. *Contributions to Indian Sociology*, 28 (1): 67–106.

Mullin, Molly, 1999. 'Mirrors and Windows: Sociocultural Studies of Human–Animal Relationships'. *Annual Review of Anthropology*, 28: 201–4.

Mukhopadhyay, Amites, 2003a. 'Doing Development: Voluntary Agencies in the Sundarbans of West Bengal'. Unpublished PhD thesis. Department of Anthropology, Goldsmiths College, University of London.

———, 2003b. 'Negotiating Development: The Nuclear Episode in the Sundarbans of West Bengal'. Paper presented at the Association of Social Anthropology (ASA), Manchester.

Nader, Laura (ed.), 1996. *Naked Science: Anthropological Inquiry into Boundaries, Power, and Knowledge*. London: Routledge.

Nandi, N. C. and A. Misra, 1987. *Records of the Zoological Survey of India: Bibliography of the Indian Sundarbans with Special Reference to Fauna*. Misc. Pub. Occasional Paper No. 97. Calcutta: Zoological Survey of India, Govt. of India.

Narayan, Kirin, 1993. 'How Native is Native Anthropology?' *American Anthropologist*, 95 (3): 671–86.

Nicholas, Ralph, 1963. 'Ecology and Village Structure in Deltaic West Bengal'. *The Economic Weekly*, 15: 1185–196.

————, 1967. 'Ritual Hierarchy and Social Relations in Rural Bengal'. *Contributions to Indian Sociology (n.s.)*, 1: 56–83.

————, 1968. 'Structures of Politics in the Villages of Southern Asia'. In M. Singer and B. S. Cohn (eds), *Structure and Change in Indian Society*, pp. 243–84. Chicago: Aldine Publishing Company.

————, 1969. 'Vaisnavism and Islam in Rural Bengal'. In David Kopf (ed.), *Bengal: Regional Identity*, pp. 33–47. East Lansing: Occasional Papers of the Asian Studies Center, Michigan State University (South Asia Series, No. 9).

Niyogi, Tushar K., 1997. *Tiger Cult of the Sundarvans*. Calcutta: Anthropological Survey of India.

Ohnuki–Tierney, Emiko, 1987. *The Monkey as Mirror: Symbolic Transformations in Japanese History and Ritual*. Princeton, NJ: Princeton University Press.

O'Malley, L. S. S., 1908. *Eastern Bengal District Gazetteers, Khulna*. Calcutta: Bengal Secretariat Book Depot.

———— 1914, *Bengal District Gazetteers: 24-Parganas District Statistics 1900–1901 to 1910–1911, Vol. B*. Calcutta: The Bengal Secretariat Book Depot (Reprinted in 1998 by West Bengal District Gazetteers Department of Higher Education, Government of West Bengal, Calcutta).

————, 1935. *Popular Hinduism: The Religion of the Masses*. Cambridge: Cambridge University Press.

Östör, Ákos, Lina Fruzzetti and Steve Barnett (eds), 1982. *Concepts of Person: Kinship, Caste, and Marriage in India*. Cambridge, MA.: Harvard University Press.

Pandian, Anand, S. 2001. 'Predatory Care: The Imperial Hunt in Mughal and British India'. *Journal of Historical Sociology*, 14 (1): 79–107.

Panini, M., 1995. 'The Social Logic of Economic Liberalization'. *Sociological Bulletin*, 44 (1): 33–62.

Pargiter, Frederick E., 1889. 'The Sundarbans'. *Calcutta Review*, 89: 280.

————, 1934. *A Revenue History of the Sundarbans from 1765 to 1870*. Alipore: Bengal Government Press.

Parry, Jonathan P., 1979. *Caste and Kinship in Kangra*. London: Routledge and Kegan Paul.

————, 1994. *Death in Benares*. Cambridge: Cambridge University Press.

Pathy, Jagannath, 1984. *Tribal Peasantry: Dynamics of Development*. New Delhi.

Peluso, Nancy, 1992. *Rich Forests, Poor People: Resource Control and Resistance in Java*. Berkeley: University of California Press.

Pokrant, Bob, Peter Reeves and John McGuire, 1988. 'The Novelist's Image of South Asian Fishers: Exploring the Work of Manik Bandopadhyaya, Advaita Malla Barman and Thakazhi Sivasankara Pillai'. *South Asia*, 21 (1): 123–38.

———, 2001. 'Bengal Fishers and Fisheries: A Historiographic Essay'. In Sekhar Bandyopadhyay (ed.), *Bengal: Rethinking History. Essays in Historiography*, pp. 93–117, ICBS Publication No. 29. New Delhi: Manohar.

Prakash, Gyan, 1999. *Another Reason: Science and the Imagination of Modern India*. Princeton, NJ: Princeton University Press.

Primavera, Honculada J., 1998. 'Tropical Shrimp Farming and its Sustainability'. *Tropical Mariculture*, 8: 257–89.

Quarto, Alfredo, Kate Cissna and Joanna Taylor, 1996. 'Choosing the Road To Sustainability: The Impacts of Shrimp Aquaculture and the Models for Change'. Submitted for the International Live Aquatics 1996 Conference, Seattle, Washington, 13–15 October 1996. http://www.earthisland.org/map/rdstb.htm, accessed on 15 January 2004.

Raheja, Gloria Goodwin and Anna Grodzins Gold, 1994. *Listen to the Heron's Words: Reimagining Gender and Kinship in North India*. Berkeley: University of California Press.

Rajan, M. G., 1997. *Global Environmental Politics: India and the North–South Politics of Global Environmental Issues*. New Delhi, New York: Oxford University Press.

Rangarajan, Mahesh, 1996. *Fencing the Forest: Conservation and Ecological Change in India's Central Provinces 1860–1914*. New Delhi: Oxford University Press.

———, 2001. *India's Wildlife History*. Delhi: Permanent Black.

———, 2003. 'The Politics of Ecology: The Debate on Wildlife and People in India, 1970–95', in Vasant Saberwal and Mahesh Rangarajan (eds), *Battles Over Nature: Science and the Politics of Conservation*, pp. 189–239. New Delhi: Permanent Black.

Rangarajan, Mahesh and Shahabuddin Ghazala, 2006. 'Displacement and Relocation from Protected Areas: Towards a Biological and Historical Synthesis'. *Conservation and Society*, 4 (3): 359–78.

——— (eds), 2007. *Making Con-servation Work: Securing Biodiversity in this New Century*. Delhi: Per-manent Black.

Rawal, V. and M. Swaminathan, 1998. 'Changing Trajectories: Agricultural Growth in West Bengal, 1950 to 1996'. *Economic and Political Weekly*, 33 (40): 2597.

Ray, B., 1961. *West Bengal, District Census Handbook, 24-Parganas, Vol. II*. West Bengal Civil Service Deputy Superintendent of Census Operations, Govt. of West Bengal.

Ray, Niharranjan, 1945. 'Medieval Bengali Culture'. *Viswa-Bharati Quarterly*, 11 (2), August–October: 45–55, 87–95.

Raychaudhuri, Bikash, 1980. *The Moon and the Net: Study of a Transient Community of Fishermen at Jambudwip*. Calcutta: Anthropological Survey of India.

Rennell, 1761. *Atlas of Bengal*. Sheet No. XX. SOAS.

Resisting the Sell-Out of the Sunderban Biosphere Reserve—An Investigative Report by PUBLIC, BEAG, & EQUATIONS, May 2004. Bangalore: Equations, Equitable Tourism Options.

Richards, John F. and Elizabeth P. Flint, 1990. 'Long-term Transformations in the Sundarbans Wetlands Forests of Bengal'. *Agriculture and Human Values*, 7 (2): 17–33.

Rishi, V., 1988. 'Man, Mask and Maneater'. *Tiger Paper*, 15 (3): 9–14.

Risley, H. H., 1981 (1891). *The Tribes and Castes of Bengal, Vols I & II* (reprint). Calcutta: Firma Mukhopadhyay.

Ritvo, Harriet, 1987. *The Animal Estate: The English and Other Creatures in the Victorian Age*. Cambridge, MA: Harvard University Press.

Rival, Laura M. 1996. 'Blowpipes and Spears: The Social Significance of Huaorani Technological Choices'. In P. Descola and G. Pálsson (eds), *Nature and Society*, pp. 145–64. London: Routledge.

Rosenberry, Robert, 1995. 'World Shrimp Farming' Annual Report, *Shrimp News International*, pp. 34–35.

Roy, Asim, 1970. 'Islam in the Environment of Medieval Bengal'. PhD thesis, Australian National University, Canberra.

———, 1983. *The Islamic Syncretistic Tradition in Bengal*. Princeton, NJ: Princeton University Press.

Roy Chowdhury, Biswajit and Pradeep Vyas, 2005. *The Sundarbans: A Pictorial Fieldguide*. Kolkata: Rupa & Co.

Ruud, Arild Engelsen, 1999a. 'From Untouchable to Communist: Wealth, Power and Status among Supporters of the Communist Party (Marxist) in Rural West Bengal'. In B. Rogaly, B. Harriss-White and S. Bose (eds), *Sonar Bangla? Agricultural Growth and Agrarian Change in West Bengal and Bangladesh*, pp. 253–78. New Delhi, London: Sage Publications.

———, 1999b. 'The Indian Hierarchy: Culture, Ideology and Consciousness in Bengali Village Politics'. *Modern Asian Studies*, 33 (3): 689–732.

Saberwal, Vasant and Mahesh Rangarajan (eds), 2003. *Battles Over Nature: Science and the Politics of Conservation*. New Delhi: Permanent Black.

Sahlins, Marshall, 1974. *Stone Age Economics*. London: Tavistock Publications Limited.

Sangwan, Satpal 1998. 'From Gentlemen Amateurs to Professionals: Reassessing the Natural Science Tradition in Colonial India 1780–1840'. In R. H. Grove, V. Damodaran and S. Sangwan (eds), *Nature and the Orient: The Environmental History of South and Southeast Asia*. New Delhi: Oxford University Press.

Sanyal, Pranabes, 1987. 'Managing the Man–eaters in the Sundarbans Tiger Reserve of India — A Case Study'. In R. L. Tilson and U. S. Seal (eds), *Tigers of the World: The Biology, Biopolitics, Management and Conservation of an EndangeredSspecies*, pp. 427–34. Park Ridge: Noyes Publications.

Sarkar, Tanika, 1985. 'Jitu Santal's Movement in Malda, 1924–1932'. In R. Guha (ed.), *Subaltern Studies IV: Writings in South Asian History and Society*. New Delhi: Oxford University Press.

————, 1987 *Bengal 1928–1934: The Politics of Protest*. Delhi: Oxford University Press.

Sarkar, Santosh K. and Asok K. Bhattacharya, 2003. 'Conservation of Bio-diversity of the Coastal Resources of Sundarbans, Northeast India: An Integrated Approach Through Environmental Education'. *Marine Pollution Bulletin*, 47: 260–264.

Scott, James C., 1985. *Weapons of the Week: Everyday Forms of Peasant Resistance*. New Haven, CT: Yale University Press.

————, 1998. *Seeing Like a State: How Certain Schemes to Improve the Human Condition Have Failed*. New Haven, CT: Yale University Press.

Sekhar, Nagothu Udaya 1998. 'Crop and livestock depredation caused by wild animals in protected areas: The Case of Sariska Tiger Reserve, Rajasthan, India'. *Environmental Conservation*, 25: 160–71.

Sekhsaria, Pankaj, 2004. 'Sundarbans: Biosphere in Peril', *Outlook Magazine*, 13 June, http://www.indianjungles.com/210604.htm.

Sen, Asok, Partha Chatterjee and Saugata Mukherji, 1982. *Three Studies on Agrarian Structure in Bengal 1850–1947*. Calcutta: Oxford University Press.

Shanklin, Eugenia, 1994. *Anthropology and Race*. Belmont, CA: Wadsworth Publishing Company.

Siddiqui, Kamal, 1997. *Land Management in South Asia: A Comparative Study*. Karachi, Oxford, New York: Oxford University Press.

Sikdar, Ranjit Kumar, 1982. 'Marichjhapi Massacre'. *The Oppressed Indian*, 4 (4): 21–23.

Sinha, Subir, Shubhra Gururani and Brian Greenberg, 1997. 'The "New Traditionalist Discourse" of Indian Environmentalism'. *Journal of Peasant Studies*, 24 (3): 65–99.

Sivaramakrishnan, K., 1995. 'Imagining the Past in Present Politics: Colonialism and Forestry in India'. *Comparative Studies in Society and History*, 37 (1): 3–40.

————, 1997. 'A Limited Forest Conservancy in Southwest Bengal, 1864–1912'. *Journal of Asian Studies*, 56 (1): 75–112.

————, 1999. *Modern Forests: Statemaking and Environmental Change in Colonial Eastern India*. New Delhi: Oxford University Press.

————, 2003, 'Conservation Crossroads: Indian Wildlife at the Intersection of Global Imperatives, Nationalist Anxieties, and Local Assertions'. In Vasant Saberwal and Mahesh Rangarajan (eds), *Battles Over Nature: Science and the Politics of Conservation*, pp. 383–412. New Delhi: Permanent Black.

Srinivas, Mysore Narasimhachar, 1965 (1952). *Religion and Society Among the Coorgs of South India*. Bombay: Asia Publishing House.

Sukumar, Raman, 1994. 'Wildlife–human Conflict in India: An Ecological and Social Perspective. In R. Guha (ed.), *Social Ecology*, pp. 303–17. New Delhi: Oxford University Press.

Trawick, Margaret, 1990. *Notes on Love in a Tamil Family*. Berkeley, CA: University of California Press.

Tsing, Anna Lowenhaupt, 1993. *In the Realm of the Diamond Queen: Marginality in an Out-of-the-Way Place*. New Jersey: Princeton University Press.

Turner, Victor W., 1974, *Dramas, Fields, and Metaphors: Symbolic Action in Human Society*. Ithaca, NY: Cornell University Press.

Uberoi, Patricia (ed.), 1994. *Family, Kinship and Marriage in India*. New Delhi: Oxford University Press.

Vatuk, Sylvia, 1972. *Kinship and Urbanization: White Collar Migrants in North India*. Berkeley, CA: University of California Press.

Vidal, John, 2003. 'It's Impossible to Protect the Forests for Much Longer'. *The Guardian*, 31 July.

Visharat, Mangaldev, Laxmi Narayan Pandey and Prasannbhai Mehta, 1979 (1993). 'Report on Marichjhapi Affairs' (MPs nominated by Prime Minister Desai to visit and investigate Marichjhanpi), 18 April 1979, no. 7 (mimeographed). In Ross Mallick, *Development Policy of a Communist Government: West Bengal Since 1977*, p. 99. Cambridge: Cambridge University Press.

Viveiros de Castro, Eduardo, 1996. 'Images of Nature and Society in Amazonian Ethnology'. *Annual Review of Anthropology*, 25: 179–200

Webster, J. E., 1911. *Eastern Bengal and the Assam District Gazeteers: Noakhali*. Allahabad: Pioneer Press.

Westland, J., 1871. *A Report on the District of Jessore: Its Antiquities, its History, and its Commerce*. Calcutta: Bengal Secretariat.

Wise, James, 1894. 'The Muhammadans of Eastern Bengal'. *Journal of the Asiatic Society of Bengal*, 63: 28–63.

Worboys Michael, 1991. 'Science and the Colonial Empire'. In D. Kumar (ed.), *Science and Empire: Essays in Indian Context (1700–1947)*. Delhi: National Institute of Science, Technology and Developemnt Studies.

Yule, Henry and A. C. Burnell, 1903 (1968). *Hobson-Jobson: A Glossary of Colloquial Anglo-Indian Words and Phrases, and of Kindred Terms, Etymological, Historical, Geographical and Discursive*. Delhi: Munshiram Manoharlal.

Websites accessed between May 2001 and May 2004:

http://www.wcmc.org.uk/igcmc/s_sheets/worldh/sundarba.html
http://www.ramsar.org/values_shoreline_e.htm
http://www.blonnet.com/2003/07/13/stories/2003071300701600.htm
http://www.zipworld.com.au/~cpa/garchve3/1032koff.html
http://www.guardian.co.uk/life/feature/story/0,13026,1008940,00.html
http://www.ejfoundation.org/reports.html

Website accessed in May 2008:

http://www.guernicamag.com/features/556/post_1/

About the Author

Annu Jalais is presently researching an Arts and Humanities Research Council project on the Bengali Muslim Diaspora led by Joya Chatterji and Claire Alexander. She is also currently Post-doctoral Associate at the Agrarian Studies Program at Yale University. She has taught and lectured at the departments of Anthropology, London School of Economics, Goldsmiths College and the School of Oriental and African Studies. Her specialisation is modern South Asia, particularly Bangladesh and West Bengal. Her research has appeared in academic journals and edited volumes.

Index